Whitewater Classics

Fifty North American Rivers Picked by the Continent's Leading Paddlers

Tyler Williams

FUNHOG PRESS
Flagstaff, Arizona

Editors
> Ginny Gelczis
> Lisa Gelczis

Additional Editing
> Todd Williams
> Bret Simmons
> Julie Williams

Book Design
> Mary Williams
> www.marywilliamsdesign.com

Rio Zimatan text written by Grant Amaral

Photography
> All river photos by Tyler Williams unless
> otherwise noted. All paddler portrait photos
> courtesy of paddler unless otherwise noted.
> All cover photos by Tyler Williams except
> open boater-Tom Stults, and aerial play boat-
> Jed Weingarten

Contributing River Photographers

Grant Amaral	Charlie Munsey
Skip Brown	Tom Okeefe
Kevin Colburn	Taylor Robertson
Katie Johnson	Tom Stults
Johnnie Kern	Jim Swedberg
Colleen Laffey	TJ Walker
Rob Lesser	Jed Weingarten
Doug Marshall	Wickliffe Walker

Printed in China
Copyright 2004
Funhog Press
ISBN 0-9664919-3-9

DISCLAIMER

Whitewater paddling is dangerous. Other dangerous activities commonly practiced while paddling include, but are not limited to: portaging, hiking, swimming, and driving between rivers. Nearly everything about going paddling is dangerous. If you don't want to endanger your life; don't paddle, don't buy this book, and certainly don't use this book.

Nature is constantly changing. Rockslides occur, floods change river and creek channels, trees fall into streams, and cataclysmic events create new river environments altogether. Therefore, any information contained herein should be considered out of date and possibly incorrect.

The author and publisher of *Whitewater Classics* claims no responsibility for any actions that might be embarked upon through the use of this book. Any decision that you, the reader, makes to climb, swim, walk, sit, stand, sleep, eat, drink, or breathe is entirely your own. You are burdened with the responsibility to take care of yourself, and any trouble you get into, before or after reading this book, is entirely your problem, and nobody else's. No amount of guidance, either from a guidebook or otherwise, can replace personal judgment.

Acknowledgements

A book like this is very much a group effort. The first thanks must go to all the paddlers in the book. They are by far the most helpful single group of people behind this project. They have provided interviews, and shared stories. Many have been paddling partners and some, good friends. This book would not have been possible without them, and I hope they are proud of their contributions. Thanks to mom, who has always nurtured my love of the outdoors, and dad, who makes me believe that I have it in me to achieve. Special thanks must go to my love Lisa. She is my primary content editor, and inspires me to do better. She is also the one who really got me into this paddling thing. It was clear from the start that I would have to learn to paddle whitewater if our relationship was going to last. I did, and it has. Thanks to Dave Shannon for brainstorming my initial paddler list, providing stories, and hosting me in Yough country. Thanks to Colleen Laffey for providing essential leads. Thanks to Jimbo and Helen for letting me hang out at their place on Durango's "paddling corner." Thanks to John Kudrna and Wildwasser-Prijon for their support, and Cascade Helmets, Adventure Medical Kits, and TEVA for their support. Thanks to Julie and Steve Jones for editing help, and donating the computer which most of this book was constructed on. Thanks to Bret Simmons and Margaret Williams for their legal assistance when our National Park tried to fine me $5,000 for paddling the Alsek. Thank you Ron Watters for leads and photos of Walt Blackadar. Thanks for the Tallulah photo Kevin Colburn. Thanks to Sutton Bacon for help with my Tallulah map, and Tom Okeefe for photos and info on the Green River Gorge. Thank you Risa Shimoda, Jason Robertson, Nick Lipkowski, and everyone who has helped at American Whitewater. Thanks to all who have paddled with me during the research of the fifty classics, especially those who allowed me to take their pictures. I promise to get you all books. Finally, thank you to the many people who provided leads and stories essential to my research: Tom and Tina Stults, Andy Corra, Tom Smythe, Andy Hutchinson, TJ Walker, Ben Gauthier, Francois Letoureanu, Bob Walker, Roger Hazelwood, John Fulbright, Eric Ohmer, Ben Gooden, Don Sessions, Rick Williams, Jean Rodman, Jed Weingarten, Kris Jonassen, Charlie Ebel, Tom Visnius, Andrew Stults, Taylor Robertson, Chuck Stanley, Richard Montgomery, Bert Welti, Lynn McAdams, John Connelly, Jeff Finley, Kent McCracken, Roger Marr, Stewart Smith, Ifor Thomas, Pete Skinner, Rick Alexander, Ron Frye, Olaf Kaler, Charlie Macarthur, Bill Bickham, Sue Negus, Claude Terry, Joann and Stan Woods, Eric Munshaw, John Cornwell, Gorman Young, Dave Kurtz, Jim Stuart, Barb Brown, Christa Kerckhoff, Payson Kennedy, and Royal Robbins.

Alphabetical Listing of Paddlers

Alphabetical Listing of Rivers

Table of Contents

Book Origins

It is probably obvious to any follower of outdoor adventure writing that the idea behind this book is not original. Long before *Whitewater Classics,* there was a well known work titled *Fifty Classic Climbs,* an excellent book first published in the '70s. Although I am not much of a climber, *Fifty Classic Climbs* fascinated me with its tales of adventure from the first time I saw it as a teenager.

When I began to write my own guidebooks, the thought of a "Fifty Classic Rivers" quickly made it onto my book ideas list. And there it stayed. I was stymied by the fact that I didn't have a broad enough range of experience to pick 50 "classic" rivers in North America by myself. A list like this would only be seen as credible were it picked by the most respected and experienced paddlers, not a retired raft guide with most of his experience limited to two states, like me.

One day while taking stock of my regional guidebooks in the local bookstore one day, I noticed an updated version of *Fifty Classic Climbs,* titled *Fifty Favorite Climbs.* This book had fifty world class climbers each select a favorite route. Like its predecessor, *Fifty Favorites* is a great book, and I recommend it. It is published by The Mountaineers Books in Seattle, Washington. Upon seeing it, the answer to my dilemma was clear: let the best paddlers pick the 50 classics themselves.

My next question was "which 50 paddlers should do the picking?" I wanted to honor the sport's pioneers, but I also wanted to keep the book contemporary. I wanted to include play boaters, expedition paddlers, and racers; open boaters, kayakers, and C-1ers. Certainly there are more than 50 "leading" paddlers in North America, and my preliminary lists included many names that could have easily been in this book. The final list is the result of a complex juggling routine of paddling style, geography, name recognition, and the vagaries of email. Ultimately, the picks were the results of my choices and decisions, which are undoubtedly imperfect.

This format of having each paddler nominate a classic run was initially chosen to give the book credibility. As I began to talk with different paddlers, however, I found a new part of the book developing. The stories behind the paddlers were sometimes inspiring, sometimes entertaining, always interesting. I quickly realized that the paddler profiles would add an entirely new and important dimension to the book.

After the paddlers and rivers were selected, the book research consisted of interviews with the paddlers, and paddling as many classic runs as possible myself. Before publication, I was able to paddle 31 of the classic runs in the book, and hiked or visited 10 more. The remaining 9 either didn't have cooperating water levels, didn't fit into my schedule, or were honestly over my head in ability.

Whether I was able to run every river or not, I have tried to get an overall accurate picture of the geography and human history on each river profiled. To this end, I relied on the paddlers in the book a great deal, but also double checked their information with several other sources. Additionally, regional guidebooks were used for basic facts, and Sue Taft's *The River Chasers* was an invaluable resource for historical information.

Despite my efforts, there will surely be some questionable facts and figures in this book. Such is the nature of documenting such a loose-knit culture as the whitewater paddling community. I am already anticipating the enlightening emails saying, "Hey! I was the first one to run that creek way back in..."

If I'm lucky, this book will help to create more wild river advocates, gain new members for American Whitewater, and maybe even inspire some to run all 50 classics. The adventure awaits. What I have tried to produce is an entertaining overview of some of North America's finest whitewater rivers and paddlers. It ain't the Gospel, it's just fun reading. I hope. Thanks for sharing in the fun.

Whose River is it Anyway?

The choice of rivers in this book is the product of the fifty paddler's suggestions, although I must admit that the final selections were swayed by my enthusiasm, or lack thereof, for a particular river. In some cases, the paddler and river match up perfectly, as the two are linked in the mind's of paddlers everywhere. Few think of kayaker Ken Whiting without thinking of the Ottawa River, for example. In other cases, however, the paddler and river are not so perfectly matched.

I made efforts to get the right paddlers with the right rivers, but this was not possible all of the time.

When it came down to it, there were certain paddlers who I felt should be in the book, and certain rivers that should be in, and the two didn't always fit. By no means should it be assumed that the river nominated by a particular paddler is necessarily "their" river. The rivers belong to no one, and everyone. We all have special connections to different places. To argue over who has the most special connection to a place is ridiculous. Every paddler in the book shares their own significant connection in some way with the river they selected, as I hope you will discover in the text.

Paddlers Are Good People

In traveling around the continent conducting research for Whitewater Classics, I visited many different rivers and river running communities. Each had its own unique flavor, and its own special cast of characters. The varied scenes all shared a common thread, however, one that I like to think of as the brotherhood of boaters.

Whenever I had a low point brought on by the everyday stresses of life, or simply an insecure moment upon arriving in a new place, the brotherhood never failed to come through to fix my attitude. There is no other arena of society that I have been a part of where you can go from total stranger to genuine friend in such a short time. Nothing cuts through the formalities of introduction like pulling a fellow human out of a gnashing hydraulic. And sometimes even the shared near-death experience is unnecessary. Upon meeting a fellow paddler, there is an instant understanding that you two are in the same groove, at least on some level.

Meeting new paddlers who quickly become new friends just makes you feel good inside, and, at least in my case, restores my wavering faith in humanity. Everywhere I've been, paddlers whom I didn't know have opened up to me, shared their stories and floor space, given their time, expertise, advice, and generally just been good folks who are fun to hang out with.

As the sport has grown, I've heard complaints about bad attitudes, and how it ain't like the good ol' days. Well, there's no debating that it's no longer the good ol' days, but basically the sport and its participants are the same as they've always been, relative to the grand scheme of things. And the attitudes? I haven't seen them. Anytime numbers increase, there is bound to be more bad apples in the bunch, but what I've seen is a lot of good fun-loving people who make me proud to call myself a paddler. It is a brotherhood I cherish.

Always Remember

"Suddenly, you were gone from all the lives you left your mark upon."

Neil Peart

Most of us who have been around whitewater for long have had to deal with unexpected death. We have experienced that moment of utter helplessness and fear when things go wrong on the river, or we have received that unbelievable phone call that puts a knot in the pit of our stomachs. When it happens, it is sad and tragic. It often makes us question whether running whitewater is worth the risk. This is a decision each of us as individuals must face.

The possibility of drowning is inherent in whitewater paddling. Without the element of risk, there is less demand for focus, less sense of accomplishment after a successful run, less reward. Speaking entirely for myself, risk is a part of my being. To not take risks, and subsequently not feel the joy that risky activities bring, would be a guaranteed slow death of another sort, a death of spirit. That is one risk I can't take.

Death is never an easy or pleasant thing, but it is an inevitable part of life. As paddlers, we are forced to confront our own mortality, which in itself is a valuable exercise, one more lesson the river can help us learn.

Let us not forget our friends who have lost their lives on the river. And for those of us who are still blessed to be paddling—let's be careful out there.

Assorted Classics

Below Big Splat on Big Sandy

A different view of 7-Foot

Charlie Munsey

Big air at Skook

An honest portage at Turnback

Pat Phillips

The secret stash of the Southwest

A peaceful respite

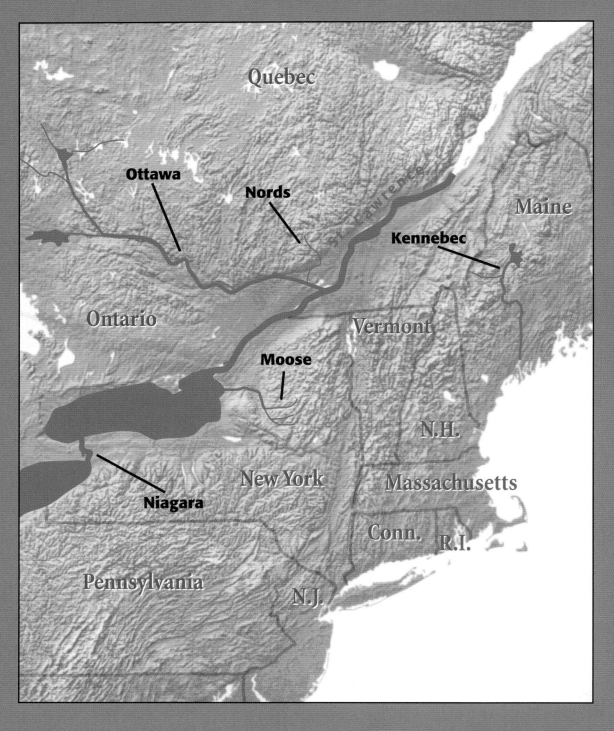

Northeast

"The river was confined between high and cragged rocks, one of which impended above the spot where the canoe rested. As these, again, were surmounted by tall trees, which appeared to totter on the brows of the precipice, it gave the stream the appearance of running through a deep and narrow dell."

James Fenimore Cooper

The Northeast is the mother land of river running in North America. Natives, and then fur trappers, traveled the waterways of this region three centuries ago, perhaps becoming the first whitewater paddlers on the continent. Canoes were their craft of choice, and open boats are still widely used in the Northeast today.

Both flat water canoe routes and whitewater runs pass through the distinguished beauty of this northern landscape, where boreal forests of spruce and pine mingle with Appalachian hardwoods. There are many wild and remote paddling locales here, but also sanctuaries of riverine solitude amidst concrete jungles of the area's urban centers.

A colder than average paddling season keeps the Northeast off the radar of many paddling vacations, despite the fact that several sub-regions offer exceptional whitewater. The Adirondack Mountains of upstate New York contain one of the highest concentrations of good whitewater anywhere. Canada's Newfoundland is a relatively unexplored resource for adventure boating, and Quebec has a multitude of rivers serving the dedicated paddling community of that enchanting French-speaking province.

A combination of snowmelt and rainfall contribute to the peak flows of spring, and dam releases offer a variety of paddling throughout the summer on many rivers. By November, freeze up begins, and it is time to stash boats in favor of ice skates, snowshoes, and skis, just as the explorers of these north woods did hundreds of years ago.

The Ottawa in summer—a play boating Mecca

Ken Whiting

As we grow up, certain places and experiences have a profound influence on us, shaping our lives from that point onward. Often these seminal moments go unnoticed at the time, only to be seen for their true significance years later. For Ken Whiting, however, one gets the impression that even at fourteen years of age, he was fully aware of the direction his life was going to take.

That is the year Ken took his first kayak class on the Ottawa River. He knew nothing about whitewater previously, being almost fanatically wrapped up with more traditional sports like basketball and hockey. When a friend of Ken's returned from a commercial raft trip raving about the whitewater kayakers he saw, it wasn't hard to talk energetic Ken into taking lessons in the new sport.

The two signed up for a five-day course with the Ottawa's oldest outfitter, Wilderness Tours, and Whiting was hooked. The following summer, Ken got a job at the rafting company so he could paddle daily. He recalls, "I cleaned outhouses, washed dishes, and picked up cigarette butts for nine hours a day so I could paddle four hours at night."

With a few seasons under his belt, Whiting had developed into one of the best paddlers on the river, and in 1994 he started competing in freestyle competitions. He won a closely contested first place at Bob's Hole Rodeo in Oregon, edging out his paddling hero Mark Lyle, and solidifying his spot among the sport's elite.

When the 1997 world championships came along, Whiting had to bear the burden of being the favorite. After all, the event was held that year on Whiting's backyard Ottawa. He calmly fulfilled expectations, and came away as world champion. The women's champ that year was another Canadian by the name of Nicole Zaharko. Whiting and Zaharko have since married, and reside just minutes away from their championship river.

Though he continued to compete in freestyle for two more years, the Ottawa victory was Ken's crowning achievement in freestyle. He soon moved on to the art of instruction, and in 2000 Whiting started Liquid Skills, now one of Canada's leading kayak schools. He has also shared his expertise through his videos *Play Daze* and *Soar*, and two books, the *Playboater's Handbook*, and *The Ultimate Guide to Whitewater Kayaking*. Most of the photos and video clips in Whiting's productions were shot on the Ottawa, naturally. Ken and the Ottawa are about as linked as any paddler and river can be. He says, "I learned to paddle on the Ottawa, I grew up in the Ottawa Valley, I won my first competition on the Ottawa. The Ottawa River is home for me, and will always be so."

Ottawa River

The Ottawa River drains much of northern Ontario and Quebec—a vast rolling landscape of forested wilderness. These are the north woods, where a dense canopy of birch, spruce, and cedar remains frozen in the grip of winter for half the year. Hacked out of this northern forest are patchworks of rural settlement, where fields of corn and wheat surround grain silos bordered by country roads that lead to quaint red brick villages.

Hiding beneath this bucolic setting is the whitewater of the Ottawa River. Raft companies have been bringing tourists to the area since the mid-'70s, and the attention hasn't gone unnoticed. The official governmental title for the region is Whitewater Township.

The name is deserved, because the Ottawa is one of the biggest, friendliest rivers on the planet, containing an astounding amount of quality whitewater in just a few short river miles. Thanks to hundreds of miles of upstream slackwater, including nearly thirty different storage reservoirs, the water of the Ottawa is relatively warm, perfect for long play sessions at one of its famous bedrock features. Between the rapids are huge pools, some of which could genuinely be described as lakes. There are few rivers anywhere that offer such significant rapids with such insignificant consequences.

The pools of the Ottawa are so extensive that first timers can easily get lost between rapids without detailed directions. Even at the put-in above McKoy's Rapid, there is no discernible current, so finding the desired channel takes a little exploration.

McKoy's alone has several good waves and holes with eddy access, making it a world class park and play location. This was the site of the 1997 world freestyle championships, and it continues to host numerous other competitions. A handful of the world's best freestyle paddlers can usually be found honing their latest moves at McKoy's. Some of those top freestylers also happen to be locals. In the '90s it was Ken Whiting and Nicole Zaharko. Now Ottawa live-ins Tyler Curtis and Brendan Mark surf McKoy's regularly as they practice for the world stage. Along the eddy near McKoy's are several riverfront houses with play boats scattered in their yards. Now *this* is paddling country.

Below McKoy's, the Ottawa morphs back into lake mode, and some flatwater touring among islands is required to reach either of the river's primary channels, the Middle or the Main.

The Main Channel contains more of the flow, and is home to numerous five-star play spots, including one called Garberator (for you south-of-the-border types, garberator is Canadian for "garbage disposal"), the Ottawa's premier low water play spot. Coliseum, also on the Main Channel, is one of the most feared rapids on the river at high water, when it develops huge crashing waves and gi-normous raft flipping holes. This is one of the few places on the river with bad swim potential, as the ledges of Dog's Leg Rapid lie just downstream. Below Dog's Leg, the channels of the Ottawa are reunited as the Middle Channel comes in from the left.

The Middle Channel is often the favored route at higher water levels because of its great surfing. The Middle is also home to Garvin's Chutes, the hardest rapid on the Ottawa. There are several difficult lines here to satisfy the class V itch.

Besides the two primary channels, there is the Lost Channel—a rarely run center route that contains a class V waterfall—and the Magical Mystery Tour channel. There are also numerous sub-channels within the Middle and Main Channels, making enough options on this five-mile stretch of river to paddle here a week and experience a virtually new river every day.

Surprisingly, this varied and relatively accessible

section of world-class whitewater wasn't discovered by whitewater enthusiasts until 1974. This raucous piece of the Ottawa had remained in obscurity dating back to the days of the canoeing fur trappers, who would portage the entire cataract-laced horseshoe bend in their race to and from the fur markets. In more recent history, the river was treated as a dark secret by the locals, who feared the whitewater due to its propensity for drowning their unlucky relatives.

It wasn't until Olympian and Madawaska Kanu Centre founder Hermann Kerckhoff heard of rapids that were "too big for canoes" that the Ottawa got a second look. Hermann and his fourteen-year-old daughter Claudia, who happened to be the Canadian national slalom champion, were accustomed to exploring the rivers of Eastern Canada, but they had discarded the Ottawa as long since lost to development. Fortunately, development had yet to reach its crowning section.

The pair put in above the Rocher Fendu Dam, and began their trip with a run through a sluice in the dam itself, which has since been reconfigured. It was an exhilarating start. Then they hit the flatwater. To determine where the barely detectable current led, they had to climb to a promontory atop a mid-lake island for a better view. With no more than an educated guess, they followed what seemed to be a sluggish line of current to the southwest, and within minutes they found themselves riding the gathering stream of the Main Channel. Slicing down the big and bouncy whitewater, the two knew they had made one of the more significant whitewater discoveries of the modern era. Claudia remembers their pioneering run clearly. "We were in ecstasy," she says.

That first run was the start of a life-long relationship between the Ottawa and the Kerckhoff family. Their Madawaska Kanu Centre began taking students to the Ottawa within the year, and their Owl Rafting Company eventually purchased the land that now serves as the standard, free-of-charge put-in for the Ottawa.

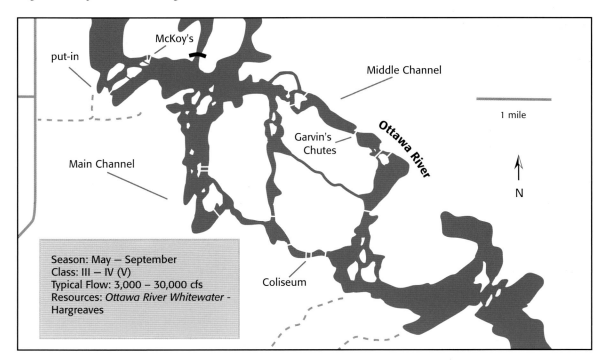

put-in

McKoy's

Middle Channel

1 mile

Garvin's
Chutes

Ottawa River

Main Channel

N

Season: May — September
Class: III — IV (V)
Typical Flow: 3,000 – 30,000 cfs
Resources: *Ottawa River Whitewater -*
Hargreaves

Coliseum

Jim Swedberg

Crystal Rapid—the grand finale to a Bottom Moose run

Jim Michaud

If you paddle frequently, you are bound to start recognizing familiar faces at the put-ins, and on the river, before long. Most of these fellow paddlers will vanish from the scene after a season or two. Some will hang around longer, becoming an integral part of the experience. A few, like Jim Michaud, will remain a fixture of the paddling arena, outlasting generations of paddlers. On the rivers of the Northeast, Michaud is an institution.

Like so many of his era, Michaud started paddling in a canoe, on a lake, with the Boy Scouts. The year was 1954. Time spent in the Air Force, and the traditional foundations of life in the 1950s, kept Michaud too busy for boating for the next decade. Having been a high school swimmer, he longed for a water sport, so in 1967 he bought a Grumman canoe. "I thought I was too lazy to paddle on lakes. I figured rivers would be easier," says Michaud.

Soon he was bombing down the rivers of New England, and discovering that "easier" is a decidedly relative term. While trying to rescue his badly pinned canoe one day, some fellows from the Appalachian Mountain Club came along and helped him extricate his boat. He joined their club, and it was a turning point, as Michaud explains: "They taught me how to paddle the *right* way."

After gaining exposure to the standard runs of New England, Michaud thirsted for more, so he built both a kayak, and a C-1, to use on harder rivers. After ten years in the C-1, he got back in his open canoe, and proceeded to paddle the most challenging rivers in the East. Michaud was among the early paddlers on Maine's Kennebec, and made first descents on both the North Branch of the Contoocook, and the Hubbard. In the early '80s, he made the first open boat descent of the Bottom Moose—one of his many favorites. Michaud has also taken his canoe down the Tareau in Quebec, North Carolina's Linville Gorge, the Narrows of the Green, and the Russell Fork, where he had his closest call during a pin on the left side of Fist Rapid.

Attempting a dry run of the infamous rapid in his open boat, he steered far to the left of the usual line, and bumped into a large, long boulder bordering the rapid. Michaud thought hitting the rock was "no big deal" until his 13-foot canoe went straight down, "as if being sucked by a giant vacuum cleaner," he says. Seconds later, he found himself in the pitch blackness of a large undercut. Fortunately, the current was slow enough to allow Michaud to claw his way along the underside of the rock until making it to daylight, and air. He says of the experience, "I didn't sleep very well the next few nights."

Once he retired from IBM in 1993, Michaud accelerated his paddling agenda even more. In his late sixties, Michaud still paddles hard. The summer of 2003 saw him on Idaho's Selway, the Grand Canyon (his 17th trip) and the lower five miles of the North Fork of the Payette. How's that for a relaxing retirement?

Moose River

New York's Adirondack Mountains are the heart of whitewater paddling in the Northeast. The plateau dominated range climbs to elevations over 5,000 feet, which wrings copious snowfall out of the moist winter airmass. By April, the region comes alive with running water falling off the uplift in all directions. There are more creeks and rivers here than one could run in a number of seasons. Of this multitude of paddling options, the Moose is the signature river.

The Moose is an especially good paddling destination because it contains two separate, yet equally attractive runs, the Lower and the Bottom.

The Lower Moose is home to several good class IV rapids, including the infamous Froth Hole, and Mixmaster. This section has been a regular stop for New York boaters since first being run in the '60s, and now it provides an avenue for commercial rafting as well. When water levels drop, the Lower run is robbed of much of its punch, and class V paddlers head downstream to the Bottom Moose.

The Bottom Moose is a series of big bedrock ledge drops separated by lengthy pools—classic playground whitewater. Fowlersville Falls is the first big slide—a fifty footer—located right at the put-in. Several technical rapids spice up the middle of the run before arriving at Surform, another long slide rapid. Besides the big slides, another classic aspect to the run is the fact that the most dramatic rapid—Crystal—comes just before the take-out, leaving Bottom Moose paddlers on high at the finish. Of course, the river is set in great New England scenery, too. However, one might not recognize the river's beauty until actually making the run, because most access points are dominated by hydro development.

The river is laced with dams and diversions that have forced boaters into political action. The Moose's gradient has been used for many years to power paper mills for local logging interests, but it was the hydro development craze of the early '80s that spurred a landmark battle for paddling interests. Pete Skinner and Chris Koll were the two most instrumental negotiators in guaranteeing the future of whitewater paddling on the Moose.

The main issue is a water diversion above Agers Falls, which is about halfway through the Bottom section. Due primarily to the efforts of Skinner, this diversion is now curtailed for twenty days a year, leaving ample water in the river to paddle the remainder of the run.

Skinner, who battled to maintain both aesthetics and water rights within the bounds of the inevitable development, says he "lost a big chunk of hide in my fight." Koll credits Skinner as "the hero for getting releases," but it was Koll himself who has organized and scheduled release dates, popularized the Bottom Moose, and essentially made paddlers a recognized constituency with a respected voice there.

Paddling on the Bottom Moose has come a long way from its beginnings in the late '70s. Before that, paddlers unquestionably took out at the Fowlersville bridge, happy to have survived the respectable Lower run. That all changed one day when Karl Lundgren's group of three paddlers were essentially shamed into running Fowlersville Falls after witnessing several local kids slide over the drop in nothing but their blue jeans, just for fun.

The next weekend, Lundgren and his crew returned, and started picking off the rapids of the Bottom Moose one by one. They took along a weighted probing pole to test for rocks at the base of the drops. Upon finding the landing zones clean, they would return to their fiberglass boats above, and prepare to huck. Surform and Crystal were the two portaged rapids initially, but Pete Skinner soon joined the probing crew, and proceeded to show that those two dramatic rapids were runnable, too.

Skinner was also the first to run Magilla—the often portaged take-out rapid at the Lyons Falls Dam. This first run was no act of calculated daring, however. After hastily launching following a scout, he missed his planned sneak route, and fell into the narrow turbulent slot that forms the meat of the rapid. Skinner emerged unscathed, but his run wasn't exactly smooth enough to encourage others to follow. It would be more than a decade before the Kern brothers began regularly cleaning the line, making it more than a rarely attempted stunt.

Although Magilla (so named because it is similar to the Green River's Gorilla) is still often avoided, the remainder of the Moose has become a destination for whitewater paddlers across the East. In mid-October, as the last of the Adirondack's autumn colors cling to the trees, Northeastern paddlers congregate for one last weekend of whitewater fun during the annual Moose fest. It is the perfect time of year to put an exclamation point on the paddling season, and there is hardly a more perfect place to do it.

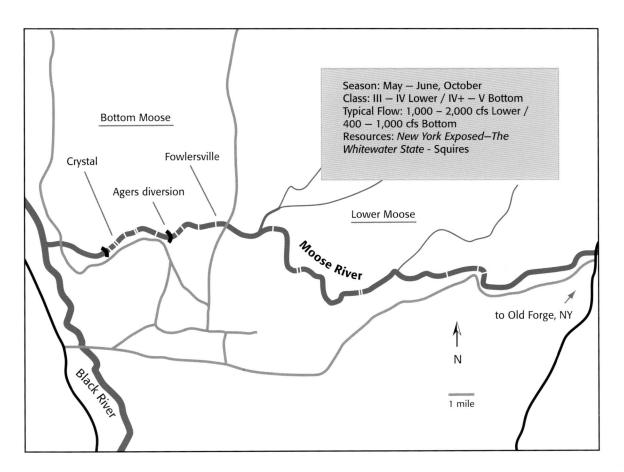

Bottom Moose

Crystal

Fowlersville

Agers diversion

Lower Moose

Moose River

Black River

to Old Forge, NY

N

1 mile

Season: May — June, October
Class: III — IV Lower / IV+ — V Bottom
Typical Flow: 1,000 – 2,000 cfs Lower /
400 – 1,000 cfs Bottom
Resources: *New York Exposed—The Whitewater State* - Squires

A classic northern river—the Kennebec

Eric Jackson

Eric Jackson is considered by many to be the best kayaker in the world. No one has excelled at as many different aspects of the sport as Jackson has. Slalom, freestyle, river running, instruction, EJ has not only done them all, he has done them all on a world class level.

Ironically, when EJ began kayaking, prevailing conservative attitudes within the sport nearly prevented him from starting at all. When Eric and his father Jim showed up at New Hampshire's Sowhegan River ready to join the regional paddling club, they were swiftly rejected with a flat "no." The eager father-son team stuck around, however, and when the next group of club paddlers (the Merrimac Valley Paddlers) came along, they were in. Within a month, Eric's father was the club president, lobbying other members to allow his fifteen-year-old son to join them on the mighty Kennebec. The Jacksons prevailed, and Eric made the most of his opportunity. He paddled so hard for four days straight that he severely pulled muscles in his back and was out of commission for months.

This kind of tenacious, competitive approach to athletics earned EJ a New Hampshire high school championship in swimming, a sport he continued to compete in after moving on to the University of Maine. Then a shift in priorities occurred. He gave up competitive swimming to focus on school, and, of course, kayaking.

He made his first United States slalom team in 1989, and a year later he was K-1 national champion. At the '92 Olympics in Spain, Jackson was the United States' top finisher in the event. EJ spent ten years on the U.S. slalom team before shifting his focus to broader venues of kayaking in 1998. His slalom days might not be completely over, however. With rule changes now allowing shorter boats to compete, Jackson plans to make a return to the racing world.

Even while maintaining top form in slalom, EJ began a career in the realm of freestyle. His first world title in freestyle came in 1993, after Jackson first learned of the event just months before it was to take place. He has qualified for the U.S. team every year since, making him the most consistent performer the sport has ever known. EJ finished second in the world in '97. In 1998 and '99, he won nearly every event he entered, and won the world title again in 2001, eight years after his first.

His freestyle and slalom training has taken Jackson to rivers around the world. EJ has paddled on every continent (except frozen Antarctica, of course), saying, "It's a focus of mine to run a new river when I can." Since EJ and family—wife Kristine, son Dane, and daughter Emily—moved into an RV full time in 1997 in order to follow the paddling seasons, Eric has paddled an average of thirty new rivers a year. His lifetime river total stands at an astounding 500-plus, a tally that will likely remain unequaled.

Jackson's breadth of paddling experience has helped him create several Wave Sport boat designs and produce a *Kayaking with Eric Jackson* series of books and videos. Next on the horizon is his own line of kayaks, not at all surprising for the man who is recognized around the world by two simple letters: EJ.

Kennebec River

The Kennebec and Lochsa Rivers are on different sides of the continent, but upon first impression, they are one and the same. Okay, there might be some over-looked technicalities here: the Lochsa is free flowing next to a highway, while the Kennebec is dam-controlled in a secluded canyon, but the feel of the two rivers is still strikingly similar. Both display a beautiful dark green hue, with water clear enough to make an inviting scuba dive. Enchanting cedar trees dangle out over the Lochsa and Kennebec Rivers, and continuous, powerful water is the trademark characteristic of both.

These kindred rivers shape the landscape of their equally remote regions as well. Like northern Idaho, northern Maine is a sparsely populated area of vast forest tracts. Logging is naturally the leading industry here. Sizable mountains wear dark crowns of conifers that perch above the hardwood forests below. The highest peaks in the area even nudge above the treeline, a rarity for most of the Appalachian Chain.

These northernmost ranges of the Appalachians gather the Kennebec's headwaters into Maine's biggest lake, Moosehead Lake. At its outlet, the Kennebec runs free for just a few scenic miles before being impounded at Indian Pond. It is at the outlet of Indian Pond where the Kennebec's best whitewater is found, as it races through a four-mile canyon.

The put-in for the gorge is located on dam property just below the base of the power generating station. To get there, boaters must pass through a gated security zone and even sign a liability waiver at the entrance checkpoint. It is an incongruous scene found here in the uninhabited wilds of Maine. The arrangement works, however, as commercial rafters and private boaters alike timely gather for the peak water releases in the canyon.

A typical release is 4,800 cfs, lasting only a few hours. Flows of about half that often surround the peak release, so lingering paddlers usually won't be left totally high and dry. Occasionally a flow of over 8,000 cfs is given. This is the level class IV and better paddlers seek, so they can run the normally class III river with some added punch.

The rapids start out quickly, with continuous and erratic class II and III wave trains leading around blind corners in the gorge. There are a couple good play spots with eddy access, but due to the river's continuous nature, several of the best waves are one-shot deals.

Magic Falls is the big rapid of the run. A large hole or two in this rapid will make class III paddlers want to scout, but more experienced boaters will be disappointed at the class III rapid with the class V reputation.

It is not far below Magic when the Carry Brook take-out stairs appear on river left. If you've come just for the river's whitewater, this is the best take-out. Downstream the riverbed widens, and the whitewater mellows for the next several miles down to the highway. If you've come to the Kennebec strictly for the whitewater, however, you're missing the point. The rapids are average, but the place is fabulous. A two-day trip could be an excellent option in the beautiful Kennebec Canyon. For the full backcountry Kennebec experience, one might start on Moosehead Lake, run the upper river, and paddle across Indian Pond before portaging the dam and continuing through the gorge.

This is precisely the route chosen for log booms before 1976, when the last log drive in the lower forty-eight states occurred on the Kennebec. The trees were traditionally logged in winter, cut into four-foot pulp wood lengths, and gathered on the frozen lakes of the Kennebec drainage. Come spring, the giant rafts of logs were sluiced down the spillway of the dam, and floated through the gorge to Skowhegen, Maine, where pulp was made for paper production.

After 1976, when the logs no longer occupied the Kennebec Canyon, paddlers and commercial outfitters began to run the river. The early raft trips featured flannel-clad north woods guides operating huge sweep oars on the backs of the paddle rafts. This crude steering technique had limited success in the gorge, especially at a rapid called Three Sisters. This rapid, which was altered by a flood in the late '80s, once held three consecutive breaking waves, the third of which often produced flips of even 20-foot rafts. The regular raft flips helped build a fierce reputation for the Kennebec. This reputation was no doubt reinforced by the river's big, continuous water, and distant locale. Most rivers of the Appalachian Mountains don't fit this profile. The Kennebec has a distinctly different feel to it. It is a unique waterway, one that fits in with its surroundings perfectly.

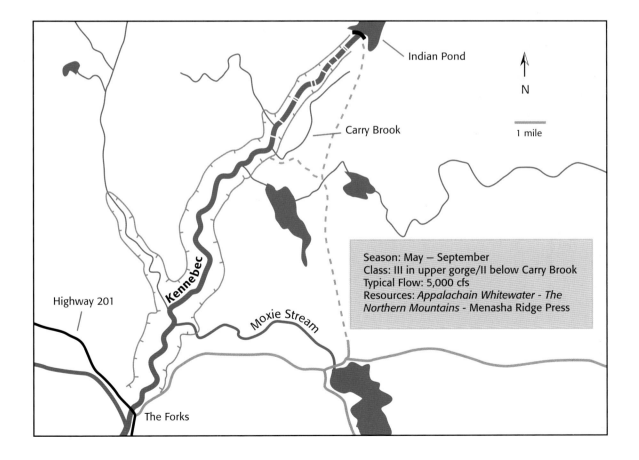

Indian Pond

Carry Brook

N

1 mile

Highway 201

Kennebec

Moxie Stream

Season: May — September
Class: III in upper gorge/II below Carry Brook
Typical Flow: 5,000 cfs
Resources: *Appalachain Whitewater - The Northern Mountains* - Menasha Ridge Press

The Forks

TJ Walker

Corran makes a pillow move on the Riviere du Nords

Corran Addison

Corran Addison would have probably been an innovative, colorful, and controversial figure in whatever field he chose to pursue. He is an original thinker who scoffs at the status quo, and thrives on the fringe of the whitewater world. However unconventional he might be, his dynamic paddling style and revolutionary designs have undeniably changed the sport of whitewater.

The South African born Addison first went on paddling trips at age eight with his father Graeme—"the Godfather of South African kayaking" as Corran describes him. Their equipment was entirely homemade, requiring Corran to be a designer before he could be a paddler. He recalls, "We'd go out and make a boat, paddle it until it was dead, and then start over and improve it for the next one." The extended kayaking trips with his father turned Corran into a paddling prodigy. At just thirteen years of age, he became the first to run a 35-foot waterfall on South Africa's Brandewyne River.

When his conscription papers came summoning him to the army at age sixteen, Corran left politically troubled South Africa for Belgium to live with his mother. Shortly thereafter, he dropped out of the prestigious private high school he was attending. The always self-assured Addison recalls, "High school seemed like something for people that were going to work for other people."

Within a year he showed up at the doorstep of Perception Kayaks in the United States with his girlfriend, backpack, and boat—a design of his called the Aqua Bat. Perception president Bill Masters was impressed enough with the plucky teenager and his

boat that he offered Addison a design job. Addison's avante-garde ideas did not fit with the mainstream company, however, and his apprenticeship with Perception ended after two years.

In 1994, Addison gained funding for his own kayak manufacturing company, called Savage Designs. With Savage, he produced several radical new models including the Gravity, the first planing hull whitewater kayak, and the Fury, another planing hull boat which forever changed the direction of play boat designs.

In 1996, Corran teamed with business partner Jeff Rivest to start Riot Kayaks. Now free to follow his visionary concepts, Addison has continued to produce novel new kayaks. Riot's Big Gun was the first whitewater kayak with a hatch, an idea Addison tried a decade earlier with Perception to no avail. "They thought I was mad," he recalls.

His innovative designs would likely not have ever been recognized if not for Addison's phenomenal paddling skill. He has raced slalom in the Olympics, run a 75-foot waterfall, (in a bat man costume, no less), and consistently remained a world class freestyle paddler. Always the inventor, Addison is credited with originating freestyle moves such as the Blunt, Ollie Oop, and Pan Am. Many of his freestyle creations were developed on the Lachine Rapids near his Montreal home.

When it was suggested to Corran that he might nominate the well-known Lachine as his classic pick for this book, he responded with absolute Corran nonconformity, "Why publish more on Lachine?" he said, "I'd rather give you a hidden gem." The North is definitely that.

Riviere du Nords

Speeding north from the bustling city of Montreal, one quickly enters a charming countryside of small French-speaking villages tucked among hillsides laced with ski runs. This is the watershed of the North River, or as they say locally, the Riviere du Nords.

The area has a distinctly European feel that is reflected in the paddlers of the region. Paddling has a long history here, where style and the subtleties of the sport are fully appreciated. As one Quebec paddler said, "It's not the size of the rapid, but the way you run it."

They have been running rivers here since the Voyageurs of the fur trade became some of the first professional paddlers in the world two centuries ago. Their trade route began at the Lachine Rapids on the St. Lawrence River, and traveled upstream to the beaver-rich wilderness of the Canadian Rockies—a journey of over 3,000 miles spanning the bulk of the continent. The first leg of their voyage, from Montreal to the western shores of Lake Superior, was completed in huge freight hauling 12-man canoes. These cargo boats were so unstable, the salty Voyageurs used to quip that "one must keep his tongue in the center of his mouth, lest the boat might tip." At Grand Portage on Lake Superior, commerce was switched to smaller six-man canoes for the remainder of the journey upstream. Following a rugged winter in the mountains, the trappers would ride the spring flush of water back across the Great Plains, returning with their loads of furs. At Lake Superior, the precious goods were transferred to the large canoes, which again plied the mostly flat waters back to Montreal.

Just as boat size dictated the navigability of waters two centuries ago, so too have rivers like the North become more runnable today with the evolution of shorter boats. Although now a classic, the North was once not even considered a worthwhile run. Following

the first descent, Francois Letourneau discussed the run with his companions at the take-out. He remembers the group concluding that, "It wasn't worth it. We won't be back."

Their assessment is understandable given the circumstances in which they ran the river. The water was too low, and their boats were too long. Letourneau paddled a British design known as an R-7 (similar to a Dancer), and the river was at a typically low June water level.

Letourneau had run the easier, lower section of the river previously, and had spied the more sporty upper section from the bike path that winds above the river. His group completed the run with only a few portages, but one of these was a thirty-minute odyssey through the woods that led them to a launch point unnecessarily far downstream. Now that the proper trail has been established, this same portage takes five-minutes.

The drop that necessitates this portage is accurately referred to as Scary Rapid. Addison is the only one to have willingly run this one, and he's not planning on trying it again any time soon. Other than Scary Rapid, the North contains only one more drop that is usually portaged. In keeping with the elementary nomenclature, this one is called Cool Rapid.

Despite these two portages, and a handful of undercuts, Addison maintains that much of the run is class IV. At normal levels, that is. According to local TJ Walker, Addison has run it "when it looks like the Zambezi." An indication of the river level might have come at the put-in, where residents of the local neighborhood were rowing boats across the street to get to their cars. A typical flow on the North is about 15 cumecs, or 500 cfs. The river on Addison's high water run was a flood of 250 cumecs, or 8,800 cfs. For a run on this kind of flow, you'd better "attach your toque," as they say in Quebec.

The North definitely has Corran's respect, though. He took his first swim in 16 years here. Fully aware of the river's hazards, Addison bailed quickly and made decisive swimming strokes for shore after backendering onto a rock and knocking himself loopy directly above a known sieve.

The undercuts of the North are naturally covered during springtime high water, but locals generally prefer to run the North in the Fall, with more moderate rain-induced flows. During the spring, a multitude of paddling options exist in the area, whereas autumn rain storms often provide the North with good water when other streams remain too low. Regardless of the time of year or water level, a run on the North is guaranteed to provide classic Canadian creeking.

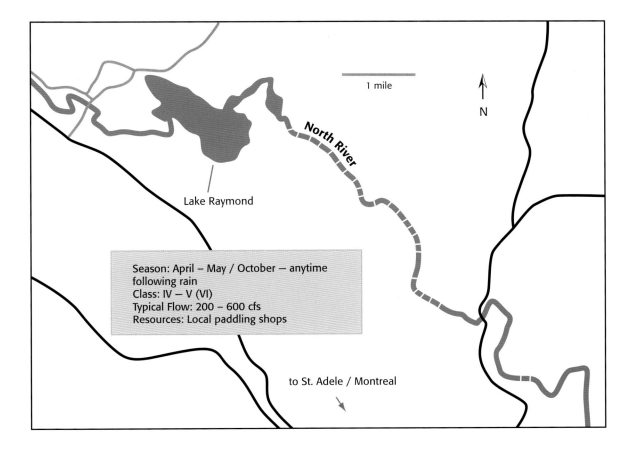

1 mile

N

North River

Lake Raymond

Season: April – May / October – anytime
following rain
Class: IV – V (VI)
Typical Flow: 200 – 600 cfs
Resources: Local paddling shops

to St. Adele / Montreal

The giant Niagara as it enters the gorge

Chris Spelius

If Hollywood ever decided to create a kayaker with star appeal, the result would probably be a lot like Chris Spelius. Tall, blond, and charismatic, "Spe" as he is widely known, was always destined to carve a remarkable niche in the world of paddling.

To start with, Spe was born with the water gene. His mom was once the Montana state swimming champion in backstroke and freestyle—the same events Chris competed in later at the University of Utah. Training for this began as a kid, when the Spelius family spent summers on northern Michigan's Isle Royale. Chris and his siblings would compete to see who could swim the farthest out into frigid Lake Superior, and return. Adventure games like this weren't abnormal for the Spelius clan.

When Spe was seven years old, his family took a 3,400-mile river trip in a 19-foot fiberglass boat that followed much of Lewis and Clark's route. Starting from Ft. Benton, Montana, they traveled down the Missouri and Mississippi Rivers to the confluence with the Ohio, then motored upstream back to their home in Cincinnati. En route, they had to run a narrow channel in bypassing the nearly completed Oahe dam. The boat momentarily went out of control in the fast currents, and spun two 360s. Most of the occupants breathed a sigh of relief once beyond the turbulence. Chris laughed with glee.

When Spe started kayaking during college, he approached it with a competitive drive, mastering a no-hands roll before setting out on the river. His strategy must have been sound, because his first season found him paddling Utah's Westwater Canyon at 30,000

cfs. This experience, combined with guiding on the Colorado River's Cataract Canyon at high water, prepared Spelius for his landmark run on the Niagara Gorge.

This descent vaulted Spelius into the spotlight, and paved the way for a career in kayaking. He taught at Nantahala Outdoor Center and Otter Bar, the leading instructional centers in the nation at the time. He refined long standing techniques, and has been credited with naming the C to C roll.

Spelius' competitiveness surfaced again in 1984, when he took a break from whitewater to make the U.S. flatwater sprint kayak team. In the late '80s and early '90s, Spelius was a major figure in whitewater rodeo just as freestyle began its explosion. Besides helping design boats for Dagger at the time, his rodeo wins in the Dagger Crossfire played a big role in popularizing that noted design.

By this time, Spelius had discovered a southern paradise in Chile, and began to develop his business there. Spe now spends much of his time running Expediciones Chile, and keeping the dam builders away from his spectacular and beloved Futaleufu. The mountainous backdrop behind his southern home is picture perfect, something even Hollywood couldn't create.

Niagara Gorge

Three of the world's five largest lakes are contained within North America's Great Lakes system. The Niagara River connects the two lowest lakes of that system—Erie and Ontario. Obviously, the scale of the river is awesome, and any whitewater boater passing through the area should stop and at least look at Niagara Falls. After discussing the hypothetical scenarios of a run with your friends, head to the gorge downstream, and you'll be amazed at how mellow class V can look when compared to the granddaddy of all drops.

The Niagara River through the gorge is full of straightforward but overwhelmingly huge water. The crux of the run is quite short, followed by an easier lower section that hosts tourist-toting jet boats. This massive but eminently runnable piece of whitewater on the outskirts of Buffalo has seen only a handful of descents due to its illegality.

The off-limits policy is likely due in part to the fact that just upstream lies the tourism Mecca of Niagara Falls itself. The history of going over the world famous falls is an interesting case study on public and government interaction with thrill seekers of all kinds.

The first to successfully plunge over the 167-foot drop of Niagara was an elderly school teacher. She took the best craft possible for the 1902 descent—a padded barrel. Upon exiting her barrel below the falls, she admonished like a true school marm, "No one ever ought do that again." That was all it took. Within the century there would be fifteen runs of Niagara Falls, five of which resulted in fatalities.

The occasional misfit going over the famous waterfall was looked on with macabre fascination in the early part of the 20th century. In the 1930s, "Red" Hill was dubbed the "hero of Niagara" after running the rapids of the gorge on three occasions. A generation later, times had changed. Red's son Major Hill was stopped by police on three attempts to run the falls and/or gorge. By the '80s, the authorities became brazen enough to quickly change the water level in the river in order to snare would-be barrel riders.

In 1977, when Chris Spelius and his companion Ken Lagergren came to run the Niagara Gorge, it was most definitely illegal. A commercial rafting venture there had ended in tragedy with four drownings after a flip the previous year. The story made headlines as far away as Salt Lake City, where Spelius read about the incident, and hatched his plan to paddle the infamous gorge.

His drive to run the "deadly rapids" was fueled by what he now calls an "infantile machoism." He reflects, "We wanted to be the best kayakers that ever existed." With his previous big water runs on the New at 65,000 cfs, and the Colorado River's Cataract Canyon at 70,000 cfs, Spelius figured he was ready for the mountainous whitewater of Niagara, and he was right.

After a nerve-wracking visit to the Daredevil Museum near the falls (in which Lagergren's kayak now hangs), the two stealthily unloaded their boats into the woods near the river. Once on the water, the trivialities of the government's rules melted away, brilliant October light filled the canyon, and the paddlers shared a few pure moments of riverine splendor as they drifted toward the rapids. Back in the rat race on the canyon rim, the alarm had already been sounded, of course, and the pursuit of the kayakers had begun.

Spe and Lagergren were vaguely aware of the commotion above, but their full attention was demanded by the whitewater they entered. Giant flopping diagonals surged and broke from both sides. Lagergren was tossed in a spontaneous aerial cartwheel, and the phenomenal currents prevented him from rolling back upright. Spelius saw his companion swimming, but was unable to offer any help as he himself was dealing with the powerful water. When a slight break in the action finally came, the two made it to shore on river left. They were past the bulk of the rapids with everything still intact.

The police, having lost track of the duo beneath the shelter of the canyon rim, assumed they had drowned. After a quick breather, Spe and Lagergren re-emerged into the mid-stream current, and the chase was on once again.

Passing the last rapid, they stashed their kayaks in the forest, and hiked out of the gorge. Upon reaching the rim, they immediately ran into one of the five police units that were now in pursuit of the dangerous criminals. Lagergren was apprehended while Spe ducked back into the cover of the forested gorge. He recalls, "it was just like playing the moose and wolf game as a kid." The only problem was Spelius was the

moose, and at six feet four inches, he was about as invisible as a moose too. Nevertheless, he climbed out of the canyon at a new location, and tried to blend with the throngs of tourists on the rim. He managed to remain undetected for a time, but when Spelius' trip photographer came by and hurriedly ushered him into the getaway car, a good citizen squealed to the authorities about the suspicious activity. Spe was smartly dropped off at a nearby restaurant, and watched as police cruisers slowly prowled by outside. "It was like being in a movie," he recalls. His accomplice photographer returned to the scene of Lagergren's bust, and was promptly arrested herself. As for Spe? The caption under Lagergren's museum-bound boat says it all: "Kenneth Lagergren was the first to kayak the rapids in 1977, with a friend known only as Charles. Lagergren was arrested afterwards while Charles escaped."

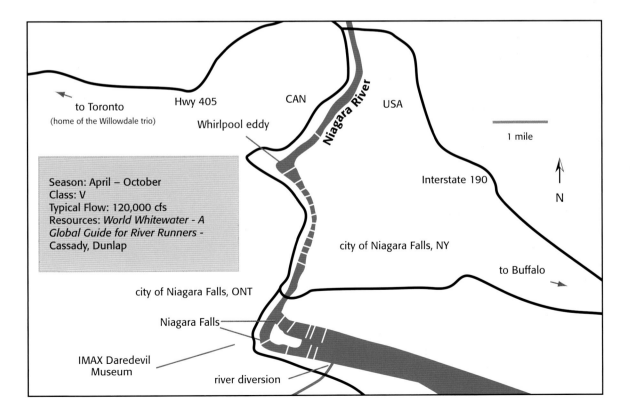

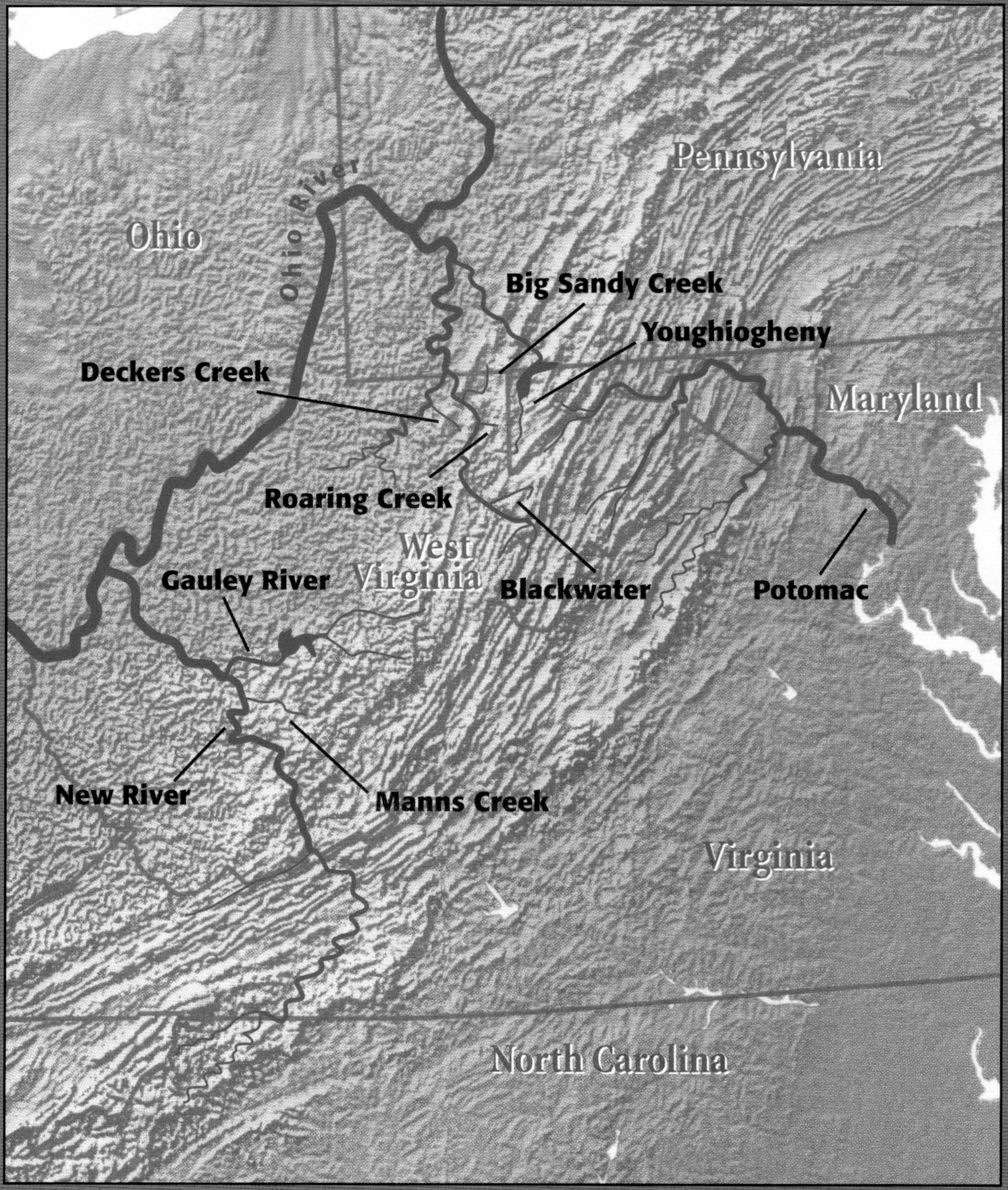

Ohio

Ohio River

Pennsylvania

Maryland

West Virginia

Virginia

North Carolina

Big Sandy Creek

Youghiogheny

Deckers Creek

Roaring Creek

Blackwater

Potomac

Gauley River

New River

Manns Creek

Greater West Virginia

"And beyond the town were the fields, the zigzag rail fences, the old gray barns and gaunt Gothic farmhouses, the webwork of winding roads, the sulfurous creeks and the black coal mines and—scattered everywhere—the woods."

Edward Abbey

This is the heart of Appalachia, where hazy blue ridgelines stack upon one another in a mysterious endless horizon. Hardwood forests of oak, maple, sourwood, and beech cover the hilltops, and dark lush grottoes of hemlock and rhododendron fill the draws. Concealed in this miasma of green mountains are innumerable springs feeding tiny creeks feeding winding rivers. If any one place in North America could claim to be the cradle of whitewater on the continent, the greater West Virginia region would be it.

The rivers here are primarily fed by the copious and evenly distributed rainfall throughout the year. Only the highest mountains (3,000–4,500 feet) hold snowpacks throughout the winter. Precipitation averages 35 to 45 inches annually in the valleys, while upwards of 50 inches is the yearly norm at higher elevations. Snowmelt from the higher ridges combined with rainfall on the leafless deciduous forest makes late winter and early spring the best time to catch high water here. A good rain can bring the rivers up anytime of the year, however, and summer offers luxuriously warm water.

Ancient sandstone slabs commonly fill the riverbeds of central Appalachia, creating well-formed hydraulics, but also prevalent undercuts. Find a local to lead you down the steep stuff here. They should be able to alert you to the known hazard spots both on the river and off. Some of the most interesting experiences for a visiting paddler to this region occur in the backwoods communities while driving shuttle. This, after all, is Appalachia.

Dave Shannon

Wonder Falls on Big Sandy

Charlie Walbridge

Whitewater boating is a dangerous sport. Every year, paddlers of all types and abilities lose their lives while running rivers. Unfortunately, the water-rock-boat-person formula is statistically bound to produce a certain number of drownings each season, but this is not a fixed equation. As decision-making paddlers, we are the X factor, and it is our job to minimize the death toll. Fortunately, progress has been made. Safer boat designs, better safety equipment, and increased rescue skills have allowed more boaters to safely run more rivers than ever before. These improvements have no doubt emerged through the exchange of information regarding river accidents. For the past thirty years, the man in charge of disseminating that information has been Charlie Walbridge.

Walbridge ran his first river at age 14 in an open canoe at summer camp. It was a humble beginning for the future chairman of whitewater safety. Paddling without even a life jacket, he nearly broached on a rock, and decided paddling wasn't for him. By the time he was a freshman at Bucknell University in 1966, Walbridge again found himself paddling an aluminum canoe down the nearby creek. This time the experience was a bit more positive for Walbridge, and despite pinning the canoe and soaking all his overnight gear, he came away from the trip thinking, "This is great. You get to see all this great country, and you don't have to carry a pack." Soon he was scanning the road maps for little blue lines, and exploring rural Pennsylvania in his canoe. He eventually chose to paddle a C-1, and still paddles a '70s fiberglass Hahn design today.

By the early '70s, the always-involved Walbridge began judging slalom events. It was at one of these races—a regional competition on Ooleout Creek in New York—when Walbridge witnessed the horror of foot entrapment for the first time. Despite a multitude of experienced paddlers at the scene, the class II rapid was enough to fatally entrap an unfortunate paddler. The tragic event spurred Walbridge to action.

He soon took over the responsibility of safety chair for American Whitewater, chronicling river accidents throughout North America, and investigating new approaches to manageable risks. He also designed a new lifejacket with better buoyancy—the appropriately named Hi-float. The style is still popular with big water river runners today. His contributions to the sport aren't limited to safety measures, however. In 1973, Walbridge authored the *Boatbuilder's Manual*. This book is still considered "the bible" for fiberglass whitewater boat construction.

When reflecting on river safety, Walbridge reminds us: "The main thing is to stay out of trouble." This is something he has been doing for over three decades of avid paddling. Charlie has paddled throughout the United States, and in Canada, but West Virginia has always been his paddling destination of choice. Since giving up his paddle sports retail business—Wildwater Designs—in the Philadelphia area, he has moved to the hill country that has always captured his heart. He and his wife Sandy now live on a breezy green knoll overlooking the Big Sandy watershed—fittingly symbolic for a man who has overseen the development of whitewater paddling ever since the days of summer campers in aluminum canoes.

Big Sandy Creek

The Big Sandy is in many ways the classic Appalachian creek. Sandstone ledge rapids, dense hardwood forests, and warm rainwater are defining characteristics of the region, and Big Sandy showcases them all. The Big Sandy drainage basin even links two of the eastern United States' most popular whitewater rivers, Maryland's Youghiogheny and West Virginia's Cheat. This is a land of big red barns, quaint white churches, grassy lots of rusting automobiles, and old men in camouflage baseball caps—Appalachia at its finest.

Big Sandy Creek gathers in this scenic rolling hill country, and emerges from the woods at Bruceton Mills, West Virginia, where Interstate 68 crosses the stream. Here it makes a progressively steeper plunge through a relatively untrammeled canyon to its destination with the Cheat River.

The Cheat is a classic river in its own right, home to legendary rapids such as Big Nasty and Coliseum, as well as numerous top-notch play spots. But the Cheat River basin has suffered its wounds. Coal mining near tributary streams has polluted the river, turning it a nasty orange color during unfavorable periods of runoff. Thankfully, the Cheat is recovering today, as mine reclamation efforts have started to clean up the basin. In 1967 however, the Cheat often cast an image of pollution too much to endure for river runners. It was this "stale apricot acid hue," says Jim Stuart, that prompted him, Norton Smith, and Chris Thomson to look for an alternate run in the area. Big Sandy Creek's first kayak descent was the result.

The trio were on a "right of passage trip," as Stuart recalls, following their graduation from high school that spring. The confident young bucks' paddling quest led them to the New, the Upper Yough, and so they thought, the Cheat. Upon seeing the clear stream of Big Sandy Creek enter the polluted Cheat however, the trio hatched a new plan.

The only information they had about the Big Sandy came from a large scale topographical map printed in 1902 that lacked detail, and a hiker's report that the creek contained "a big waterfall." What could be more enticing to a threesome of teenage whitewater paddlers? After a quick check to see if the water level was adequate, the enthusiastic threesome went on a search for a put-in.

They headed up the "ancient and mostly unused road" as Stuart says, that led out of the Cheat River Canyon to the east. Once on top, the maze of Appalachian back roads required diligent navigation as the trio searched for an abandoned mountain outpost called Rockville, which they hoped would serve as the put-in. In the end, they had to "go off through some fields to find it" Stuart remembers. When they finally reached the creek, it was like finding Shangri-La. A beautifully clear stream ran through a corridor of fragrant blossoming rhododendron, and there was just enough water to paddle on.

The trip began uneventfully enough. The group cautiously portaged around spectacular Wonder Falls, and marveled at the pristine scenery. Their pleasant afternoon adventure rapidly turned into high drama however, when Stuart nonchalantly dropped into a hole that "didn't *look* too hairy."

Stuart began an unexpected surf, and found that he was being fed toward an undercut rock that swallowed the left side of the hole. He tried to push away from the shallow cave, first with his paddle, then with one hand, then with both hands. He fought the current for a moment, but then the dominance of the river was decisively established as he flushed under the boulder. He reflects on the moment in a reserved tone, saying, "I wasn't pleased with the situation."

Youth was certainly on his side as he endured several blows to his helmet before emerging on the downstream side of the rock. When he noticed sunlight once again illuminating the water, he rolled up thinking the ordeal was over, but then he immediately pinned at the lip of a chute.

Meanwhile, Thomson had fallen into the same trap. Stuart, while trying to extricate himself, noticed his partner's inverted blue kayak hull squeezing out from beneath the undercut that they would later name "The Esophagus." Stuart saw Thomson was still in his boat, and probably in deep trouble, so he lunged for Thomson's hull as it drifted near, and tried to flip his partner upright. Just as Stuart nearly had the boat flipped up, Thomson unexpectedly thrust back under the water.

Thomson, you see, had learned to paddle in Roger Paris' school in Colorado, where he was trained to keep his eyes closed while underwater in order to protect them from silt. Because of this, Thomson failed to realize when he was beyond the undercut. Worse yet, he thought Stuart's attempt at righting was a sieve grabbing his boat, so he reached for the bottom of the river to pull himself free.

On Stuart's second try, he got Thomson upright, and Chris finally opened his eyes. The tug of Thomson's boat had pulled Stuart from his pin also, and the two washed over the chute backwards and paddleless to the pool below.

Following this close call, all three unquestionably portaged a falls they named Big Splat, and safely made it to the take-out at the Cheat River confluence.

Big Splat is Big Sandy's signature class V rapid, featuring a complex lead-in to a vertical 12-foot drop with a dangerous block at its base. Below Big Splat, the river weaves through large chunks of sandstone and past a gorgeous waterfall as it courses through the forested canyon. The whitewater remains good nearly all the way to the take-out. It requires one's full attention at times, but the river also offers enough respite to look around and soak up the scenery of this most classic Appalachian creek.

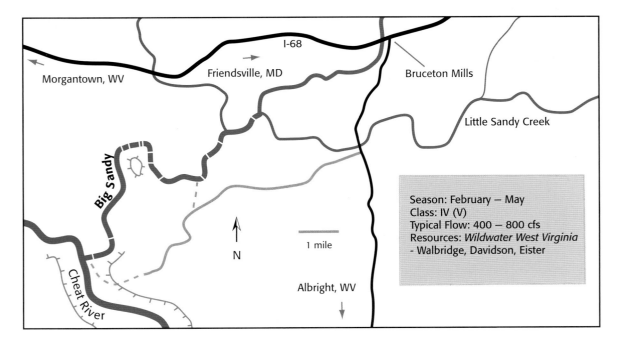

Morgantown, WV • Friendsville, MD • I-68 • Bruceton Mills • Little Sandy Creek • Big Sandy • Cheat River • N • 1 mile • Albright, WV

Season: February — May
Class: IV (V)
Typical Flow: 400 — 800 cfs
Resources: *Wildwater West Virginia* - Walbridge, Davidson, Eister

A moody day on the Upper Yough

Jesse Whittemore

Although the boats that most people paddle have transformed in the past two decades, Jesse Whittemore still uses a full length fiberglass kayak. Thank goodness he does, because seeing Jesse Whittemore paddle one of his sleek, fast boats down the river is more like watching a graceful dance on water than simply watching a kayaker.

He weaves back and forth, slicing across currents, and darting through slots with a speed and precision that is unattainable with today's short plastic boats. Whittemore's style of paddling is a lost art. Ironically, it is this unique paddling style that was the seed for freestyle boating as we now know it.

Whittemore's introduction to whitewater came through an explorer post (sort of a teenager's Boy Scouts) in the Baltimore area. As a requirement, explorers had to make their own boats and sprayskirts. Whittemore recalls, "We were always gluing neoprene on the way to the put-in." The boat building triggered a creative side in Whittemore that would blossom in future years with the first squirt boat.

He built the revolutionary Millennium Falcon in 1982. Based on contemporary slalom designs, the Falcon had less volume in the hull, which aided the sub-surface moves that Whittemore had recently developed. His patented stern squirt was the basis for nearly all play boating to follow. Jim and Jeff Snyder joined Whittemore regularly for experimental freestyle runs on West Virginia's Cheat River throughout the winter of '82. Jim Snyder reflects on the evolutionary period, "Before long, it seemed we were going boating to watch Jesse. We knew that we had to get into the act before we fossilized."

Besides the Snyders, Jesse also paddled with C-1 racer Jon Lugbill, who had simultaneously but separately mastered the stern squirt for the purposes of faster race times. The two exchanged ideas, and challenged one another to attempt new and creative ways of paddling. Their friendly competitions inspired Whittemore to perform the first rock splat—still a staple of every playboater's tool kit.

The Lugbill connection led Whittemore to Europe in 1985 as the United States slalom team boat repairman. He was the natural choice for the job, having designed and built several of the most sought-after race boats through his business Whittemore Laminates.

Today Jesse feeds his artistic engineering drive by designing products for Immersion Research. After work, he can usually be found making a speed run down the Upper Yough, which runs past his front door. At latest count, he has made over two thousand runs on this classic. Jesse is credited with being the brainchild behind the Upper Yough race, the first organized extreme race on the continent. The Youghiogheny served as breeding ground for his boat designs, and his play moves that were seminal in the growth of the sport. Perhaps more than any paddler and river, Whittemore and the Yough are inextricably linked.

Youghiogheny

Few rivers have more significance to North American whitewater than the Youghiogheny. The Lower Yough (pronounced Yock) is the birthplace of American commercial rafting, and home to The Loop—the best class III run with no vehicle shuttle required anywhere. The Upper Yough is the classic class V run—short and beautiful, with reliable flows and memorable rapids, host to the continent's first extreme downriver race, and stomping grounds for some of whitewater's most influential paddlers.

Top boaters have been flocking to the Upper Yough in increasing numbers ever since the run was first explored by Bill Bickham, Dave Kurtz, and Tom Smythe in 1959.

After a high water day on the Lower Yough, the trio headed for the Sang Run put-in with their 15-and 17-foot long Grumman canoes. The water level was low, which was good for an exploratory run, but it also might have played a part in Bickham's pinning on a log in the rapid now called Meat Cleaver. Bickham escaped unhurt, but his canoe remained stuck, forcing him to hike out. Smythe finished the run with Kurtz, who wrote in his notes of the rocky river, "probably the last time it will be run."

With Smythe's descent, the gap was bridged between river running's origins, and the modern era of whitewater sport. Smythe had learned to canoe in Boston, where the back-ferrying technique he was taught was known as "setting," because it was a derivative of the ancient setting pole which was once used to maneuver downstream. By the time Smythe ran the Upper Yough, his skills had come a long ways from the setting pole. His Upper Yough run helped usher in the new age of whitewater paddling. Forty-five years later, the Upper Yough is still considered a class V run.

The drops these pioneers first ran now all have names familiar to paddlers throughout the East Coast: Charlie's Choice, National Falls, and a true classic—Heinzerling.

The rapids begin following a brief flatwater stretch beneath the Sang Run put-in. Gap Falls is the first real drop, where a series of broad ledges forms some nice play holes. Perfect warm-up water follows for the next mile, then the meat of the run begins with Bastard. From here until the major rapids end at Double Pencil Sharpener four miles downstream, the gradient is over 100 feet-per-mile as the river is broken into a multitude of runnable lines in every rapid.

At higher water, the wide array of options begins to diminish. Such was the case when John Regan, Jeff Snyder, Jesse Whittemore, and Roger Zbel took on the river at the highest ever attempted level of seven feet. Several thousand cfs in the smallish riverbed of the Upper Yough can create some amazing features, as the Friendsville foursome quickly discovered. The most impressive indication of the ridiculous water level might be in the fact that hair boater John Regan opted out at the sight of the first major rapid, Bastard. The other three had their adrenaline goggles on, however, and pushed on.

At Tommy's Hole, a good scout was difficult, but Zbel was convinced a line existed by launching off a giant midstream pourover. Whittemore went first, and got trundled in the hole he was trying to boof. In the midst of a cartwheeling circus, Whittemore says he "finally got it slowed down, and managed to get out of there." Snyder went next. In his tiny squirt boat, he completely disappeared for several seconds (even a squirtist would consider this a "major meltdown") before re-emerging 100 feet downstream with gashes streaked across his mid section beneath his armpits. After watching those two chaotic runs, Zbel still gave it a shot. Maybe he learned from his compadres' runs, or maybe he really did see a good line. In any case, he cleaned it.

At triple drop, the fun included paddling beneath a rhythmically swinging tree trunk that guarded the entrance to the rapid. Heinzerling at seven feet was too much even for the macho men of Friendsville. Whittemore remembers it as "just giant holes everywhere." They made it their only portage of the day.

At normal levels (1.8 to 2.3), the Upper Yough is much more hospitable than the high water class VI run Whittemore and the boys saw, but it still has plenty of pop. Most of the rapids are class IV or IV+, but a few standouts remain in the V- category, and the run taken as a whole is considered easy class V. There are several

undercuts. One in particular carries the macabre title of Tombstone Rock, and it has claimed the life of at least one paddler.

Once past the major rapids, the Upper Yough run is a pretty float past arching hardwoods and graceful white pines before floating under the freeway bridges at Friendsville. Mountain Surf—a leading manufacturer of paddling soft goods—is headquartered at the take-out, just one more example of the Youghiogheny's long-standing relationship with the sport of whitewater.

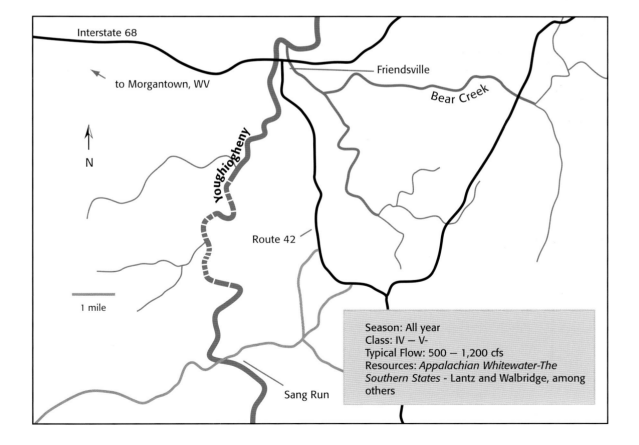

Interstate 68

to Morgantown, WV

N

Youghiogheny

Friendsville

Bear Creek

Route 42

1 mile

Sang Run

Season: All year
Class: IV — V-
Typical Flow: 500 — 1,200 cfs
Resources: *Appalachian Whitewater-The Southern States* - Lantz and Walbridge, among others

Deckers Creek, West Virginia

Jeff Snyder

After spending time with Jeff Snyder, one gets the impression that he sees the world through different lenses than the rest of us. Where we see limits, he sees opportunity. Where we see chaos, Snyder sees patterns. His keen, ethereal analysis of moving water, and the way he interacts with it, has changed what is deemed possible in the sport of river running.

Jeff Snyder's destiny was clear from the time he launched himself onto Lake Erie in the family Klepper kayak at age five. A rope connecting the boat to shore came undone, and little Jeff was suddenly floating free, headed for open water. The adults nervously implored him to backpaddle, and after a few tense moments, he returned to the safety of the beach.

By the time he was eight years old, he had paddled the Lower Youghiogheny loop, and at twelve he was attempting the class V Upper Yough, led by his older brother Jim. Jeff speaks of the time with unflagging loyalty, "I knew he would keep me out of trouble. He was my big brother."

In the years that followed, he took creek boating to its logical extreme, making several first descents and running rivers at levels previously considered off-the-chart too high. He once ran the Gauley when it was at its maximum release of 16,000 cfs, and the tributary Meadow River was, according to Jeff, "pushing the Gauley aside." The 24-mile run took only an hour to complete on the high water. This flood stage run is impressive enough of its own accord, but even more staggering is the fact that it was done in true Jeff Snyder style—solo, in a squirt boat.

Feats like this were standard for Snyder during the period, as he served as chief test pilot for his older brother's nascent boat designs. He paddled squirt boats regularly until one day when a passing rafter quipped that he'd be better off without his barely buoyant boat. Snyder began swimming the Gauley soon thereafter. "I started with a boogie board, but then I realized even that was unnecessary."

His next challenge was abruptly conceived after he injured his back kayaking a waterfall on Mexico's Agua Azul. Snyder needed a challenge for class II water while his back slowly healed. Reflecting on the Mexican native's stand-up paddling style in their wood carved Kayukos, Snyder began experimenting with the stand-up technique as soon as he returned home, and the sport of striding was born. Snyder now strides inflatable kayaks almost exclusively, unbelievably standing amid class V turbulence. "The knee goes under the spine by design," he proudly proclaims.

Although they harbor distinctly different personalities, the Snyder brothers share a common streak of genius. It's as if the laws of nature that the rest of us accept as limitations are a fountain of potential to them. There is no doubt that Jeff Snyder honestly believes himself when he looks you in the eye with beaming intensity and says, "There are no limits. There are no rules." For Jeff Snyder, maybe there aren't.

Deckers Creek

Deckers Creek is the typical West Virginia stream. It embodies all that is good and bad with the different watersheds of this whitewater-rich region. Before flowing directly through the city of Morgantown, West Virginia, Deckers Creek runs through scenic hill country that features both idyllic rhododendron grottoes and hillsides devastated from pollution.

The wheels of industry began to roll through Deckers Creek when railroad track was first laid in the canyon in 1899. Coal mines, rock quarries, and the rapid unplanned development that accompanied them flourished along the shores of Deckers Creek and its tributaries in the early part of the twentieth century. This voracious development helped build the nation's infrastructure, but it also despoiled the once lovely Deckers Creek.

By 1935, the state health department issued an official warning to the city of Morgantown to clean waste from the stream, as Deckers reportedly smelled of sewage as it ran through the streets of the city. It was 1962 before the economically depressed area finally could build sewer lines to help protect the creek. In the next two decades, the slightly cleaner stream began to gain popularity as a high water canoe run.

A new era was starting in West Virginia, but it wasn't until 1995 when Friends of Deckers Creek—a nonprofit organization based in Morgantown—was created to help restore the creek to a place of clean swimming holes and fishing eddies. Roadside trash, acid mine drainage, and industrial runoff still present challenges to a completely healthy creek, but Friends of Deckers Creek is working hard to make the legacy of human impact on the creek a more positive one in the next century.

Part of the initial impetus for Friends of Deckers started with a boater's offhand comment at a local put-in one day. The paddler commenting on the shameful pollution of Deckers was one of its most frequent visitors—Jeff Snyder.

In the mid-80s, Snyder first paddled the lower half of the infamous Pioneer Rocks section of Deckers Creek. The creek was at flood stage, and Snyder was in a squirt boat. The run was entertaining to say the least, and Snyder was intrigued enough to return for an attempt at the rest of the run upstream.

He first attempted the entire run in a high performance inflatable about the time he was near the apex of his limit-seeking phase of paddling. He refers to his initial run on Deckers as "a solution to a testosterone problem." This unflattering self-assessment sheds light on the mental approach that certainly must have been in place for the creek's first descent, because even with today's established lines, Deckers takes unfaltering confidence to be safely paddled. The reason Deckers is such a mind game? Undercuts.

Deckers' 200-foot-per-mile Pioneer Rocks section is notoriously sievey, a fact that any aspiring Deckers Creek paddler has to come to grips with before putting on. Snyder knows the hazards all too well.

While making a solo winter run in a hard shell kayak, Snyder came to grief beneath a slab of ice and rock in an incident he refers to as his "glacier pin." Attempting a left side sneak run at a rapid called Eyes, Jeff missed his boof due to an ice-altered channel, and slid into a vertical pin, where he was forcefully sucked out of his boat, and through a three-foot diameter hole. Standing up beneath the "glacier," he found that the water reached up to his chin, with just a few inches of air space available in the cave. He quickly spotted a chimney crack leading up through the ice and rock, and began climbing out of the frigid water. Following a difficult fifteen-minute climb, Snyder emerged on the top of the ice flow with one of his nine lives cashed in.

Following an incident like this, one might think that Snyder was done with Deckers, but this event served as a re-evaluation tool for Snyder. He chose to back off the hair-raising stunts in favor of more personally challenging new techniques, like striding. Since learning his new paddle sport, of course, he has returned to Deckers Creek, and successfully strided it.

Deckers has a faithful following in the nearby paddling community. This is most likely because it is a short class V creek run close to the population center of Morgantown. There is a special aura about Deckers Creek, however, that might also have something to do with its popularity. Despite its biting, dangerous riverbed, or perhaps because of it, it offers a unique paddling experience. Despite the environmental wounds it has suffered, it still provides refuge, and offers hope for a better future. Deckers Creek, in short, is a survivor.

Jeff Snyder striding in the vertical realm

John Russel

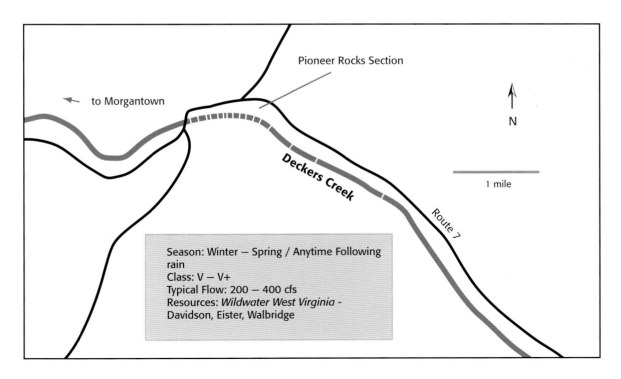

Pioneer Rocks Section

← to Morgantown

N

Deckers Creek

Route 7

1 mile

Season: Winter — Spring / Anytime Following rain
Class: V — V+
Typical Flow: 200 — 400 cfs
Resources: *Wildwater West Virginia* - Davidson, Eister, Walbridge

Blackwater Falls just above the put-in

John Regan

John Regan is one of the most prominent and charismatic figures in the sport of whitewater paddling. His trademark enthusiasm is infectious, energizing others wherever he paddles. Anyone who has been on the river with John will likely agree with the following observation made by a fellow paddler as John sped by on the Upper Yough, "When he is on the river, Regan looks like he's been plugged into a 220 volt socket."

This electrifying life of paddling began for John at age thirteen, when he was introduced to whitewater through a prominent explorer post (a sort of teenage Boy Scouts) near his Baltimore home. The year was 1975, and whitewater paddling, as Regan says, "was a hard core thing...you had to make your own boats." Regan was slowly learning the sport, but his passion for it had yet to be ignited. Then while watching the national slalom championships, he saw perennial champ Eric Evans gracefully surf a wave across the river to make a gate, and the synergy between river and paddler was suddenly crystal clear. Says Regan, "That's when I decided that kayaking was *it*."

At seventeen, he lied about his age in order to get his first raft guiding job. For the next seventeen years, John would travel up and down the East Coast between different raft guiding gigs. He paddled religiously, and his aggressive and smooth style soon became a fixture on the rivers of Appalachia. In 1979, Regan traveled to West Virginia's Gauley River for the first time.

It was an exceptionally high water year, skewing Regan's initial impression of the river. He recalls, "They had to turn the river down to 2,500 cfs every weekend from 8,000 cfs during the week." Most paddlers were scared away from the high water. Regan camped at the put-in and ran the river every day, guiding rafts on weekends, and kayaking all week. Besides guiding rafts on the Gauley, Regan also photo-boated there.

When commercial rafting became established on the Upper Youghiogheny in 1981, Regan was quick to follow. "I realized this was the place to be, Friendsville, Maryland," he says. Although he no longer guides rafts (Regan now drives a truck around the continent for a living. The truck is loaded with boats, of course.), he still lives on a hill overlooking the town of Friendsville.

Regan has pioneered many of the creeks in the area. Seneca Creek, Red Creek, and Otter Creek are all classics of today in which Regan either led the first descents, or played an essential role in their development as viable runs. The Blackwater, however, is where he feels an extra special connection. He has an estimated 500 runs on the river. When access to the put-in at Blackwater Falls was made illegal by the state park, it was Regan and friend Matt Putz who gained permission for all boaters to use the fisherman's trail across the river. Apparently, even the formal park officials aren't immune to the enthusiasm of John Regan.

Blackwater

The Blackwater River originates in a magical part of Appalachia known as Canaan Valley. Perched on the backside of the Allegheny Front, this high country basin is a rich wetland of spruce and alder thickets more reminiscent of northern Minnesota or Alaska than the typical hardwood forests of West Virginia. Entering Blackwater country is like going through a portal to a new world, where the colors are richer, the air fresher.

Over 50 inches of precipitation fall each year on this elevated landscape. This snow and rain sponges into the watershed before emerging as the tannin-brown Blackwater. The color is attributed mostly to the interaction between the underlying rock and the organic acids of the lush mountain valley. After meandering through the high swamps of Canaan, the river falls off the plateau into an uninhabited river canyon. For whitewater paddlers, this is where the full-on adventure begins.

The put-in is a dramatic whitewater scene, with majestic Blackwater Falls as a backdrop. The roar of the falls and rapids below can be heard as you make your way down the steep quarter-mile trail through a dank setting of hemlock and rhododendron.

Once at the river, paddlers better be warmed up, because any reasonable put-in eddy is in the midst of solid class V action. After surviving the first couple hundred yards, the gradient relents for a bit before reaching Tomko Falls.

This rapid was named in 1984 when Dean Tomko, one of the most noted expert paddlers in the East, was unable to make a crucial eddy at the entrance to the rapid. John Regan and Roger Zbel were on the run with Tomko, and Regan recalls hearing Tomko yell "I can't stop!" as he flushed by his two companions in the eddy. Regan continues, "We went down there to see what

happened, and Dean's in the hole swimming, and his boat's all busted." Tomko made it to shore, but his day of boating was finished. He hiked out of the rugged canyon, and Regan and Zbel finished without him.

Regan has had his own bit of unfortunate rapid naming on the Blackwater. Flatliner Falls was coined after John had the closest call of his paddling career there. He vividly remembers, "It was your classic vertical pin. I had water rushing over my head, I had an air bubble, and I was getting violently thrashed around." His partner Marty McCormick had lost sight of him, he could only see an unnatural rooster tail of water that he assumed was John. Just as Regan had delicately moved his knees into a position where he could exit the boat, it shifted, and McCormick was able to grab the kayak enough to haul it to shore. Regan named the rapid after recalling his thought process during the emergency. He says about his pin, "I had time to think, 'Hey, I might drown.'" Fortunately the situation didn't end in tragedy, but the cryptic Flatliner Falls name remains.

The upper Blackwater isn't always a carnage fest, however. The run is blitzed by locals these days, some of whom log up to sixty descents a year. Jeff Snyder has even strided the upper Blackwater, although he admits he was "pretty matched up against the learning curve" the first time he tried the stand-up technique on the run.

Many paddlers now end their Blackwater runs at the confluence of the North Fork, where the lower run begins. This take-out offers a short shuttle with a quick class V stretch of whitewater, but paddlers who take out here miss the stupendous lower section, where the rapids are only slightly easier than above, and the scenery remains excellent.

The lower Blackwater has been described as "West Virginia's longest continuous set of rapids." Since this description was written, however, the continuous character has changed somewhat. A massive flood in 1985 changed the river dramatically, and the lower run now has more of a pool-drop nature. The rapids that remain, of course, are steeper than before the flood. Several more smaller flood events in the last decade have kept the riverbed in an almost constant state of change. Blackwater regulars know to expect the unexpected on this dynamic run.

The wild "upper B"

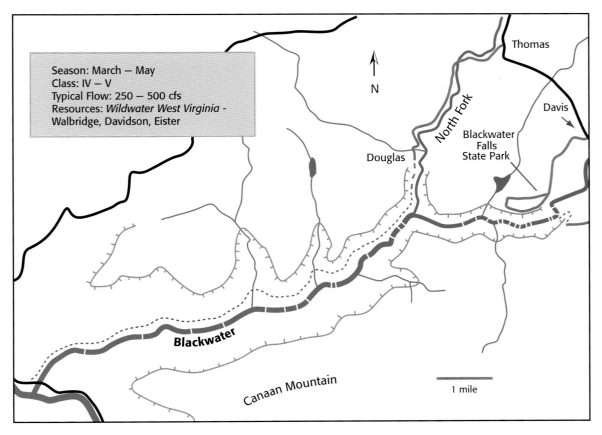

Season: March — May
Class: IV — V
Typical Flow: 250 — 500 cfs
Resources: *Wildwater West Virginia* - Walbridge, Davidson, Eister

Jim Snyder sluices down Roaring Creek

Jim Snyder

Jim Snyder might be the most influential paddler in the modern era of whitewater paddling. He approaches the sport with a creative genius that has led to new horizons in steep creeking, paddle design, boat design, and paddling technique. He is indisputably the father of paddling's misfit cousin, squirt boating. When one considers his development of short boats and avant-garde freestyle moves, it is reasonable to consider him the father of play boating as well.

For such a storied career, it started rather inauspiciously. His first experience in river running came with his father at the age of eleven. They flipped their aluminum canoe on the first eddyline they encountered, resulting in an icy cold swim. Ever the engineer, Jim modified his boat, and next went paddling with a covered canoe, and a kayak paddle. He naturally gravitated to a kayak soon after, and was guiding rafts on the Youghiogheny, and racing slalom while still a teenager.

It was through his connection to slalom racing that Snyder developed his first theories on squirt boating. As early as 1970, Snyder recalls watching slalom champion Eric Evans use a counter-intuitive outside lean in order to shave seconds off his race time. Jim says of the innovative move with classic Snyderism, "Eric was a victim of his realm of superior speed, and could not travel the beaten path."

The top racers adopted and refined the stern-pivot technique during the '70s before the Snyder brothers, along with companion Jesse Whittemore, began using the move to toy with sub-surface currents in their everyday recreational paddling on the Cheat River. In 1983, Jim designed the Arc—a short, radical kayak that was the precursor of today's play boats. In the Arc, Snyder performed the first ever flatwater cartwheel—a move that is the bread and butter of today's freestyle menu.

Through the '80s and '90s, Jim continued churning out new squirt boat and surface boat models, along with his legendary *Squirt Book*, the bible for three-dimensional boating. Snyder's stewardship of the squirt sub-sport is so universally recognized that one of the most prestigious squirt competitions of today is honorably called the *Jimi Cup*.

Snyder's influences on paddling aren't limited to squirt boating. In 1975, he apprenticed under the king of wood paddle making, Keith Backlund, and Snyder has been producing his own highly sought custom sticks ever since. Snyder's paddles brought the now customary 45-degree offset into the mainstream.

In the creek boating realm, Snyder has been years ahead of his time. In the late '70s he ran West Virginia's Quarry Run, a creek dropping up to 650 feet-per-mile. He and his brother Jeff probed many other small steep streams of northern West Virginia too, but their accomplishments were often kept a secret between brothers. Jim's classic pick—Roaring Creek—is one of those local runs. It is just one of the many threads in the fabric of whitewater paddling that Jim Snyder has weaved.

Roaring Creek

Paddlers from all points on the compass have a backyard creek. Whether it is the drainage ditch out back that only rarely has enough water to float a boat, or a nearby classic that attracts boaters far and wide, local runs have a special place in the hearts of paddlers everywhere. Roaring Creek is such a run.

It is like many small streams that crisscross the scrambled rolling hills of Appalachia. Gathering in farmer's fields, and tumbling down dark forest glens, the innumerable creeks of Appalachia provide an intimate avenue of exploration amidst this semi-settled region. Creeks like Roaring are so small that paddlers from other parts of the globe might not believe them runnable when seeing a base flow like Roaring's 7 cfs. Just add water, however, and these quiet little trickles turn into non-stop rides of fast corners and tight slots. Streams this small are unrunnable across much of North America due to log strainers, but here in Appalachia the creeks are generally cleaner, (although small creeks still get log-choked), and the rocks fit the riverbed, so paddling can be done on just about anything that floats a boat. Jim Snyder's backyard Roaring Creek just barely does that.

The put-in for Roaring is on 40 to 60 cfs. When Jim showed the run to visiting British paddlers, they called it "a dew-dampened ditch." Maybe so, but with Roaring's ten to twenty-foot wide bed, there is plenty of "dew" to make holes, one of which comes at the base of the put-in slide.

The operative word for the first couple of miles of this five-mile run is *busy*. Action is continuous and fast, with plenty of blind corners to keep you grabbing for riverbank bushes unless you are following someone who knows the run. Delicate yet furious paddling is necessary to stay off the rocks in between drops, and well planned rock boofs are needed to keep from pin-ning in the rapids. Given the prevalent boat-to-rock contact on a run of this size, I asked Snyder how he and his partners were able to negotiate a creek like Roaring in years past, without breaking their fiberglass boats. He replied honestly, "We broke 'em."

The first bit of boat abuse took place here in 1984. Though the class II lower part of the creek had been run previously, nobody had considered putting in upstream where the gradient is 200 feet-per-mile. No one except Snyder, of course.

On a high water winter day, Snyder talked friends Paul Marshall and Diana Kendrick into making an exploratory on upper Roaring. They drove up the hill from Snyder's home in Albright, West Virginia, looking for the closest access point to the creek. Their explorations took them down a dirt road covered in sloppy wet snow. As they stuck their heads out the window to hear the creek rushing along in the hollow below, their 4-wheelin' Saab gave a disgruntled whine, and they realized they were stuck in the heavy rain-soaked snow. A lengthy battle for tire traction ensued, and after getting the truck rolling again, the trio had to re-summon their energies to slosh down to the aptly named Roaring Creek.

Grabbing overhanging rhododendron branches above the one-boat eddies offered the only respite from the fast-paced action of Roaring. After scouting several significant ledges, they found everything to be runnable, and emerged at the mouth of Roaring several hours later with a classic new creek behind them.

Since then, Snyder has run Roaring dozens of times, and at all levels. There is no gauge on Roaring to report the exact level, but Snyder has his own system. It starts at zero—the minimum flow—then gets progressively higher with levels fun, fu, free, fo, and mo. Mo level has actually never been attempted, but being keenly aware of the innate human ability to explore new horizons, Snyder has included it in the system anyway.

The creek's flow is boosted about one-third of the way down when a tributary nearly equal to the size of upper Roaring comes in from the right. Below this confluence, the creek is anywhere between 80 and 120 cfs, and some of the bedrock slides make it seem like more. The creek here doesn't feel quite as tunnel-like as it does higher up, where it burrows under a canopy of hemlock boughs and rhododendron thickets. A few ledge falls up to seven feet in height are the run's whitewater highlights. Shortly below these ledges, things start to mellow, and paddlers will find a fast, continuous paddle out to the roiling brown Cheat River.

Roaring Creek is barely more than a trickle most of the time

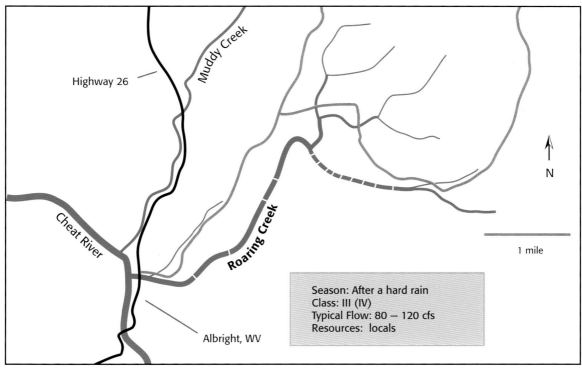

Season: After a hard rain
Class: III (IV)
Typical Flow: 80 — 120 cfs
Resources: locals

The New River girls approaching the bridge

Anna Levesque

Anna Levesque (pronounced La vek) is quickly becoming the leader in whitewater development for women. Perhaps her most significant contribution to this end is her video *Girls at Play*—the first kayak instructional film designed specifically for women. Anna brings a unique perspective to the feature, because before she was running some of the burliest whitewater on the continent, she saw the sport from the perspective of a non-paddler working at the local raft company.

While still a teenager, Anna got a job as receptionist at New World Rafting on Quebec's Rouge River near her home. She recalls the time as one of youthful naiveté: "I remember being surprised at seeing guides openly change their clothes in the parking lot," she says.

Following her early introduction to the world of whitewater, Anna attended the University of North Carolina, where she competed on the rowing crew, and graduated with an honors degree in International Studies. Her professors at North Carolina probably had no idea that their pupil would embrace the international part of her major quite so earnestly. Since college, Anna's paddling has led her on a tour including New Zealand, Australia, Chile, Ecuador, Costa Rica, Spain, and Austria, as well as her native Canada and neighboring U.S. and Mexico.

Levesque set the wheels in motion for this life of international study immediately after receiving her degree, when she used her graduation money to buy her first kayak. To maximize paddling time, she got a raft guiding job on West Virginia's New River, where she remembers being "in awe" of the region's top boaters. Soon she was on par with those she had been emulating, even though Anna herself was the last to realize it. It took the encouragement of a respected acquaintance to get her to take a shot at the Canadian freestyle team. She tried out, and has been near or at the top ever since.

Her proudest freestyle finish to date is third at the 2001 worlds. She also consistently medals in the Gorge Games down river race. But these events are merely competitions that go with the job of being a professional paddler. Most of Anna's paddling is pure recreational fun. A sampling of her good times paddling is seen in videos such as *Aerated* and *Gush*. California's Tule River is home to a set of drops that bears Anna's name. Anna's Tazitas was appropriately coined after she became the first to clean the falls.

Anna Levesque continues to travel the world in search of quality whitewater, but she often seems to find it right back at her beloved New River. She learned the basics of kayaking on the New River Gorge, and now she practices cutting edge aerial maneuvers on the Dries of the New. When Ms. Levesque surfs one of the giant waves of the Dries, there is no doubt we are seeing one of the sport's leading Girls at Play.

New River

West Virginia's New is everybody's river. Countless paddlers have learned on the New, and even the top experts are still entertained here. It is *the* big river of the Appalachians.

Starting from numerous springs and small feeder creeks in the high country near Blowing Rock, North Carolina, the New runs north for over 250 miles through the small towns and wooded valleys of Appalachia. It runs across the foot of southern Virginia, where it passes some of the oldest rocks in the eastern United States, evidence of the ironically titled New River's old age. It is believed to be the oldest river in North America, relatively maintaining its course while the Appalachian Mountains around it have built and eroded to their current form.

The New is runnable almost from its very source, but the most interesting boating for the whitewater paddler comes in its lower reaches, where it runs through the New River Gorge. Once considered a benchmark for difficult whitewater, the Gorge by today's standards would more aptly be described as a pleasant and scenic run, but with enough action to keep it interesting for any paddler. Even when water levels are low, deep channels down the gut of the rapids provide some punch. At moderate levels, the average rapid contains a half dozen different lines, from big and juicy to creeky slots. This diversity is what makes the New such a great river to develop skills on. The warm water and big pools tend to take the hard edge off the learning curve as well. High water on the New creates the biggest water in the East outside of the Niagara Gorge. Grand Canyon-style waves are commonplace above seven feet on the New, and things just get bigger from there. High water events usually cause the best boaters to head for the New River Dries for a surfing safari. The truly epic waves of this normally diverted and dry riverbed are in prime form when it is over 30,000 cfs.

While freestylers throw down amazing aerial maneuvers on the giant waves of the Dries, the opposite end of the riversport spectrum has also seen its logical extreme on New high water. The year was 1976, and renowned paddler Barry Tuscano was getting his first meaningful lessons in water hydraulics.

The New was high, very high—over thirty feet on the gauge, which translates to something in the neighborhood of 100,000 cfs. Tuscano says the river "looked like the ocean." His assessment of the water level carries considerable credibility given his broad experience on rivers like the Ottawa and Grand Canyon. Those experiences, however, came years after his first flood stage run on the New. In 1976, Tuscano and his three companions launched with little more than guts, adventuresome spirit, and blissful ignorance. Their preparedness for the high water was evident in their equipment—a $99 Sears raft and a truck innertube with homemade paddles. In case of a flip, the paddles were permanently tethered to the raft via a few feet of parachute cord! At least their lifejackets were adequate, or we'd have never heard their story.

After they "paddled like hell to get out through the trees," things smoothed out. Tuscano relates, "Having negotiated what I thought would be the only threat on the river, I began a short discourse on how easy this was going to be." Then came the hole.

Whale Rock is normally a house-sized boulder towering twenty or more feet above the water, but at 100,000 cfs, it is...well, you can imagine. Tuscano says, "I remember thinking, 'Now I know what a hole is.'" Needless to say, the novice rafters were given a quick lesson in the power of water, and when they each surfaced from their respective rag-doll thrashings, it was time to swim for their lives. Tuscano climbed back in the empty raft, but, "All the paddles were either broken or gone. Suddenly being in the raft seemed less than secure," he recalls.

A second hole sent Tuscano deep again, and this time he surfaced near two of his inner-tube-clutching companions, who had luckily missed the second hole. They swam the tube to shore, where they re-united with the fourth member of their party, Tuscano's sister. She had made the bank by grabbing onto a tree upstream.

Following the experience, Tuscano says, "for a time I had a hard time finding folks to take rafting." He and his wife Kitty—a fellow survivor of the New debacle— went on to become expert kayakers. And like many, they still enjoy the New.

Paddling toward Whale Rock at a moderate level

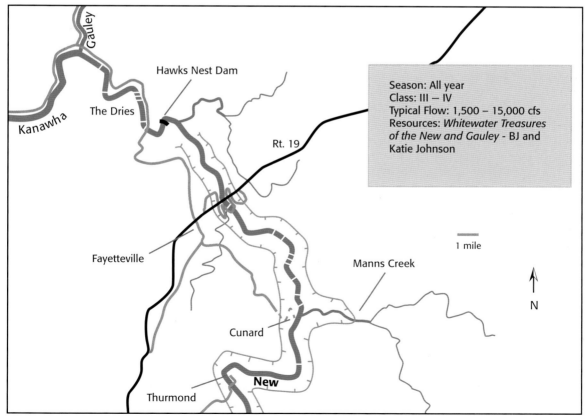

Season: All year
Class: III — IV
Typical Flow: 1,500 – 15,000 cfs
Resources: *Whitewater Treasures of the New and Gauley* - BJ and Katie Johnson

Gauley

Hawks Nest Dam

The Dries

Kanawha

Rt. 19

Fayetteville

Manns Creek

1 mile

N

Cunard

New

Thurmond

Katie Johnson

Little Dave and Josh in the Gladiator's arena—Manns Creek

BJ Johnson

South central West Virginia has always been a hot bed of whitewater paddling. In the 1960s, the New River was a popular destination. The '70s saw the adjacent Gauley come into favor, and by the '80s major tributary streams of the two rivers started to be run regularly. Every generation of whitewater development in this region has had a leader, someone who explores the new runs, refines the old rapids, and defines their era. That leader in the 1990s was BJ Johnson.

BJ grew up in the whitewater hub of Fayetteville, West Virginia, a town perched on the rim of the New River Gorge, well known to rock climbers and paddlers alike. BJ's involvement in the town's budding water-jock culture came at age sixteen, when he began working for a local raft company.

Soon after learning the basics of reading water from the back of a raft, he took up kayaking, and tore into the sport with fanatic teenage enthusiasm. After learning the standard lines on the rivers of the area, he next made a concerted effort to master the many obscure slot moves as well. His paddling improvement reflected his intense focus, and by his second year of kayaking, he started exploring unrun creeks in the area, many of which he had fished as a kid.

When asked, the humble BJ will discard many of his firsts as merely "little stuff," but the impact that his explorations had on the new age of the sport proved otherwise. There was Laurel Creek, Keeneys Creek, the falls on Wolf and Panther Creeks, and his most significant first—Mann's Creek. BJ made several scouting hikes into this one before finally running it in February of 1994.

Besides exploring new creeks, and running several previously unrun waterfalls in the area, Johnson also played a major role in facilitating the growth of the region's world class play boating. He methodically recorded water levels for the various play features of the New and Gauley, cutting out the guess work and optimizing surf time. Much of BJ's intimate knowledge of the area is conveyed in *Whitewater Treasures of the New and Gauley*, a guide he co-wrote with his wife Katie.

BJ and Katie met on the rodeo circuit in the mid-'90s, and promptly formed their own video production company called Falling Down Productions. Their successful debut title, *Fallin' Down*, of course featured the cutting edge of West Virginia creek boating. While competing in freestyle through the '90s (BJ was 6th in the world in '97, and Katie was 3rd in the world in squirt that year), the duo produced four more whitewater films.

With their freestyle touring days behind them, BJ and Katie now live just minutes from the New River Dries in Ansted, West Virginia, with their two young children. The youngsters' favorite pastime is an activity not the least bit surprising given their genetic background. It entails climbing to the top of a steep grassy slope in the backyard, jumping on a slick plastic pad, and sliding at breakneck speed to the bottom. It appears West Virginia's next generation of whitewater leaders are already getting started.

Manns Creek

Manns Creek is such a fine example of an Appalachian country stream that photos of it have been used worldwide to portray an image of rural America. Although many have seen the picturesque grist mill with a peaceful book running beneath it on postcards and calendars, few realize that just downstream the creek turns into one of the best whitewater runs on the continent.

For many years, Manns Creek was out of reach for whitewater paddlers. Although a few hairball boaters pushed into Manns in the early '80s, most of the tight corners and constricted channels of the creek were simply not runnable before the advent of shorter boats. The creek was generally regarded as a disappointing portage fest. It wasn't until BJ Johnson and Kent McCracken ran it in 1994 that Manns began to be regarded as a worthwhile run, and at that time it was still considered outer-limits paddling. Johnson's first run included twelve portages. His second descent cut that number in half, and by the fifth full descent of the creek, everything had been run. Most mortals still portage a handful of the rapids on Manns, but the fact that everything does have a line (albeit sometimes a very thin line) makes this a truly classic creek.

Johnson had hiked the length of Manns before his first kayak run, so he knew generally what great rapids were in store for him and McCracken. More importantly, he knew the lay of the land. Should any problems occur, their escape route from the wooded river canyon lay in the form of a dirt road that traversed high above creek left. This was only contingency information, though. Their goal was to run the length of Manns into the New River and the take-out, before dark of course. Even though they were making the run during the short days of February, they weren't overly concerned with running out of daylight. McCracken recalls, "We thought we'd be done with it in no time."

Six hours, and about thirty rapids later, they were still on the creek, and it was getting dark. Both paddlers knew it was unsafe to keep going in the fading light, but they also knew that they were almost out, so they decided to run "just one more." Four rapids later, it was *really* dark, and they were forced to call it quits. They left their boats in the woods, climbed up to the road, and wisely walked to the take-out. The next day, they hiked back in, ran the last couple of rapids, and opened a new era for Manns Creek.

Now Manns is done by lots of paddlers, but the demanding and deceptively long 5-mile run continues to produce a number of unplanned epic adventures. Key advantages for a successful run on Manns include an early start, an experienced guide, and knowledge of the hike-out options. When Roger Marr attempted Manns in July of 2001, he had none of these.

Marr's first clue that he was in for a memorable day came when the only person he could find to paddle with was a fellow nicknamed "Sketchy" Steve. Steve had reportedly been a Hollywood stuntman before turning to whitewater, and had made BASE jumps off the 876-foot high New River Gorge Bridge. Running a new class V creek was probably a relatively safe undertaking in *his* eyes.

Manns Creek was still high following 100-year floods that had ravaged the area just weeks before. Anticipating some good action from the high water, Sketchy packed his video camera. He and Roger put in at a prompt 3 P.M., and started down the creek slowly, with plenty of filming in the dramatic 400 fpm first mile. When they noticed it was getting dark, they finally picked up the pace, and started bombing off the unrelenting horizon lines in a race to beat darkness. Sketchy began living up to his title as he led over several blind drops in the waning twilight. Roger tried to follow the Sketch-man, but as he recalls, "I could barely see him in front of me." At a rapid called Lunatic Fringe, the line is a boat-width slot next to an ugly pin rock. Roger was inches off his line here, and the inevitable carnage finally occurred. Luckily, he banged through the rapid with only a bloodied elbow, and prudently got off the creek. Not knowing where they were, Steve and Roger began dragging their kayaks downstream through the rhododendron thickets by the light of the video camera bulb. When their meager light source gave out hours later, they called it a night. At least Sketchy had a dry lighter in his "medicine kit" that they could use to make a warming fire. The damp forest offered little combustible fuel, however, and they struggled to get anything going. Salvation came from Roger's first aid kit, where he kept tampons as bleeding control devices. The dense cotton tampons lit up wonderfully, and the two be-nighted paddlers sat back and burned all night long.

In the morning, they ran the last big rapid— Liquid Drain-O. Roger got drain-o'ed, appropriately finishing his Manns Creek christening, and matching his bloody elbow with a bloody nose. While surveying his wounds below the rapid, Roger heard a whistle, and looked around inquisitively. It was doubtful that Sketchy would have a whistle, so who was it? His friend and shuttle driver Ted suddenly appeared. Ted had been on an all-night search for the two. He gave them food that he had hiked in, and sent them on their way downstream to the New, where Steve and Roger proudly finished the first-ever Manns Creek overnighter.

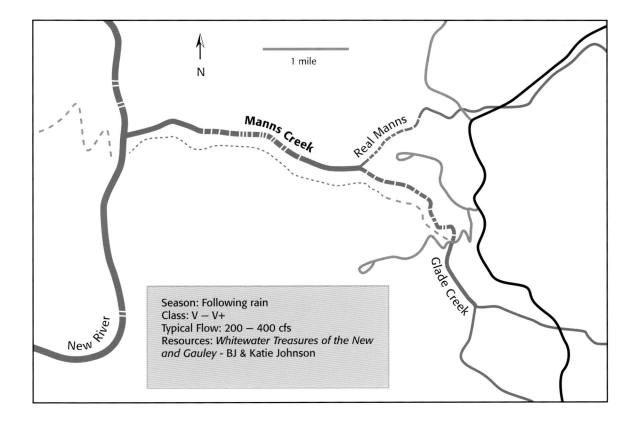

Season: Following rain
Class: V — V+
Typical Flow: 200 — 400 cfs
Resources: *Whitewater Treasures of the New and Gauley* - BJ & Katie Johnson

The Gauley in autumn

John Sweet

The 1960s and '70s were, in many ways, the golden age of whitewater paddling. Boats had developed beyond the crude designs of the '50s, racing had organized, and paddling clubs were flourishing. Despite paddling's growth, the sport was still in a carefree and adolescent stage. Crowds on rivers were unheard of, and major classic runs still awaited first descents. This was the era when John Sweet flourished in the sport.

In 1963, John Sweet was a graduate student at Penn State University whose primary outdoor interests were rock climbing and caving. It wasn't until Sweet's housemate started building a canoe in the basement that Sweet took an interest in paddling. Come spring, John and his friend gave the finished canoe a test run, and Sweet knew he'd stumbled onto something good. After finishing up a major cave mapping project in Pennsylvania's Hosterman's Pit, he set his sights on whitewater.

Running with the Penn State Outing Club, Sweet quickly developed his skills in the C-1, and within a year he was paddling the cutting edge of whitewater rivers at the time—the Upper Yough. Sweet and his contemporaries made regular outings to many runs that are the standards of today, like the Cheat, Tygart, and New. We now take these weekend jaunts for granted, but in the mid-'60s, reliable information was hard to come by, and even the guidebooks were often written based on assumptions, rather than experience. Adventuresome paddlers like Sweet studied their own maps, and went prepared for anything.

Such was the case when he led the first decked boat descent down the Gauley. The river had caught his eye a few years earlier, while en route to the New River. Sweet was inspired to launch on the alluring river right then, but his group's planned rendezvous on the New prevented a spontaneous run. In retrospect, it was a good thing that the under-prepared group waited, as Sweet reflects, "We probably saved some lives by not doing it then." On Labor Day weekend of 1968, Sweet finally got his chance.

Though the river had been run by Sayre Rodman's rafting party several years earlier, it was still basically unknown, and Sweet's group regarded any information about the run as hearsay. He says, "We'd heard stories of rafts getting sucked under rocks and popping up 100 yards downstream, but we dispelled that as overblown rumors." Overblown, perhaps, but Sweet and company—Jimmy Holcombe, Norm Holcombe, Jim Stuart, Miha Tomsic, and Jack Wright—found plenty to keep them on their toes nonetheless. The level was 1,200 cfs, making for a very long 24-mile day, and requiring the group to keep the scouting to a minimum. Sweet was the only one to run Iron Ring that day, and another particularly steep rapid that still bears his name—Sweet's Falls.

It was a big year for Sweet. Besides the Gauley descent, he also ran the Colorado through Grand Canyon, made a first descent of Washington's Icicle Creek, and won the national C-1 wildwater title. He would go on to win several more national racing titles, and run many more rivers (including a first on Maryland's Savage), but Sweet's legacy will always be linked to that river he helped pioneer—the Gauley.

Gauley River

The Gauley is timeless. Even though it was first run in the '60s, a trip on the Gauley is still a benchmark for many. The river has so much character, nearly anyone who has paddled here just once has a Gauley story. Simply the name "Gauley" has been ingrained in the whitewater vernacular worldwide, "This one time, on the Gauley..." This river's broad popularity is likely related to that six-week period every autumn that is known to paddlers everywhere as Gauley Season.

The fall draw-down of Summersville Reservoir serves as the centerpiece for the greatest gathering of river runners in the world as commercial rafters, guides, and all types of whitewater paddlers converge every September to float on the scheduled dam releases. Not only is the Gauley often the only whitewater around at that time of year, it is also some of the best.

The riverbed is made up of giant sandstone blocks, which create both excellent whitewater, and dangerous undercuts. Initiation Rapid, within a half mile of the put-in, contains one of the more dangerous spots on the river. Despite the rapid's class III appearance, a sieve tunnel on the right has been the cause of fatalities, and several more close calls.

Although hazards are present, the Gauley is home to numerous classic rapids. The big five of the upper run—Insignificant, Pillow Rock, Lost Paddle, Iron Ring, and Sweet's Falls—are the most talked about rapids, but many other interesting class IV drops intermingle between the biggies. The slightly easier lower Gauley has a handful of great rapids too, like Koontz's Flume, Mash, and Diagonal Ledges. Experienced rafters claim there is no bigger bang for the buck than the Gauley, and tens of thousands run the river every season. Today's often busy Gauley is a far cry from the first trip down in 1961.

The primary impetus for that initial exploration came from adventurers Sayre and Jean Rodman, a couple who demonstrated that one doesn't need high tech equipment to have high adventure. Starting in the mid 1950s, the Rodmans made a series of weekend river outings in first generation military surplus rafts. Their boats were 13 feet long, steered with 6-foot-long makeshift oars that rested in under-equipped rubber oarlocks. Both Sayre and Jean rowed their own boats, evidently quite well. Their weekend outings took them to notable whitewater rivers like the Cheat and Upper Yough.

On Memorial Day weekend of 1961, the Rodmans, along with friends David Barbour, Ken Hawker, and Kay and Ralph Kirschbaum, launched above the town of Summersville for a 3-day trip down the unknown Gauley. Sayre had attempted the run the previous Fall, but high water had thwarted the effort, forcing an early exit. This time, he was determined to lead a successful descent, despite arriving at the put-in during a spring snowstorm.

The first day's float traveled a river never to be run again, as this section is now lost under Summersville Reservoir. Jean Rodman recalls "several miles of really very nice whitewater," including one drop that some of the group portaged. They camped for the night at the approximate site of today's Summersville Dam.

Day two began with an eerie mist enveloping the river that proved to be a harbinger of the day's events. The group successfully ran several big rapids in the morning, and had yet to portage when they arrived at what is now known as Iron Ring.

Ken and Dave were the first to run the rapid, choosing a line down the right. They each flushed through upright, following somewhat wild rides. Next was Kay. As she entered the rapid, her boat nudged up against a large table rock just to the right of the rapid's gathering tongue of water. Her raft instantly rose on edge against the rock, and Kay looked down to see a powerful vortex of water sucking underneath the huge boulder. In the next instant, Sayre recalls seeing Kay and the boat get swallowed under the rock "like a trout taking a fly." Following an uncomfortably long and helpless interval, Kay surfaced downstream of the rock, followed by the still-intact raft. The remaining boaters portaged.

Kay had injured her knee in the swim, and the ominous misty weather continued, so camp was made early. The next day, the party lined their boats through the yet unnamed Sweet's Falls, and rowed the remainder of the river without mishap. It would be another seven years before the river was run again, this time by John Sweet and company in hard boats.

Following Sweet's descent in '68, trip participant Jim Stuart organized another trip now known as "The Lost Paddle Trip." Besides naming Lost Paddle Rapid after spending a dangerous 45 minutes searching in undercuts for the missing blade, many other drops were given titles as well, including Insignificant. When Stuart was asked, "What's this one like?" he responded, "I don't know, something insignificant." Stuart recalls the scene at the bottom of the rapid, "I looked over my shoulder to see the helmets of several swimmers bobbing down...Peter yelled angrily as he went by, 'Insignificant huh?' I wrote the name down. Then we fished everybody out."

The rapid naming might be over these days, but new Gauley stories are still being played out every day of every season. This river, despite the impacts man has wrought, has never lost its charm.

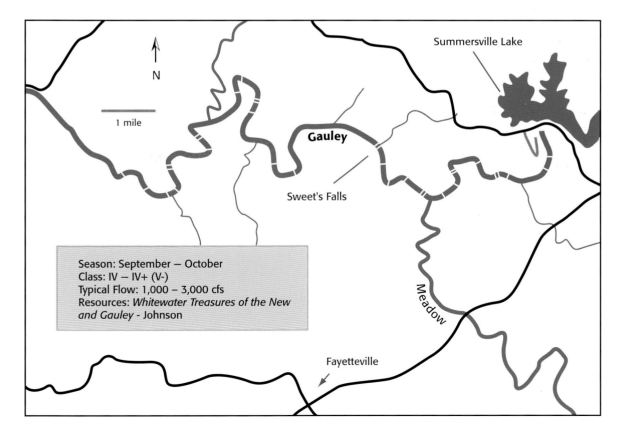

N

1 mile

Summersville Lake

Gauley

Sweet's Falls

Meadow

Fayetteville

Season: September — October
Class: IV — IV+ (V-)
Typical Flow: 1,000 – 3,000 cfs
Resources: *Whitewater Treasures of the New and Gauley* - Johnson

Skip Brown

Great Falls of the Potomac

David Hearn

Every sport has a figure who rises to the pinnacle of his craft through an almost obsessive will to succeed, maintaining a sheer determination that few of us have, and even fewer are able to take to the top. Exemplifying this model of success through hard work, football has Jerry Rice, baseball has Cal Ripken Jr., and whitewater has David Hearn.

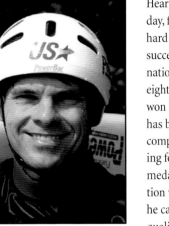

Hearn was introduced to whitewater paddling primarily through his father Carter—an avid canoeist who still paddles in his seventies. At age five, Davey and his older sister Cathy went on a three-day family canoe trip through the Missouri Breaks in Montana. The early exposure to the art of river travel evidently made quite an impact on the impressionable youths, because their lives have been mostly dedicated to the sport of paddling ever since.

Encouraged by his father's enthusiasm for down river racing and his sister's involvement in organized paddling, Davey began training with the C-CATS, a youth racing arm of the Canoe Cruisers Association, or C.C.A. Besides Hearn, the Washington, D.C. area C-CATS included Kent Ford, Jon and Ron Lugbill, and Bob Robison—a group whose eventual impact on the sport was monumental. The C-CATS were the first to make the stern squirt an essential skill in the world of slalom racing, emulated worldwide primarily due to the success of Hearn and Lugbill. The duo completely dominated C-1 competition through the '80s, and into the '90s, bringing the decked canoe class into the racing spotlight.

At seventeen years of age, Hearn won the C-1 slalom in the first national championship he entered.

Hearn trained twice a day, nearly every day, for the next two decades, and his hard work paid off with unprecedented success. He would go on to win the national championship an astounding eighteen more times. In 1985, Hearn won his first world championship. He has been in three Olympics, and also competed in C-2 and wildwater, accruing fourteen world championship medals in the process. His determination was perhaps most evident when he came back from shoulder surgery to qualify for his third Olympic team in 2000. His sweetest victory? A world championship at Nottingham, England, in 1995—ten years after his first world title. Simply put, Davey Hearn helped redefine the sport of slalom racing.

The vast majority of Hearn's racing success can be traced to his estimated 7,000 runs on the Potomac. He has run the river from all-time lows of 150 cfs to flood stages in excess of 300,000 cfs. Today he still frequents the Potomac, now as the most sought after slalom coach in the racing realm.

Potomac River

If the United States were to have a designated national river, the Potomac would be the natural choice. Along its entire course, if fills the many different roles of an American river. It grows from both pristine mountain streams and polluted industrial sources, winds placidly and thunders angrily, and is used for recreation, drinking water, and commerce. Even the governmental management of the river is emblematic of both the good and bad found in America's bureaucratic structure.

As the Potomac approaches its dramatic transition from flatwater to whitewater at Great Falls, it enters a relatively healthy riverine ecosystem that provides habitat for wildlife as well as rejuvenating solace for the thriving human population of the surrounding metropolis. Hikers and bikers enjoy pathways lining the river, fisherman relax along its banks, and boaters ride its mighty flow. Paddlers can be thankful that this section of river is protected from overdevelopment by the presence of the National Park Service. At the same time, the primary hindrance paddlers face in enjoying this wonderful natural treasure is, well, the National Park Service.

The unnecessary yet ever-present conflict between the uniform-wearing sect and the generally independent paddling community was never more clearly illustrated than during the arrest of distinguished Potomac paddler David Hearn.

It was January 1996, and widespread rain following a record snowfall produced the highest water the Potomac had seen in years. The river roared along at over 200,000 cfs. The flood inundated towns, and reshaped long-standing canal walls along the Potomac's banks. It also happened to create a rarely seen surf wave of epic proportions. Being a dedicated Olympian, Hearn promptly went to the river to test his skills on the 15-foot high wave.

After a few minutes of surreal high speed action, his surf fest was interrupted by a blaring loudspeaker from a circling helicopter. They were broadcasting some sort of message. It sounded something like this: "foo hoss shoo haave." Mr. Hearn figured the obnoxious static was directed at him, so he paddled toward shore, where he was greeted by an irate shouting policeman. Paddling close enough to speak with the fulminating officer, Hearn tried several futile attempts at communication, then returned to the relative peace of a raging 200,000 cfs. Next, the world champion paddler was promptly ordered off the river, because in the officer's esteemed opinion, it was unsafe.

Davey paddled a few hundred feet downstream to a parking area, where he began talking with a waiting park ranger from his boat. Just as the first rational conversation of the day had begun, Hearn was blind-sided by the infuriated policeman from upstream. He tried to grab Hearn's paddle. Like any good paddler, he refused to relinquish his lifeline to river survival, and a struggle ensued. Next they grabbed the ends of his boat, and lifted him out of the water in an attempt to shake him loose. Tipping over, Hearn put out a hand to stabilize, and sprained a wrist in the process. He was handcuffed, taken to a nearby police station, and fingerprinted.

This fine display of American civil servitude was caught on videotape, and seen on news channels from Japan to Switzerland. Thankfully, the judge hearing the case possessed considerably more reason than the agents who created it, and the charges against Hearn of "disobeying a lawful order" and "resisting arrest" were thrown out of court before Hearn's defense even had to make an argument.

Despite using a kayak display as part of their visitor's center attractions, the Park Service maintains a somewhat surreptitious policy with regards to running the Great Falls. It is allowed, but only when the tourist-filled park is relatively empty, so as to not create a spectacle that contributes to overcrowding at Falls overlooks.

Assuming your interactions with the park are pleasant, the Potomac offers a wealth of nice paddling. Besides Great Falls, the hardest rapid on the river is Little Falls. Here you can negotiate class IV, then gaze downstream at traffic gridlock on the Chain Bridge, and smile, because you are on the water. Most of the river has a much more natural feel than this, however. Wary herons suspiciously eyeball you from the bank, and lush forests hang over the eddies.

The most unique feature of the Potomac is the availability of no-shuttle river runs. The Chesapeake and Ohio Canal runs along river left, offering a flat water paddle back to the put-in. Sometimes certain sections of the canal are dewatered for various reasons, but even then there is a wide, flat trail known as the tow path (because mules used to walk here while towing barges up the canal) that provides hassle-free portaging.

There is no disputing that Washington, D.C. is the premier paddling city on the East Coast, and the Potomac is the reason why.

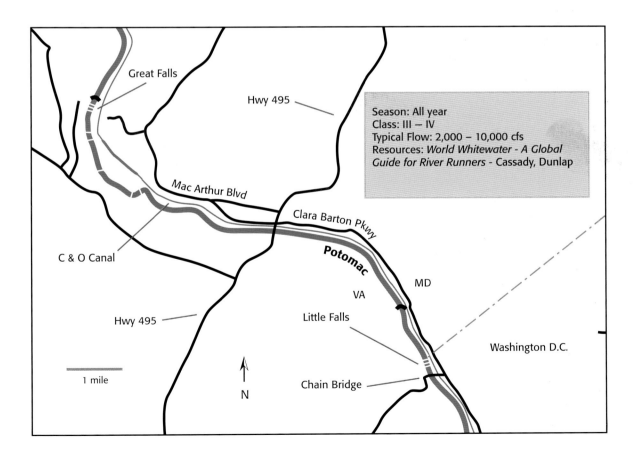

Great Falls

Hwy 495

Season: All year
Class: III — IV
Typical Flow: 2,000 – 10,000 cfs
Resources: *World Whitewater - A Global Guide for River Runners* - Cassady, Dunlap

Mac Arthur Blvd

Clara Barton Pkwy

Potomac

C & O Canal

MD

VA

Hwy 495

Little Falls

Washington D.C.

1 mile

N

Chain Bridge

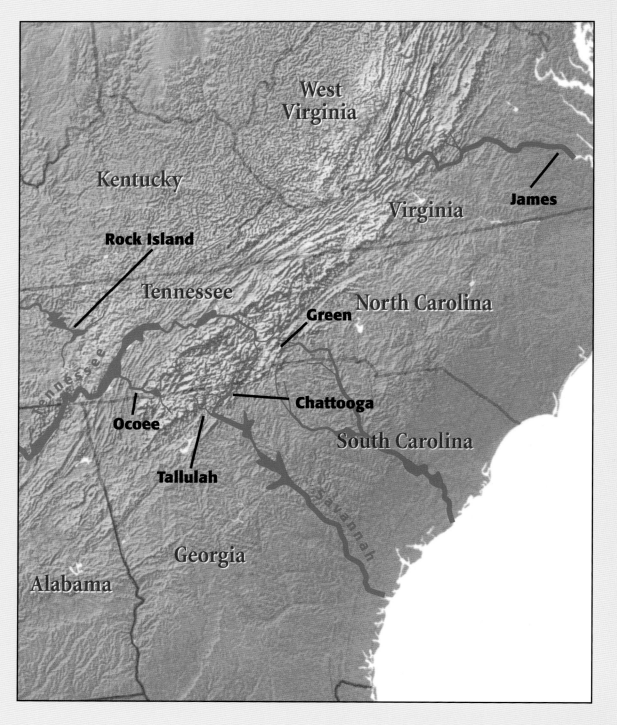

The South

"We went down, picking up speed, and the step-up in sound, like a dial being tuned, brought up the old terror, but also excitement: the sensation Lewis was always describing: I felt it, tired as I was."

James Dickey

If one were to create a whitewater paradise, the southern Appalachians might be a good model to follow. Plentiful rainfall, a warm temperate climate, and a myriad of steep mountains make this region prime for paddling. Maybe that is why the South is home to so many paddlers.

The South has always been renowned for its top-notch open boaters, and several difficult rivers of the region were run first in canoes. Today, both canoes and kayaks continue to explore new steep creeks that are hidden deep within the misty mountains of the South.

The paddling season here lasts throughout the year. Summer brings a hot and humid airmass that helps produce heavy thunderstorms, which can make creeks rise rapidly. Summer is also the season when the lowest water of the year occurs, as dense forests use much of the available ground water. Hurricanes occasionally come in the Fall, often rejuvenating parched watersheds overnight. With the deciduous forests bare in winter, the ground water recharges. During this season, paddlers can often enjoy high water combined with relatively mild temperatures. Not much snow falls in the South, but the highest mountains of the entire Appalachian Range are found here (North Carolina's 6,684-foot Mt. Mitchell is the highest), and a modest snowpack does occur. Snowmelt can contribute to springtime flows on a multitude of mountain creeks of the Southeast.

Paddling doesn't stop at the foot of the mountains in the South. Several large rivers contain whitewater stretches far beyond the convoluted landscape of the Appalachians. The James River, for instance, has great whitewater at the junction of the Piedmont and the coastal plain, right at the city of Richmond. There aren't many cities in North America where paddling can be a lunch break activity, but here in Richmond, and in Atlanta, Georgia, on the Chattahoochee, it is a regular occurrence. Welcome to life in the South.

Nailing the middle line at Gorilla

Woody Callaway

Woody Callaway has always had an addictive nature, and this is a good thing. As a child growing up in the South, his addiction was team sports, and the obsession eventually produced a college athletic scholarship. When he was introduced to boating, that quickly became his passion, bringing him a funhog's lifestyle and prominence in the sport. Now, as he directs one of the continent's leading kayak manufacturers—Liquidlogic—it is clear that his latest fix is satisfied by creating new boat designs for the ever-changing sport. Thank goodness for addictions.

In fourth grade, Forrest Callaway was diligently chasing his baseball dreams as bat boy for the local high school team when it was decided that he needed an obligatory baseball nickname. Forrest became woods, which begot Woody, and a persona was born. The name became synonymous with Callaway's friendly smile in every arena of his life.

The 6'4" Callaway starred in basketball during high school, landing him a scholarship at Western Carolina University. This is where Woody was first exposed to whitewater paddling. On a trip offered to the university through a local outfitter, he went tandem canoeing on the Missinabie River. It was clear from the very moment he felt the glide of current beneath the boat that river running was going to be his next life-defining endeavor. He remembers that first day vividly. "I was instantly hooked," he says. A raft guide friend of his helped him keep the momentum going, and Woody was soon catching eddies with the same grace he displayed while taking a jump shot.

His uncommonly smooth style combined with his noticeable stature made him one of the more recognizable paddlers in the South, especially when his endless legs would come crawling out of the tiny squirt boat he often paddled. His cordial Southern manner became a fixture of the boating scene, too. As contemporary Risa Shimoda says, "Woody has never met a stranger."

This easy-going nature helped Woody become a technical representative for Perception Kayaks in the early '90s, when Callaway helped create the "Pied Piper" concept of product promotion. He traveled extensively with a trailer load of new boats, visited river festivals, and had a new group of boaters sampling his products at every stop. Woody and his quiver were seemingly everywhere at once, and he was paddling all along the way.

It was during this period when Callaway first ran North Carolina's Green River. Bob McDonough and open boater Dave Simpson (a.k.a. Psycho) were his regular paddling partners. This trio named the Green's signature rapid, Gorilla, on Woody's first time down. After inspecting the vertical sluice for potential lines, they came to the conclusion that it was indeed runnable, but anyone who tried it would need "nuts the size of a gorilla," as Callaway recalls.

Callaway has such an attachment with the Green that when it came time to select a headquarters for Liquidlogic, the choice was obvious. The company is based in Saluda, North Carolina, just off the road to the put-in for Woody's classic pick—the Narrows of the Green.

Green Narrows

It is probably safe to say that North Carolina's Narrows of the Green is the most difficult regularly run piece of whitewater on the continent. Normally a creek like the Green, that drops over 350 feet-per-mile, is firmly in the realm of only the most hairball exploratory boaters. The Green, however, will see dozens of paddlers hurling themselves down it on a typical summer weekend. Hundreds of paddlers run the Green in a year, and there is even a downriver race that takes place here. Despite its popularity, the Green contains class V+ whitewater. The phenomenon of the Green is clear testament to how much the sport of whitewater has developed in the past two decades.

One of the key factors contributing to the Green's popularity is the reliable flow. Water is released almost daily from the upstream reservoir of Lake Summit, providing consistent flows throughout the year. Rather than a foot gauge or cfs value, water levels here are reported by Duke Power as a percentage of release capacity. One hundred percent or two hundred percent with minimal natural inflow are the standard levels. Typically, this translates to summer levels around 200 cfs, while springtime flows are usually 300 to 400 cfs.

Whatever the level, anyone planning to run the Green should expect plenty of tight slots and sheer drops. With today's short, round boats, the run is doable, but challenging. When it was first attempted with the 13'2" boats of the late '70s, it was off the scale of runnable whitewater. A group of five tried it anyway.

Scott Pendergrast and Andrew Stults were among the quintet that was lured to the unknown Green in 1978 on the advice of local open boater Michael Rainey, who told of "a neat canyon that was like the Chattooga." To compare the Green with the Chattooga is a stretch to say the least, but after running the warm-up rapids, the group thought their guide in the canoe had indeed turned them on to a pleasant new river.

Then they hit the gorge. Stults recalls, "He [Michael] had hiked it before without a boat, which is essentially what we did, but with boats." He continues, "It was way beyond what any of us had seen before." The portage fest turned semi-epic as Stults recalls, "hugging poison ivy, and doing whatever we could to arrest our descent." After the steepest part of the canyon, they were able to paddle some more, and narrowly made it off the river before dark.

A decade later, boats had shortened, and new creek boating techniques were developing. The Green's time had come. By 1988, groups of instructors from Nantahala Outdoor Center were probing the Green, and chipping away at the portage total. Then in November of that year, the definition of running the Green changed quite suddenly from a portage-laden canyon exploration to an entirely runnable steep creek. The paddlers responsible for this change in perspective were Tom Visnius and John Kennedy.

The duo had been on a tear that month already, as Kennedy followed up on an alluring threat he had made to Visnius earlier in the season. When faced with Tom's possible departure for a winter of skiing out West, Kennedy promised, "If you stick around here, I'll show you some creekin'." Visnius stayed. Kennedy produced. They ran all the known steepest runs of the region, and a few unknowns too. By the time they reached the Green, they were on the top of their games, ready to run seemingly anything. And they pretty much did.

At the rapid that would become known as Squeeze, they ran the insanely tight line now fondly referred to as "Go left and die." Their planned route at signature rapid Gorilla was to make the eddy at the lip of the final drop, then ride the rock shelf on river right, avoiding the middle of the falls. Kennedy eddied out at the lip and waited for Visnius to join him, but Tom had blown his boat angle in the entrance, and wasn't going to make the eddy. He shouted as he blew by the waiting Kennedy, "I'm running it!", and paddled hard off the dreaded middle hump of water. Not knowing his partner's fate, Kennedy quickly peeled out, ran his right-side boof, and was greeted by a smiling Visnius in the surging eddy below. When asked about their reaction to the landmark moment, Visnius remembers simply, "We screamed." The elated pair then gleefully proclaimed to the lonely river canyon, "We're gonna call that Zoom Flume!" Fortunately, that title never stuck. Rather, it was coined Gorilla shortly thereafter by Woody Callaway and friends. Visnius and Kennedy were so bent on running everything, they stranded

themselves in the middle of the river amidst a log-choked sieve that is now considered the one mandatory portage on the run. After walking and swimming themselves to shore, they re-grouped below the sieve for Sunshine. The must-make boof hardly gave them pause in their focused states of being, as Visnius understates, "we were feeling pretty good at that time."

As word of the ground-breaking descent spread, the Green quickly became the place to go for the top creek boaters to test their skills. Paddlers like Bob McDonough and Woody Callaway became so enamored with the place that they made it their regular training ground, running it hundreds of times. Even though the Green now sees several hundred paddlers every season, it is still a benchmark run to any serious creekboater. As Callaway says, "while many consider it an afternoon jaunt, others feel it is a rite of passage."

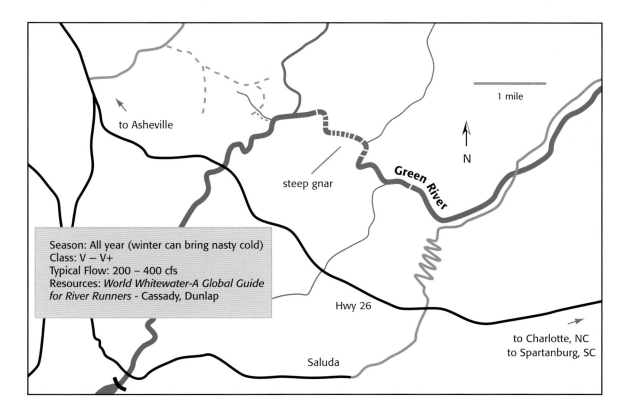

Urban whitewater on the James

Jon Lugbill

Some athletes take their performance to a higher level when faced with pressure situations. In the sporting world, these exceptional competitors are known as game players, and Jon Lugbill is certainly one. Throughout the 1980s, Lugbill always raced his C-1 at a high level, but when it came to the biggest competition of them all—the world championships—Lugbill dominated.

The youngest of three boys, Jon was led into the world of whitewater by his older brothers, Ron and Kent. Learning to paddle with their father Ralph in a C-2, the boys quickly embraced the new sport. Jon recalls, "We would beg our parents to take us on river trips every weekend." On days when they couldn't make it to the river, the brothers would paddle around on a pond near their home. With this fanatical paddling schedule, it's no surprise that at ages fourteen and fifteen, Jon and Ron made the national team in C-2 as the youngest members ever.

In 1979, Lugbill raced at his first world championships, and won the gold medal. For the next 12 years, Lugbill was a one-man dynasty, winning five out of the next six biannual world championships.

His crowning moment came at the '89 worlds on Maryland's Savage River. Lugbill's first of two runs was so fast that he knew the race was already his, allowing him to relax and attack the course on his second run. What followed was the most impressive display of power and grace ever witnessed on a race course. Those who were there still speak of Lugbill's Savage run with reverence. When Lugbill himself says, "I was very dialed in to the Savage," it is still an understatement.

Part of his Savage success can be traced to the difficult whitewater of that particular course. Lugbill always excelled on challenging courses, because he regularly ran difficult whitewater. While attending George Mason University in Washington, D.C., Lugbill would often make a morning run over the Potomac's Great Falls before heading to class.

In the early '80s, he paddled with river runner Jesse Whittemore. The two had each independently developed the revolutionary stern squirt, but Whittemore had to work for months to finally emulate Lugbill's bow squirt technique. Paddling together offered the two an opportunity to exchange new paddling theories. "We would talk about moves and then go try them," Lugbill says. Their experimentation sessions are regarded as the most serendipitous fusions of paddling minds in whitewater history.

Lugbill is recognized as one of the most athletic paddlers ever. For the past several years, he has used that athleticism to direct the Richmond Sports Backers, a non-profit organization that attracts events like off-road triathlons to the city of Richmond, Virginia. Sometimes, Lugbill-designed courses lead participants swimming across the James River, where Lugbill first came to paddle at age twelve. "The thing I love about the James is that at high water, it retains definition," says Jon. The highest level Lugbill ever ran it was 18-feet, which translates to over a quarter million cfs. At that level, it is only an advisable endeavor if you are truly a game player. Lugbill is.

James River

The James River winds placidly for many miles through rich Virginia farmland before tumbling off the Piedmont to the coastal plain below. Today, the whitewater of this geologic boundary provides outdoor recreation amidst the concrete of a medium-sized city, but historically the James' rapids were primarily viewed as an impediment to regional commerce.

The whitewater that breaks up the monotonous smooth surface of the James also disjointed the smooth movement of goods along the James in the 1700s, causing shipments to be taken off the river at the site of the rapids. The resulting break in the line of trade is partially responsible for the existence of the city of Richmond, whose downtown now perches above the enduring rapids.

While the sight of skyscrapers looming over class IV whitewater adds a certain surreal quality to the river, the James is more than just a novelty urban run. This river actually has quality whitewater.

Locals divide the several miles of James whitewater into two sections—the upper and the lower. The upper run starts at Pony Pasture, which is part of the James River Park system.

This extensive greenbelt runs along much of the river with a broad path that can lend itself to bicycle shuttles for those inclined. The greenway and its center piece—the river—provide sufficient habitat for bald eagles and river otters to survive in the center of this capital city. The river corridor sanctuary is also host to an off-road triathlon promoted by Jon Lugbill's Sports Backers. Participants swim the river in between rapids, and bike and run on the trails of the park.

Boaters exercise their skills by logging some time at the Pony Pasture put-in, where several ledges produce decent play spots at varying levels. Many paddlers park and play here. Those venturing downstream will

find several more good surf spots before reaching Reedy Creek a few miles downstream. High water makes the play better, including a broad ledge feature called Ten Boat Hole—it can hold at least that many.

Reedy Creek, besides being a runnable urban steep creek during storms, serves as the put-in for the more difficult lower section. Many of the rapids on this downtown run have been altered by dams. Paddlers new to the James will have to proceed cautiously or go with a local to avoid the nasty hydraulics caused by the artificial ledges. Where the dams have broken away, however, there are easily runnable channels, sometimes with good surfing. Okay, maybe it isn't the most pristine waterway, but it's still pretty damn fun.

The *big* rapid of the James is called Hollywood, as it is adjacent to the river left Hollywood Cemetery. Belle Isle, the island on river right, has its share of grave sites too. This was a POW camp in the Civil War, and numerous Union soldiers are buried here. Don't get distracted by the aura of the graveyard now, though, or the class IV drops of Hollywood Rapid will snap you back to attention. There is a hole in Hollywood called Stripper, because, as a local Richmond paddler will tell you, "it'll rip yer britches off."

Below Hollywood the river passes underneath the Robert E. Lee bridge, then tumbles through another broken dam that can offer decent surfing when high, and threatening chunks of concrete when low. The last drop on the James is divided into five channels, with a different amount of water and difficulty level in each. At low water, the far left Pipeline is usually preferred. At higher levels, the middle channels create class IV+ creek lines. River right is known as South Side, the widest of the channels.

The most commonly used take-out on the James is a unique re-entry into urban life from the cleansing sanity of the river. After passing by the bridge-sheltered residence of an established Richmond resident who most would consider homeless, paddlers emerge onto the pavement of the Mayos Island industrial zone. Nowhere is the importance of a river's powerful lifeblood more evident than here on Virginia's James.

Class IV in downtown Richmond, Virginia

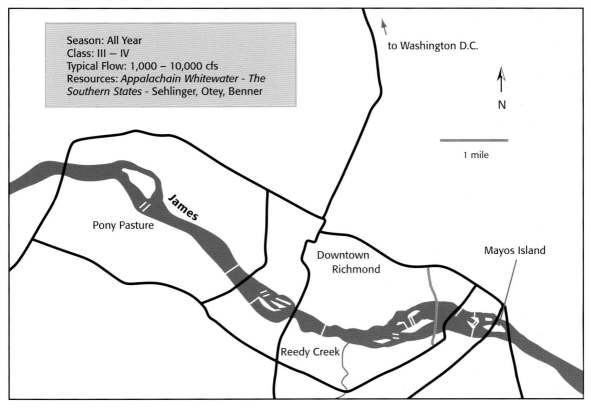

Season: All Year
Class: III – IV
Typical Flow: 1,000 – 10,000 cfs
Resources: *Appalachain Whitewater - The Southern States* - Sehlinger, Otey, Benner

to Washington D.C.

N

1 mile

James

Pony Pasture

Downtown Richmond

Mayos Island

Reedy Creek

Canoes have a long history on the Chattooga

Nolan Whitesell

From the fur trappers of the 1800s, to the first recreational whitewater boaters in the early 1900s, the open canoe was the most instrumental craft in the early development of whitewater paddling. As the sport grew, however, many paddlers favored decked canoes and kayaks for difficult water. Open canoes often took a back seat to these smaller craft, and a belief spread in many parts of the paddling community that open boats were unsuitable for whitewater. No single paddler has done more to change this uninformed attitude than Nolan Whitesell. Through both his forward thinking designs, and his landmark descents, he has remained the leader in the realm of open boating.

There was some indication that Nolan would become the leading canoeist of his time when he eagerly jumped into the family canoe on Lake Erie before he was even big enough to hold a paddle. These early signs of promise were not so evident, however, when in college he took his first canoe trip on section III of the Chattooga River. Nolan and his partner were struggling to make their boat go straight when a helpful bystander offered some advice. "It'll work better if y'all put your paddles on opposite sides of the boat," he exclaimed. "Ah hah!" thought Nolan. It was a simple start, but it would not be his last revelation in whitewater canoeing.

While still a relative beginner, Whitesell began toying with different rolling techniques while he and his kayaking friends practiced on Georgia's Lake Lanier. His experiments eventually led to a new, more efficient canoe rolling technique that is now accepted as the standard method. During the same period, Whitesell searched for an alternative to the bulky, loose, and decomposing Styrofoam that was used for water displacement in canoe hulls. He found a discarded waterbed liner on the side of the road one day, crammed it in his canoe, and blew it up. The first float bag was born.

He never intended to become a revolutionary boat designer, but as he says, "nobody was doing what I wanted to do." What he wanted to do was run harder, bigger rivers, and he needed a new boat design to do it in. His answer was the Piranha—a radically short design that changed the face of whitewater canoe manufacturing. He continued to produce some of the most sought after canoes on the market until he finally stopped taking orders in 2000. Now, Whitesell says of the canoe industry, "I'm trying to be un-involved," a tough task when you're the preeminent figure of the business.

Credibility for his designs came largely from the ground-breaking descents he made paddling them. In 1984, Whitesell became the first open canoeist to run every rapid in Grand Canyon. He followed that with descents on Idaho's North Fork of the Payette, and the Niagara Gorge—both big water runs thought impossible for open boats. Despite his noted big-water accomplishments, most paddlers are more familiar with seeing Whitesell's graceful style on the more technical waters throughout the East. One of his favorite haunts is a place not too far from his North Carolina home, a place that inspired thousands to take up canoeing, a place where Nolan himself learned to paddle—the Chattooga.

Chattooga River

The Chattooga has a special charm that makes it one of the most beloved rivers anywhere. The river seems to cast a spell over its paddlers, and many have moved to the region to live near the Chattooga.

It is an inviting clear stream babbling over sinuous potholes of ancient river-worn bedrock. Graceful white pines angle out over the water, and side creeks form picture-perfect waterfall backdrops. The river drains the southeastern tip of the Appalachian chain, and catches the full brunt of moist sub-tropical air masses. The result is a verdant landscape of uncommon plant diversity where annual precipitation totals are as high as 90 inches. From its first spring sources in North Carolina to its final flurry of action above Tugaloo Reservoir, the Chattooga offers something special every step of the way.

The Chattooga's charm reached congress in 1974, when the river was granted official Wild and Scenic status. Contributing to this decision by Congress was no doubt the recognition the river received two years earlier when millions were exposed to the Chattooga through the book and movie *Deliverance*.

For better or worse, no other book or film has ever done more to popularize the sport of whitewater. In the decade following the release of *Deliverance*, nearly twenty drownings occurred on the Chattooga, many of which were the result of under-prepared canoeists trying to emulate their big-screen heroes.

The primary actors in the film were Ned Beatty, Ronny Cox, Burt Reynolds, and Jon Voight. The real whitewater experts, however, were behind-the-scenes paddlers Payson Kennedy, Claude Terry, and Doug Woodward.

These three men were among the top whitewater paddlers of the region in 1971, so it was logical that their skills be used in the filming of the river-based story. They might have been overlooked, however, were it not for the recommendation they received from fellow canoeist Lewis King—a primary inspiration for the story.

In *Deliverance*, the fictional Cahulawassee River is the centerpiece for a story about three suburbanites led on a weekend canoe trip by their rugged bow-hunting friend named Lewis. There is little doubt that author James Dickey's fictional Lewis stems from archery champion Lewis King, an acquaintance of Dickey who once had a real life adventure on Georgia's Coosawattee River. Ironically, the real life Lewis was merely a shuttle driver on the canoe trip that eventually led to the book and movie.

While looking for a shortcut to the river where he hoped to pick up his friends, King ran into two shotgun-wielding locals who menacingly questioned what, exactly, he was doing out there. When he told them he was going to the river to pick up his friends, the older of the two hillbillies told his younger companion to escort King to the river, and "don't bring him back without them." His meaning, it was assumed, was that King was to be killed if no canoeists showed up like he had claimed. King was likely suspected to be a "revenuer," a regional name for authorities searching the back woods for illicit stills. Appalachian bluegrass music is rife with songs about dead revenuers, and King was about to become fodder for the next lyric. Fortunately, the paddlers arrived, King was spared, and the story developed into a masterpiece of film.

Acclaimed director Sam Peckinpaw almost directed the film with Charlton Heston as the Lewis character, but when Warner Brothers bought the rights from author Dickey, John Boorman got the nod as director, and Lewis, of course, was played by a fiery young Burt Reynolds. Reynolds' unforgettable character was partly gleaned, according to Claude Terry, from a flamboyant and athletic Navy seal that was on the movie set to handle river logistics. When a boat guided by the Navy man flipped over and drowned expensive camera equipment, the real whitewater experts were called in. Kennedy, Terry, and Woodward handled the boating for the remainder of the filming.

Kennedy recalls that the actors became "fairly proficient" at paddling, although they had trouble at Raven's Chute. With repeated flips, actor Jon Voight's make-up was washing off, and the script supervisor demanded that he have blood on him for the scene. It was late in the day, and the make-up artist had left. The director's temper was getting short when Claude Terry came up with a very Southern solution to a Hollywood problem. He picked some wild riverside grapes and mashed them up into juice. The grape juice was used to simulate blood on Voight, and they finished the shot.

Most of the filming for *Deliverance* was done on the lower portions of the river, known as sections III and IV. This is where the most difficult whitewater is, culminating with the spectacular Five Falls—Entrance, Corkscrew, Crack-in-the-Rock, Jawbone, and Soc-em-Dog. Like the rest of the Chattooga, these rapids have such character that even a tenth of a foot of change in water level can make a noticeable difference in their features, making for many intricate and different runs. It's just one more part of the mystique of the lovely Chattooga.

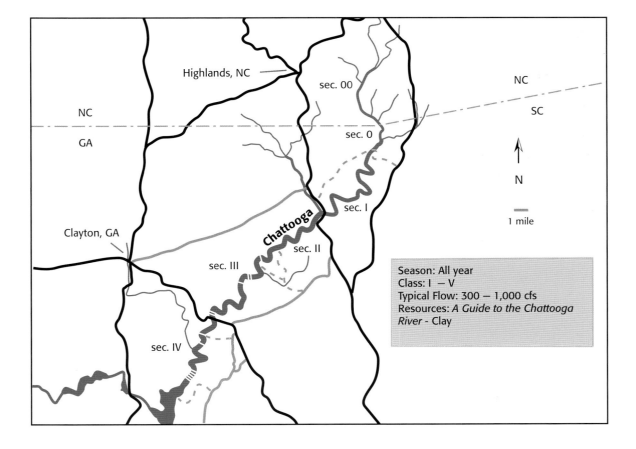

Season: All year
Class: I — V
Typical Flow: 300 — 1,000 cfs
Resources: *A Guide to the Chattooga River* - Clay

Katie Johnson

Surfing it up at Rock Island

Clay Wright

From the river cruising of yesteryear to the gymnastics play boating of today, Clay Wright transcends the old and new schools of whitewater. "I just like whatever's new and interesting," says Wright. For the past thirty plus years, he has been vitally involved in the "new and interesting" aspects of whitewater paddling.

Clay began paddling at the age of seven under the tutelage of his mother and extended family, who were all avid paddlers as members of the Tennessee Scenic Rivers Association. His first boat was a fiberglass Klepper that had a broomstick for a bulkhead. Clay naturally took to the sport despite his basic gear, and soon he could Eskimo roll consistently. By the time he was twelve, Clay was running the Ocoee, and his destiny as a world class kayaker was beginning to come into focus.

When squirt boating emerged as the progressive wing of paddling in the '80s, Wright quickly took to it. For several years a squirt boat was his craft of choice. He climbed to the top of this sub-culture of paddling with a world championship in the class in 1997. Even though Wright rarely paddles a squirt boat these days, he still manages to finish among the best in the world whenever he competes.

Competition paddling has taken different forms for Wright, from squirt to freestyle to extreme races. He has logged victories in down river races on the Green, Watauga, Gore Canyon, and Cherry Creek to name just a few. His abilities at racing down class V no doubt stem from his experiences of exploring new and difficult runs.

Along with his cousin Howard Tidwell, Wright pioneered several new runs in the Southeast, then teamed with BJ Johnson to explore new possibilities in West Virginia. He and Johnson worked as a team both on and off the river, as Wright would glean important information from the locals, while Johnson pored over the topo maps.

In all, Wright has logged first descents in 11 different states, and 5 different countries. Much of his paddling antics have been captured on film. He has appeared in an astounding 25 different videos, and the list is still growing.

Many of Clay's video clips have him running big drops, but he has also been a major player in the world of freestyle. Not surprisingly, he is inspired by the newness of it all. "When I first saw a helix," he says, "I thought I'd never do it. But six months later, there I was." Clay's backyard playground—Rock Island—has played host to several U.S. team trials. The competition hole is in the same rapid he used to ride in his inner tube as a kid. Clay Wright may have changed with the times, but the spirit behind his paddling has remained the same.

Rock Island

Tucked amid the rolling green hills of central Tennessee, there is a whitewater enclave developing. The place has everything a professional whitewater paddler would want—world class play waves and holes, consistently runnable water levels, class V falls, and big water rapids. Adding to the mix is a scenic waterfall backdrop. It's no wonder why paddlers Clay Wright and Eric Jackson have both made this place base camp for their various kayaking adventures. It might sound like a paddler's fantasy island, but its real name is Rock Island.

Rock Island is located northeast of McMinnville, Tennessee, on the Caney Fork River. Wayward boaters who have a hard time finding this out-of-the-way paddling destination can stop in a nearby roadside market to ask, and the friendly locals will usually be able to direct them to Rock Island. Maybe it hasn't always been a play boating Mecca, but the location has been recognized for its whitewater for a long, long time.

In the early part of the 20th century, the town of Great Falls grew up around the power of the Caney Fork River. The town's lifeblood was a sawmill powered by a large water wheel, and the wheel spun in response to the terrific current pouring over the cataract of Great Falls. When the Great Falls Dam was constructed just upstream of the drop in 1916, the waterfall itself was dewatered. The town's unique energy supply was suddenly gone, and soon after, so was the town.

As the 92-foot-high impoundment backed water upstream filling the canyons of the Caney Fork and its tributary Collins River, the surrounding hillsides began soaking up the standing water like a sponge. It infiltrated the porous limestone of the reservoir's banks, and began creeping through the subterranean cracks of the faulted geology. When it reached the cliffs of the river canyon below the dam, the water came pouring

out in an unnatural but spectacular series of curtain waterfalls that remain today. Despite its origins, the reservoir seepage forms a remarkable backdrop to some of the best kayaking at Rock Island.

Typically, paddlers put in across from the waterfalls, just downstream of the powerhouse that releases water back into the river. The quality play boating starts immediately, with nearly perfect surf waves leading downstream to the Rock Island Hole. This is a big frothy tumbler that has been the site of three (at latest count) national team trials. Though flows are normally 2,500 to 3,500 cfs, the hole remains good up to 5,000 cfs before it washes out. At that level, anyone still looking for action will want to head downstream to the "Brave Wave." This is a relatively new feature at Rock Island that could be gone with the next flood. Perched above a potentially hazardous undercut (hence the name), Brave Wave is huge and rowdy up to 15,000 cfs. As Clay Wright says, "Big air is a regular occurrence here."

Below the Brave Wave, the high-speed surfing is over, but a couple of class II rapids spice up a pleasant float around the corner and down to a public take-out on the left.

Upstream of the powerhouse put-in, the river is often dry. When the lake behind Great Falls Dam fills up, however, the Tennessee Valley Authority opens the flood gates, creating an impressive display of big water. The first rapid immediately below the dam is 20-foot-high Great Falls. There are two relatively easy lines leading over the drop, and several more difficult routes for those in search of true gnar. If you really want class V though, your best bet is to head just downstream to the next rapid. This one "gets heavy above 6,000 cfs," says Wright, and he speaks from experience.

His first run of Rock Island's most difficult rapid

came in the days when a 12-foot-long Mirage was a hot boat, and Clay was fifteen years old. He scouted the drop thoroughly before dropping in, but at fifteen he didn't quite have the big water experience to know just how powerless a kayaker can be in the throat of 5,000 cfs. He made it cleanly through the initial part of the rapid, but wound up involuntarily surfing in a second big hole downstream. Fortunately, his sprayskirt popped during the ride and water poured in, sinking his boat enough to flush him out of the sticky hydraulic. Since that first less-than-graceful run, Clay has learned the nuances of the rapid, and paddled it up to 16,000 cfs. Even at levels of 7,500 cfs, he says it is "One of the most powerful big water drops I've run."

Big water, world class play, scenery—Rock Island has it all. It makes you wonder why a whitewater addict would want to go anywhere else.

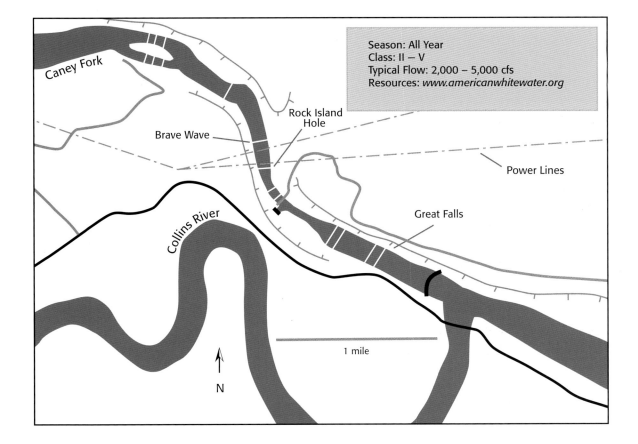

Season: All Year
Class: II – V
Typical Flow: 2,000 – 5,000 cfs
Resources: *www.americanwhitewater.org*

Caney Fork

Rock Island Hole

Brave Wave

Power Lines

Collins River

Great Falls

1 mile

N

Getting ready for instant action on the Ocoee

Mark Lyle

Mark Lyle has built a life around white-water. To support his river lifestyle he has guided rafts, driven shuttles, won freestyle competitions, represented manufacturers, and designed new kayaks. Looking back on this varied whitewater career, he believes he can trace it all to his first kayak run down the Ocoee River. He says facetiously, "I can plot the start of my life going downhill to right then."

Even before his Ocoee experience, however, the seeds of Lyle's whitewater growth had begun. As a senior in high school, Lyle first went kayaking with his older brother on the Hiawassee River. In a classic display of first-timer's gear, Mark wore a football helmet, and used a crude non-offset paddle. Despite the basic equipment, Lyle enjoyed it enough to make a return to the Hiawasse, this time solo. After multiple swims on the run, he loaded his boat on his car and immediately drove to an indoor pool where he tried to learn the Eskimo roll.

Tenacious Lyle flailed around in the pool for hours. He recalls, "I came closer to drowning in the pool than on the river." By the time the pool attendants kicked him out at midnight, Lyle had a roll.

His first Ocoee paddling came shortly thereafter, while Mark attended the University of Tennessee at Chattanooga on a wrestling scholarship. The quickness and strength that made him an all-star wrestler are still evident in his paddling today. Few paddlers can move a boat with as much explosive power as Lyle. His aggressive style is a natural fit for freestyle boating. Ironically, Lyle says he "never thought about doing a rodeo" until he was cajoled into competing just weeks before the 1993 U.S. team trials at the Ocoee.

He was working as manager for Sunburst Raft Company when he received a call from Dagger Kayaks. A Dagger spokesperson suggested that Lyle's raft guides had better start becoming more visible at rodeos if they wanted to keep their discounted boat arrangement with the company. Unbeknownst to Lyle, the phone call was a set up by friend and Dagger president Joe Pulliam, who wanted to lure Lyle into competing at the upcoming event. The ploy worked. Lyle entered, made the U.S. team, and was soon a leader in the growing sport of freestyle. He won the Ocoee Rodeo the next three years in a row, finished first in the pre-worlds in '96, and was national champion in 1997. His success in freestyle led to a design job with Dagger, where he has made his most significant mark on the sport. Lyle has been the principal designer on almost every whitewater boat Dagger has made since the mid '90s, including proven designs such as the Ego, CFS, and the best selling whitewater kayak ever, the RPM.

If you happen to see a stocky bright-eyed southerner wickedly throwing his boat into the latest freestyle move on the Ocoee, chances are its Lyle. He may look like he's just having fun, but he's actually testing his latest design. For him, it's just another day of working life on the river.

Ocoee River

With nearly 300,000 river travelers annually, Tennessee's Ocoee River is the most popular whitewater run in the East. Most of this traffic comes in the form of commercial rafts that parade down the busy run throughout the summer. The rafts flock here for the Ocoee's twenty named rapids, its easy access next to the highway, and its convenient location. It sits within an hour of Atlanta, Georgia, and Chattanooga, Tennessee. If ever there was a made-to-order recreational river, this is it.

For most of the twentieth century, the Ocoee was nothing more than a dry riverbed of bedrock ledges. In 1913 a dam was built that channeled the Ocoee's flow into a wooden flume feeding a powerhouse, and the whitewater-forming boulders of the riverbed were left high and dry. By 1976, the old flume was leaking so badly that power production was being impacted, so water was re-directed back into the river while repairs were made. The Ocoee suddenly leapt back to life, and paddlers quickly took notice.

National races were held on the temporarily restored river, and a commercial rafting industry began to form. When the Tennessee Valley Authority tried to divert the river back into their repaired flume, a battle naturally ensued between river advocates and industry officials. Whitewater interests had many locals on their side. Not only did area residents recognize the positive economic impact of river recreation, they were also familiar with the results of careless extractive development.

Much of the Ocoee basin had already been poisoned by mining and its resulting acid rain. The denuded hillsides of the upper Ocoee's Copper Valley are such an obvious scar on the landscape, that the deforested area is one of the few man-made impacts that can be seen from space.

After a heated negotiation process, the U.S. congress finally passed an appropriations bill that mandated the TVA to release water into the river, provided that they are compensated for their lost power revenue by river users. As long as commercial rafting remains intact on the Ocoee, the releases should continue.

Although the main Ocoee's water politics were basically settled in the early '80s, the absurd battle to maintain water in the river persisted on the dewatered upper run. This section upstream of the standard run came into the limelight in 1996 when the Atlanta Summer Olympics held whitewater slalom events there. To accommodate an Olympic slalom course, 1,700 feet of riverbed were modified. The wide riverbed was channelized to half its original width, and sandstone boulders were grouted to the bedrock. Completing the development, a whitewater visitor center was built on the banks of the Olympic race course. Ironically, the whitewater center overlooked a rocky channel that rarely ever contained whitewater. Negotiations in 2003 resulted in an agreement to allow water to again flow through this part of the river for 54 days a year.

When water does flow down the upper Ocoee, paddlers find rapids with slightly more push than those on the standard middle Ocoee run. The biggest rapid, Humongous, features a large artificial rock and a sticky hole. Even a few Olympic paddlers swam out of their boats here. The upper run finishes at a powerhouse where the emasculated river is normally returned to its natural bed just in time to gather behind the diversion dam that supplies the once-leaky flume. When releases occur (weekends only March to October/Thursday through Monday June through August), the diversion dam spills over in a sheet of white that serves as a dramatic backdrop for the put-in.

The action begins right away with Entrance Rapid, and remains fairly continuous for the first couple of

miles downstream. Broken Nose and Double Trouble
are standout rapids before reaching a flat section called
the Doldrums, located a little more than halfway
through the run. Tablesaw and Diamond Splitter are
the big rapids below the Doldrums, then several small
drops lead to Hell Hole. There is almost always a line-
up waiting to jump into this famous play spot, where
several major freestyle events have taken place.

Most of the Ocoee's rapids are class III, with play
spots interspersed liberally throughout. Every rapid has
a handful of different eddies to catch, waves to surf, and
holes to play. The lively nature of the river makes it a
favorite destination for intermediate and advanced paddlers alike. Even world class paddlers like Mark Lyle still
find plenty of entertainment on the familiar Ocoee.

Dodging a moving undercut on the Ocoee

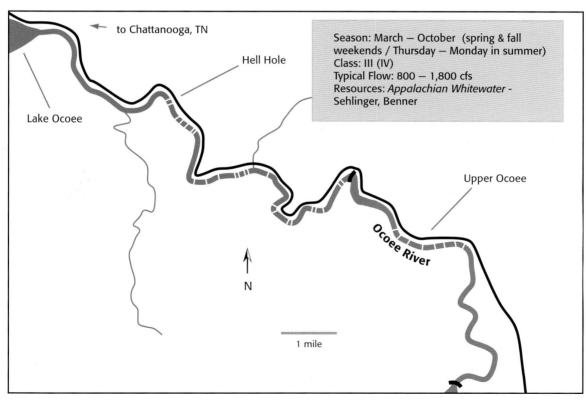

to Chattanooga, TN

Hell Hole

Lake Ocoee

Upper Ocoee

Ocoee River

N

1 mile

Season: March — October (spring & fall
weekends / Thursday — Monday in summer)
Class: III (IV)
Typical Flow: 800 — 1,800 cfs
Resources: *Appalachian Whitewater* -
Sehlinger, Benner

Kevin Colburn

Oceana Rapid on the Tallulah

Risa Shimoda

One of the things that drew Risa Shimoda to whitewater was the diversity of the paddling community. She remembers characterizing the first group of paddlers she met as "smart, independent people whose other personal interests were completely eclectic." No one fits that profile more than Risa herself.

In college, her spry energies were focused on tap dancing and musical playwrighting—hardly springboard activities to whitewater addiction. After college, she was working in Cincinnati as a design engineer for Proctor & Gamble when a co-worker randomly invited her to the ubiquitous kayak pool session. She met her first group of diverse paddlers, and her interest in the sport was sparked.

Soon she was spending every weekend on Tennessee's Ocoee River, and paddling was quickly becoming more than just a hobby. She attacked the sport with the same vigor that had thrust her into corporate America. "I would spend every day of my two week vacations paddling," she says. By her second season, Risa had tackled the Gauley, and her confidence was soaring.

In 1983, Risa made her first paddling trip to the West, where she became the second female to run the North Fork of the Payette (Kathy Blau was the first), at a juicy 3,000 cfs, no less. The same trip took her to California, where she ran infamous Bald Rock Canyon.

Her diminutive 100-pound frame bombing down raucous class V was serving as inspiration to other female paddlers, and certainly turned heads throughout the paddling community, but Risa really found her paddling niche when she tried on her first squirt boat.

The low volume Jim Snyder designs were perfect for petite Risa, and the new sub-sport invigorated her passion for paddling even more. She ran things in her squirt boat that she admits "I probably shouldn't have," including the Watauga Gorge, and the Russel Fork. In 1987, she became the only person to squirt the massive water of the Niagara Gorge. Canoeist Nolan Whitesell describes Risa's squirt boating antics at the Niagara's Whirlpool Rapid as "The most eerie thing in the world. She disappeared for many, many seconds."

Risa has competed in four world championships in the squirt class, but her biggest contribution to freestyle paddling has been her founding of NOWR—the National Organization for Whitewater Rodeo. Although now disbanded, NOWR played an important role in the blossoming of freestyle throughout the '90s.

Risa's primary legacy to whitewater sport is undoubtedly her leadership of American Whitewater, *the* advocacy group for whitewater paddling in North America. She first volunteered for AW in 1984, and took over as executive director in 2001. AW has protected and restored scores of rivers, the Tallulah among them. Risa first paddled here during an AW-directed flow study to sample the river's viability as a whitewater run. She then played a major role in securing scheduled releases on the river. There's no doubt Risa Shimoda has traveled quite a distance on the winding stream of life since her days of tap dancing.

Tallulah Gorge

In the movie *Deliverance*, four canoeists find themselves trapped between dramatic waterfalls in a deep vertically-walled gorge. The film reaches its defining moment here, as the protagonist is forced to face his primal instincts in the unyielding wild canyon. Jagged cliffs lurch out over the river, and gnarled pine trees cling to gullies on the black walls. The setting is a perfect backdrop for the story's portrayal of the struggle between civility and instinct. In the movie, this moment of deliverance takes place on the fictional Cahulawassee River. In reality, the scene was filmed in the Tallulah Gorge.

The Tallulah is not quite as remote as we are led to believe in the movie, but beneath the canyon rims, there is still a distinctly untamed feel to the place. The dramatic waterfall rapids and scenic vistas attracted enough tourists to sleepy north Georgia that in the late 1800s, the community of Tallulah Falls thrived. The Tallulah was known as the "Niagara of the South," hosting the same waterfall-based tourism as its famous cousin in the North.

In 1913, however, the Tallulah was dammed. Almost overnight, Tallulah Falls Lake filled the upper reaches of the gorge, water was diverted into tubes for power production, and the spectacular waterfalls of the canyon were reduced to a trickle.

The river remained virtually dry for the next eighty years, the only exceptions being flood surges when the dam operators were forced to spill extra water, and the brief flows that Hollywood purchased for the filming of *Deliverance*.

Then in the early 1990s, the seeds of the river's re-birth were planted when paddler/activist Pete Skinner spread the word to other politically active boaters to look for dewatered riverbeds in their regions that might benefit from the federal relicensing process.

The Federal Energy Regulatory Commission (FERC) must re-evaluate licenses granted to hydropower projects every fifty years. In 1991, the Tallulah license was up. Through the efforts of local paddlers, American Whitewater, the Georgia Canoe Association, and several other groups, momentum for scheduled recreational releases was begun, and all interested parties were brought together to discuss proposals. The result was a flow study in 1993 in which Risa and other top paddlers of the region were sequestered to make a run of the gorge.

The event was quite possibly the most publicized first descent in history. Four Atlanta-based television stations showed up to film the run, newspapers from around the region sent reporters to the scene, and a bevy of local police and Georgia Power representatives scuttled about the put-in. Completing the media circus, a helicopter circled overhead. Several of the paddlers declined requests from the media to attach cameras to their boats for the run. Apparently the cameramen were unaware of the inherent violence contained in class V rapids like Oceana, the Tallulah's signature drop.

This rapid lies near the start of the run. The only warm up paddlers receive before Oceana comes in the form of two relatively small ledge drops, and a 592-stair descent to the canyon bottom. Oceana's most noticeable feature is a giant exploding rooster tail of water in the middle of the 50-foot slide known as "The Thing." Encounters with "The Thing" are shockingly severe, earning the rapid its fierce reputation. Below Oceana, there is the class IV Gauntlet, then Bridal Veil Falls, the last true class V of the run.

Despite its impressive gradient of over 300 feet-per-mile, the Tallulah is a remarkably moderate run, dominated by a host of class IV rapids. The runnable nature of the pool-drop Tallulah was a pleasant surprise for Risa and the rest of the crew of paddling probes. Following their first run down, they knew that the spectacular Tallulah would be fully utilized if releases were indeed granted.

Before a final agreement was reached, a second test run was conducted in 1995. This time, three different water levels were sampled by the paddlers: low, optimal, and high. As the group lingered in the gorge on their final, highest run of the day, they were surprised to notice the river unexpectedly rising. The quick rise hurriedly got the group paddling for the mouth of the canyon, and they rode well over 1,000 cfs through the last of the gorge. At the take-out, they learned that the dam operator had assumed they were off the river, so he had released extra water in order to flush debris out of the canyon.

Paddlers aren't likely to see any more debris-flushing

flows these days. As a result of the test runs, the established flow regime is now 500 cfs on Saturdays, and 750 cfs on Sundays. These releases are scheduled for the two weekends in April every year, and the first three weekends in November .

Like the tourists of a century ago, paddlers now flock to the hamlet of Tallulah Falls for weekend getaways. For five weekends a year, the local economy gets a boost, while paddlers and non-paddlers alike are free to enjoy the splendor of the river canyon. The same thing cannot be said for a certain cousin of the Tallulah in the north called Niagara. Maybe that river's governance will someday evolve enough to allow paddlers to run the gorge. If they play their cards right, the regulators of Niagara might someday gain an attraction that could be called the Tallulah of the North.

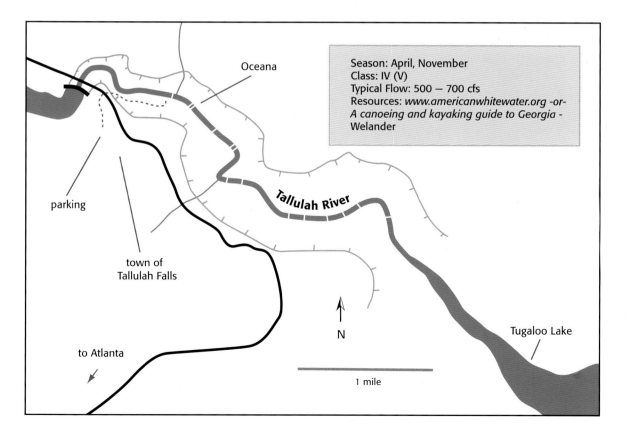

Oceana

Season: April, November
Class: IV (V)
Typical Flow: 500 — 700 cfs
Resources: *www.americanwhitewater.org* -or-
A canoeing and kayaking guide to Georgia -
Welander

parking

Tallulah River

town of
Tallulah Falls

N

to Atlanta

Tugaloo Lake

1 mile

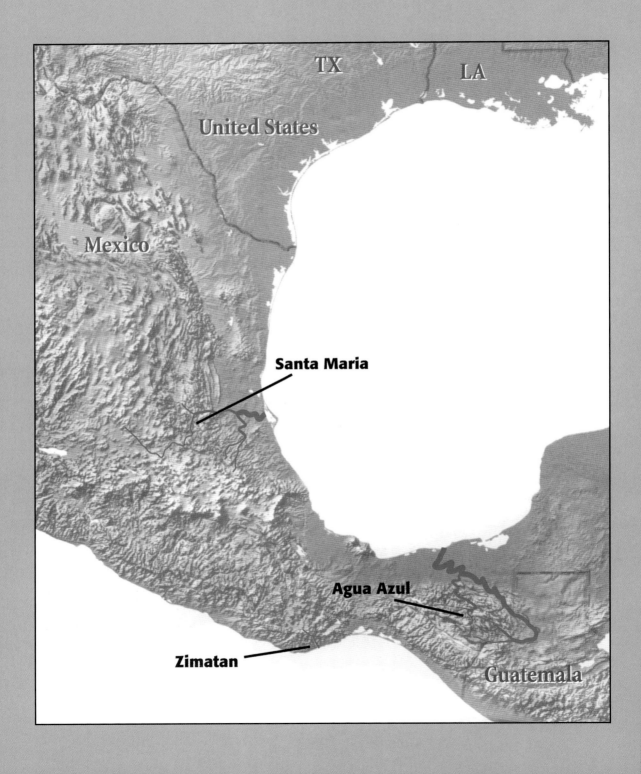

Mexico

"One should not forget that though the Sierra Madre is in fact a sister to the Rocky Mountains, it is in the tropics. There is no winter, no snow and ice, and consequently all plants, shrubs, insects, and animals keep alive all the time, and very much alive at that."

B. Travern

Mexico is a diverse country with warm weather, plentiful water, and varied cultures. A few regions of the country are savvy to river runners, but locals throughout much of Mexico still look at whitewater boaters as if they were from Mars. Paddling in Mexico can be an exotic foreign adventure, even if it is just across the border from the U.S.A.

About half of Mexico lies within the tropics. This southern half of the country receives the most rainfall, and subsequently is home to most of the rivers. The three selected *Whitewater Classic* rivers in Mexico each fall south of the Tropic of Cancer, but each is in its own unique paddling region.

In the far south, the Agua Azul is a perfect example of the travertine rivers in the remote jungle-covered province of Chiapas. Farther north, the Santa Maria displays tropical characteristics within driving distance of the U.S. The Rio Zimatan, and unknown jewel, is located in the Pacific coastal state of Oaxaca, which harbors perhaps the finest whitewater, and most colorful culture, in all of Mexico.

Northern Mexico has its share of rivers, too, but the climate is drier, and many attempts at exploration here are stymied by wildly erratic flows. For the patient explorer, first descents in the Copper Canyon region still await.

Paddling trips in Mexico are generally easiest when done with someone who knows the place. Beyond that, bring a good attitude, at least a little knowledge of Spanish, and some sunscreen, because there are plenty of rivers to be run south of the border.

Wickliffe Walker

Paddling downstream of Tamul Falls on the Santa Maria

Kent Ford

Kent Ford is passionate about paddling, period. It doesn't matter if it's multi-days, park & play, ocean surfing, downriver racing, sea kayaking, whitewater kayaking, surf kayaking, C-1, C-2, or open canoe, Ford does them all.

Ford's life of paddling was conceived in a time and place that served as genesis for the sport's modern era—Washington D.C. in 1972. Jamie McEwan's bronze medal in C-1 at the Munich Olympics had instilled a confidence in U.S. paddlers that led to unprecedented growth in the sport. No place thrived on McEwan's success more than the D.C. area, home to McEwan and the U.S. national team. It is no wonder that a paddler like Kent Ford came from such a harmonic convergence of paddling forces.

His introduction to paddling came in a C-2 with his father. Kent was initially enthusiastic about the sport, but the fourteen-year-old was understandably chagrined at being stuck in a boat with dad all the time. At fifteen he got his own boat, and in Kent's words, "As soon as I got my drivers license, that was all she wrote."

The subsequent paddling frenzy took Ford to 27 different countries, and over 350 different rivers. He has paddled in Turkey, Tasmania, Australia, Japan, throughout Europe, and of course Mexico, where his classic Santa Maria River is located. During the winters, Ford worked and skied in Colorado before returning East in the spring to teach and race on whitewater.

His racing exploits are nearly as varied as his recreational paddling. He competed in downriver, was on the national champion C-1 team twice, and finished fifth in the world in C-1 in 1985. As his competitive racing years have drifted into his past, Ford has taken up announcing duties at the major world events, becoming the standard whitewater race announcer for the Olympic games.

Although he has quite a history in racing, Ford's greatest impact on the sport has probably been through his instruction. He has taught paddling for over twenty years, including several seasons as the manager of instruction at Nantahala Outdoor Center—one of the United State's biggest instructional centers. Today, paddlers continue to benefit from Ford's mastery of technique by watching his instructional videos. He has produced over sixteen of them to date, including: *The Kayakers Edge*, *Breakthru*, and *The Kayak Roll*. Whether we've seen him race, taken his lesson, or watched one of his films, there are few paddlers in North America that haven't been touched by Kent Ford's passion for paddling.

Santa Maria

Not only is the Santa Maria River one of the closest tropical rivers to the United States, it is also one of the best. The Santa Maria offers dramatic scenery, rapids of all levels, and of course, the warm turquoise water of Mexico.

The turquoise comes largely from the limestone geology of the area, a substrate that lends itself to springs, caves, and surreal travertine formations. One of the strangest of these formations is located just beyond the last whitewater on the river. As a final obstacle to running the canyons of the Santa Maria, boaters must portage the Puente de Dios (Bridge of Gods), a travertine bridge that forces the river subterranean for 200 yards. This is just one of many amazing features of the Santa Maria, a river that neatly sums up the Mexican paddling experience.

There are five canyons on the Santa Maria, each with a slightly different flavor. The first two canyons are both the least visited, and the most difficult of the five. Congested boulder piles usually force a handful of portages here. When the water is low, there are a number of unrunnable sieves, and when it is high, both gorges turn into gripping class V.

The addition of the Rio Verde sometimes boosts the flow of the Santa Maria before it enters its third and fourth canyons. Located below the village of La Boquilla, the third canyon (also known as Canon Rincon Grande) is run together with the fourth canyon. The fourth canyon is the heart of the Santa Maria, with a series of class IV to IV+ rapids, and the otherworldly spectacle of Tamul Falls.

A side stream pouring into the main river is normally of little consequence to river runners, something to gaze at as you drift by. Tamul Falls changes this definition completely. This thunderous cascade is an obstacle to be avoided. When Kent Ford first arrived at

Tamul in 1986, he was completely astounded. "We'd heard about this waterfall blocking the river," he recalls, "but I thought it would be a falls on the Santa Maria that we would portage." The power of the Rio Gallinas crashing into the Santa Maria was so great, however, that the spray, noise, and wind created by the falls was too much to penetrate. Ford wanted to try it anyway.

Wick Walker, who had portaged around Tamul the previous year, matter-of-factly told Ford that there was, "No way you can go through there." Ford was unconvinced, and somehow coerced team member Doug Gordon to probe into the mist first.

With Ford prodding him along from behind, Gordon paddled into the hurricane-like sheets of water. Not knowing what lay ahead, the two strained to see downstream as they cautiously forced their way through the liquid atmosphere. Several paddle strokes in, their visibility was reduced to a few feet. Communication was impossible, and even paddling forward was a challenge. They retreated.

From the relative calm where their companions waited upstream from the falls, it didn't look that bad. They went in again, but the result was the same. There was just no way to know what lurked beneath the spray. Paddling full-bore under the waterfall might lead them into a terminal hole, or a rock sieve. It was time to portage. They laboriously roped their boats up a steep gully to the rim of the canyon, and emerged two hours later in a tropical paradise.

The Rio Gallinas sluiced between perfect flower-rimmed pools before dropping forever into the mist below. To continue their portage, the paddlers had to ferry across the Gallinas just above its 345-foot final plunge. As Ford recalls, "It was an honest-to-God 'don't miss your ferry!'" Of course no one blew their ferry, and they made their way back into the canyon of the Santa Maria below the falls. The next day the group ran through the fifth canyon of the Santa Maria (actually called the Tampoan below the falls), crossed the Puente de Dios, and took out.

They were celebrating their successful trip with a few cervesas at the local cantina when someone noticed a picture on the wall. It was a photo of the Santa Maria, with a low water Tamul Falls in the background. The unknown stretch of water that they had portaged was clearly visible in the photo. Ford and companions scrambled over to the picture to see what they had elected to not run blind. It was flat water.

The Santa Maria left an unforgettable mark on Ford. With the Santa Maria in mind, he explains what a classic means to him: "To qualify as one of my favorites, a river must have spectacular scenery. So spectacular that it threatens to draw my attention from the excitement of the whitewater. Meanwhile, the whitewater is intricate, playful, or overpowering, so it diverts my attention from the scenery. These competing natural dynamics make for a fabulous experience." Intricate whitewater and spectacular scenery defines the Santa Maria—undoubtedly a classic.

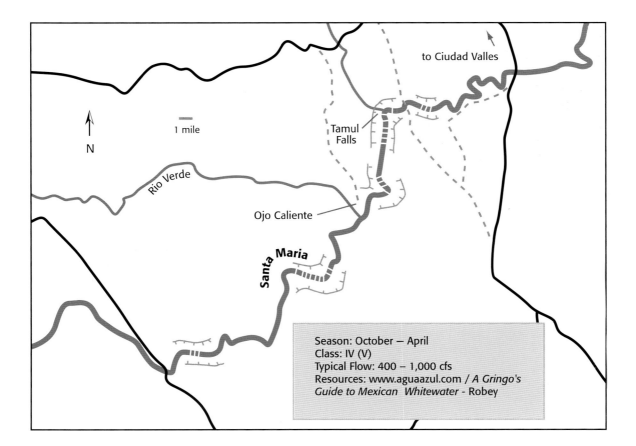

N

1 mile

to Ciudad Valles

Tamul Falls

Rio Verde

Ojo Caliente

Santa Maria

Season: October — April
Class: IV (V)
Typical Flow: 400 – 1,000 cfs
Resources: www.aguaazul.com / *A Gringo's Guide to Mexican Whitewater* - Robey

Grant Amaral

California granite? Nope, this is Oaxaca's Rio Zimatan

Grant Amaral

Grant Amaral never intended to be the expert on Idaho whitewater. In fact, when he first came to Idaho in 1977, he wasn't even that interested in being a kayaker.

Like most paddlers in the '70s, Amaral took up the sport the hard way—without any real instruction. At sixteen, the California native and his brother learned how to roll from the pages of a book. It was a constant struggle, and Grant thought maybe kayaking wasn't all that great. Then he moved to Idaho.

Enthusiastic friends urged him back onto the water, and soon Grant realized that he had stumbled into a treasure chest of paddling. The map-studying Amaral recognized that sparsely populated Idaho held heaps of virtually unknown rivers and creeks, and kayaking was the best way to explore them all. When he asked the few veteran paddlers of the area about different rivers, they were often tight lipped in their responses. Either they were being secretive, or, as Amaral remembers, "there just wasn't that much known." While earning two degrees at Boise State University, Amaral created his own systematic inventory of the state's potentially runnable rivers, and proceeded to go see what each one held.

Along the way, his paddling skills improved, allowing exploration of ever more obscure and difficult runs. In 1990, thirteen years after moving to Idaho, Amaral published *Idaho—The Whitewater State*, one of the most thorough and successful whitewater guides ever written.

By the time he finished the guidebook, Grant had fully embraced the whitewater bum's lifestyle: safety boating for commercial raft trips, instructing, and traveling to Central and South America for more boating in the off season.

Mexico became Amaral's favorite southern locale, as he went on annual paddling safaris there en route to a kayak guiding job in the southern state of Chiapas. Today he runs his own kayak business in Mexico. Expeditions Agua Azul runs trips both on central Mexico's Santa Maria and Micos Rivers, and in the southwestern state of Oaxaca. This culturally-rich region has the best whitewater in Mexico according to Amaral, who ought to know. He has likely done more river running south of the border than anyone.

Oaxaca is home to Grant's classic pick—the Rio Zimatan. He now owns property on the river's banks, so there is a chance you might run into him if you're down there. Unless he is back in Idaho, that is. After all, there is still plenty of exploring to be done there, too.

Zimatan

The Zimatan. I dreamed of the Zimatan years before I laid eyes on it. I saw it years before I realized it was the jewel of the Pacific and Mexican whitewater. Typical of the myths of Mexico, the Zimatan at first presented me with a dry riverbed and a brittle gray forest. Later—years later when I returned, I expected an easy class III run.

Once again I was fooled but far from disappointed. This isn't the dusty desert cantinas of Mexican dreams and misconceptions. The Zimatan is warm water, big waterfalls and a climate made for kayaking. Not out-of-this-world hair, but clean-cut fun in a remote canyon.

Oaxaca is a mix of tropical opulence and end-of-the-world adventure. This is the poorest state in Mexico in terms of income, but the richest in culture and a way of life that we all dream of. Geographically, Oaxaca is the perfect blend of the pine forests and wilderness of Idaho along with the white granite canyons of California. Only in Oaxaca, the canyons are within a stones throw of the Pacific Ocean, and the pine forests are 3,000 feet above sea level.

On the map the Zimatan looks like little more than a small stream. But as a creek it has more than enough water for kayaking. Viewed from the Coastal Highway, the Zim looks promising. Towards the ocean a small class II drops around the bend into fields of papaya and groves of bananas. Upstream looking towards the green mountains of Oaxaca and the abandoned coffee fincas, it looks even better. The canyon closes in and steep cliffs impinge on the riverbed.

Just upstream the road climbs the canyon wall and then takes a sharp bend creating a natural overlook for some of what the Zimatan holds. A thousand feet below, the river has carved a narrow gorge in a polished canyon of white granite. Upstream is a straight-away of what appears to be a half-mile-long succession

of technical class III drops. Directly below the overlook, the river takes a sharp bend to the left and disappears into the granite gorge. The roar of the river reaches all the way to the road, but the source of the sound is hidden behind the curve in the river.

A group of us (Grant Amaral, Peter Arthur, Trevor Hudson, Rich Wensel) probably made the first descent of all the rapids, but not the river. Eating sushi in the nearby resort of Huatulco, we ran into an expatriot German river guide, Andreas Weigelt, who was more than happy to share his Zimatan knowledge. Andreas had indeed run the river, but we were later to learn at extremely low flows. His estimates of the difficulty of the rapids were short by a grade or two across the board. Years later he told me that his first descent had so little water that he had to drag his boat at least a dozen times and "wheelchair" down several of the bigger drops.

Equipped with the former, but ignorant of the latter bit of river info, we put in at a high flow armed with play boats. Trevor Hudson complainingly took a Blunt as the play boats were snatched up in anticipation of a play run.

We paddled across the gravel shoals below the put-in and down a couple hundred meters where the river abruptly dropped into a six-foot-wide slot and over a twelve-foot drop. My first thought after struggling out of my tiny play boat to scout the drop was not to scout, but to run back upstream and see if I could stop the truck. I looked downstream, and could see another drop, then another. I couldn't tell how difficult they were, but one thing was very obvious, they certainly weren't class III. They weren't even Class IVs. These were textbook class Vs.

The whole canyon had an another-world type of feel, in 1997 Hurricane Paulina had cleared the canyon of almost all the vegetation. What remained was a flat expanse of slick white-granite with a narrow gorge cutting the plain in two like what it was: a crack in the earth. This was indeed what we had come for, but the shock of class III expectations and a class V reality gave me more of a start than looking over the lip of a powerful waterfall. That too was to come later in the day.

We regrouped, I didn't run back to the truck, and Trevor ran the first two drops without incidence. The rest of us rethought our play boat schemes and shleped ourselves down to a nice flat pool above a simple class IV.

With all the scouting, we arrived at the toughest and last rapid of the Zimitan in a shadowy tropical dusk. The time and our group's fatigue made me force Trevor to wait for another day to attempt the class V entrance and walled-out falls of El Chorro. We portaged on the left. There was no way back down to the river. The cliffs forced us to throw our boats into the canyon and leap into the calm pool below. It was dark by now, and we paddled out a series of class III shoals to the coastal highway where our driver had built a campfire to help us find the take-out.

The next day we encountered an old friend of mine, Carlos, one of the few Mexican kayakers. We told him of our Zimatan adventure. He took us into his store and showed us a photo of the first descent of EL Chorro. He had a yellow Mirage and was sliding over perhaps 1 cfs of water into the deep canyon of El Chorro. We rallied for an afternoon run of the Zimatan, this time with creek boats, and a bank-full descent of El Chorro.

Grant Amaral

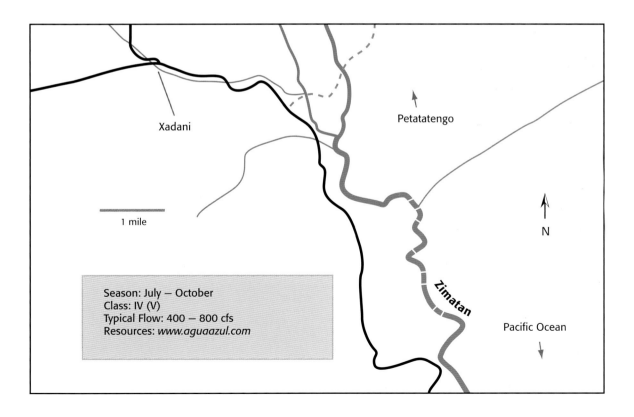

Xadani

Petatatengo

1 mile

N

Zimatan

Pacific Ocean

Season: July – October
Class: IV (V)
Typical Flow: 400 – 800 cfs
Resources: *www.aguaazul.com*

Dropping in on the travertine heaven of the Agua Azul

Cully Erdman

Cully Erdman was a fearless twenty year old athlete on the ski team at Vermont's Middlebury College when he first joined the school's paddling club in 1971. It was a time when getting started in whitewater paddling took a little more perseverance, and a little less money, than it does today. Cully proudly remembers building his first boat, a Prijon special slalom, for under $40.

As was customary at the time, Erdman didn't learn to roll until after his first season, but that didn't stop him from paddling any river he could find. He recalls, "trying to run all sorts of rivers in Vermont and New Hampshire." Without a roll, he learned the hard way. "Needless to say, I swam them all," he remembers.

The school of hard knocks paid off in the next few years as Erdman acquired uncommon river savvy that propelled him to the cutting edge of the sport. By the mid-'70s, he was one of America's most renowned paddlers.

In 1976, he was invited north to Alaska to participate in a made-for-TV descent of the Susitna River. Walt Blackadar, the most high-profile paddler of the period, had arranged the trip with the intention of making the first full descent of legendary Devil Creek Rapid, a monstrous big water drop that according to Blackadar, "made Lava Falls look like a mill pond."

Blackadar ran first, was back-endered in a giant breaking wave, and continued through the rest of the rapid in a rolling frenzy. "Rollups and rollups, flips on flips, blurred my mind into a drunken stupor," Blackadar himself recalled. At the bottom of the rapid, he finally swam.

After seeing this drama unfold, filmmaker Roger Brown radioed down from his helicopter that no one else was to run the rapid, because it was suicide. Erdman, however, was poised and ready. He shoved off from shore anyway. Cully entered farther left than Blackadar had, and hit the giant waves with an angled bracing technique perfectly suited for the big water. Erdman flipped twice, but unhesitatingly rolled up both times, and confidently paddled to shore below. He had become the first to successfully run ominous Devil Creek Rapid.

With this success, Erdman was asked to join more filmed endeavors. His most notable moment of high water fame was unfortunately a bad swim on the Yampa's Cross Mountain Canyon. Rebounding from this, he traveled to Mexico's Jataté River for a first descent in 1981. It was the start of a storied career of exploration south of the border in which he was the first to run the Tzaconeja, Santo Domingo, and of course the Agua Azul.

Chiapas, Mexico, was Erdman's winter home for many seasons, giving him the opportunity to explore several uncharted sections of his idyllic Agua Azul. Besides being the first river runner to explore the well-known cascades of the lower river, Erdman also probed the maze of waterfalls above the standard put-in, and has run the rarely traveled upper reaches. Today he still spends winters in the tropics with his company Slickrock Adventures. Most of the time he can be found on a Caribbean isle surrounded by turquoise waters reminiscent of his favorite river, the Agua Azul.

Agua Azul

Seventy-five degree turquoise water, a riverbed of soft travertine ledges, long slide rapids, sheer curtain waterfalls, deep pools, a warm tropical setting; these are all attributes one might create in a whitewater fantasy. This is also precisely what you'll find on the Agua Azul. It is a river straight out of a dream. This is no dream, however, this is just another river in Chiapas, Mexico.

Chiapas is the southern-most state in Mexico, a mountainous tropical land that harbors tremendously diverse habitats, from pine forests, to arid scrub lands, to lush jungle. It is on the moist jungle-covered eastern slopes of the state where the Agua Azul is located. The geology of the region is predominantly limestone, and a labyrinth of caves and sinkholes lurk beneath the green canopy of the surrounding mountains. The limestone also lends itself to the formation of travertine, a deposit of calcium carbonate that is primarily responsible for the stalactites found in caves. When a watercourse runs through this travertine-rich environment, the result is a surreal series of perfect waterfalls.

Unlike the conventional chaos of boulder strewn riverbeds, travertine forms uniform natural dams, domes, and ledges across a river. Cover this sculpted riverbed with water the color and temperature of your local swimming pool, and you've got a Tolkien-esque wonder world of whitewater.

Chiapas contains an array of travertine rivers, but the Agua Azul is the ultimate example. As Cully Erdman says, "No other river that I have seen, of a scale big enough to kayak, has such fantastic formations, water colors, and exotic backdrop as the cascades of Agua Azul. We call it kayaker's Disneyland."

The put-in for the standard run is not quite as overwrought as Disneyland, but it is still a comfortable lawn-adorned park. Upstream, multi-channeled tiers of dramatic falls weave through a myriad of tree islands that stubbornly cling to outcrops in mid-stream.

This was the first section of the Agua Azul to be explored by Erdman and friends. He recalls, "It was rather epic, we had to back track when we got to big waterfalls, and portage around sections, all the while not knowing where we'd end up, or even where we were in that maze of channels."

The riverbed downstream of the park continues to be split into multiple channels for the first part of the run, and paddlers will find themselves either in creeky sluices, on the brink of dam-waterfalls, or in a tangle of strainers, depending on their route selection. Guess wisely!

The river eventually gathers itself, and the impressive travertine horizon lines loom larger. Most of the drops have picture-perfect pool landings, but there are some hazardous spots, so launching in the wrong place can produce very ugly results. Shore scouting from the steep vine-covered slopes can be a pain, but fortunately most of the falls have shallow or dry spots on the lip of the drop where one can get out of their boat and scout. Be forewarned. If the river is higher than base flow, these scouting platforms can disappear, making the Agua Azul a whole different ball game.

The most dramatic part of the run comes as the river makes its final plunge into the Rio Shumilja (Shoo mul ha'). Here the Agua Azul tumbles over five big falls, the last one being a 35-footer dumping into the Shumilja. All of the falls have been run, but number four—the biggest—is normally a portage.

Once on the Shumilja, a few more traditional rapids lead to the long scenic paddle out, and the footbridge take out. Unless you drove your own shuttle, a doable but healthy uphill walk to the highway remains, where you might find a bus back to town.

Another class III waterfall

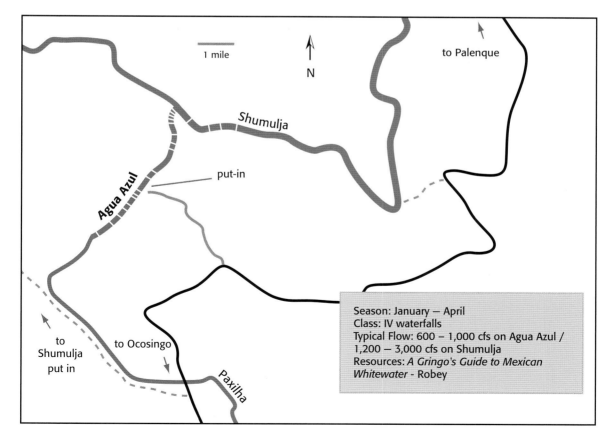

1 mile

N

to Palenque

Shumulja

put-in

Agua Azul

to
Shumulja
put in

to Ocosingo

Paxilha

Season: January — April
Class: IV waterfalls
Typical Flow: 600 – 1,000 cfs on Agua Azul /
1,200 – 3,000 cfs on Shumulja
Resources: *A Gringo's Guide to Mexican
Whitewater* - Robey

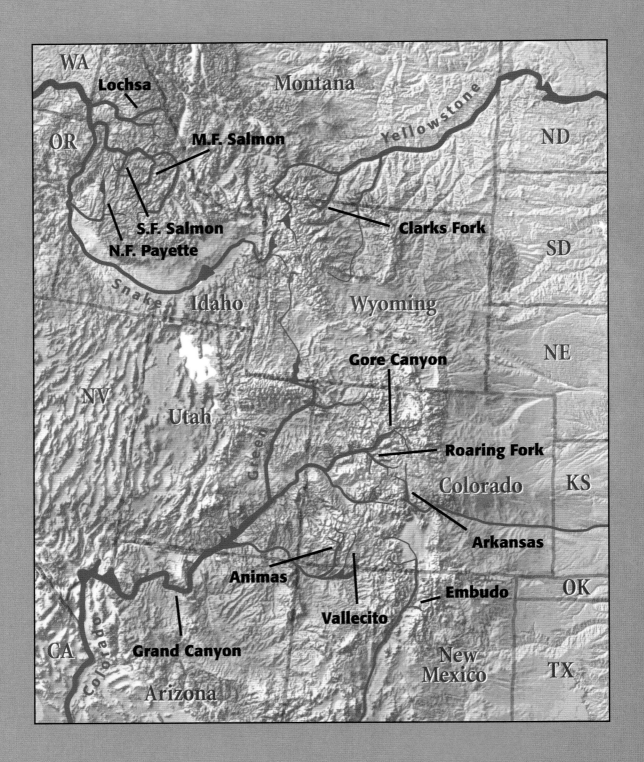

WA

Lochsa

Montana

OR

M.F. Salmon

ND

Yellowstone

S.F. Salmon
N.F. Payette

Clarks Fork

SD

Snake

Idaho

Wyoming

NE

NV

Gore Canyon

Utah

Green

Roaring Fork

Colorado

KS

Arkansas

Animas

Embudo

OK

Vallecito

CA

Grand Canyon

New
Mexico

TX

Colorado

Arizona

Rocky Mountains

"We top a ridge and real mountains reveal themselves on the eastern horizon, towering beyond red mesas and purple buttes and blue plateaus—country so beautiful it makes a grown man weep."

Edward Abbey

Ahh, the great American West, this is the place of wide open spaces, unforgiving deserts, and big wild mountain ranges. This region contains more *Whitewater Classics* rivers than any other, a fact owing more to the large area encompassed than to a high concentration of whitewater.

The Rocky Mountain region is generally an arid place, relying on its vast geography and high mountains to gather enough snowmelt to produce runnable rivers. Most of the region is entirely dependent on winter snowfall for its water, although summer thunderstorms can sometimes give the hydrology a boost in the south. In the northern state of Idaho, rainfall often helps saturate the snowpack, extending the paddling season.

The rivers here are as varied as the region itself, ranging from pool-drop to continuous, creeks to big water, crystal clear to muddy brown. The only constant is water temperature, which is almost always cold.

Cold water, arid climate, and vast distances—not exactly a recipe for an ultimate paddling destination. But this is the American West, a breathtakingly scenic region unique to the rest of the world, and paddling here can offer an equally unique experience. Whether it is the big crystalline rivers of Idaho, the wilderness streams of Wyoming, the creeks of Colorado, or the desert rivers of the Southwest, the Rocky Mountain region offers a little something for every paddler.

Deep in the Muav Gorge—Grand Canyon

Dana Chladek

"I'm not a big thinker. I just paddle," says Dana Chladek. The words ring with humility when one considers that the person speaking them knows four languages, runs her own business, and owns two Olympic medals. Considering her background, it's easy to understand how these extraordinary successes seem perfectly natural to Chladek.

Her parents were racers themselves, competing for the Czech national team in C-2 mixed. In 1969, five-year-old Dana and her family fled Soviet-controlled Czechoslovakia, escaping just five months before the border closed for good.

Like many influential European paddlers who crossed the Atlantic, the Chladeks brought their advanced techniques to America with them, and it wasn't long before Dana was paddling her own kayak behind her parent's C-2 on Michigan's Huron River. When asked what her earliest memory of paddling is, Chladek replies with a revealing chuckle, "It was probably terror." Although she has certainly outgrown the paralyzing fear of childhood, class V whitewater has never held great appeal for Chladek. Fortunately for American medal hopes, her focus has always been on racing.

Dana's parents entered her in numerous slalom competitions as a youth, and by the time she graduated from Dartmouth in 1986, Chladek had made the decision to pursue the K-1 slalom event seriously.

With her energies focused, it wasn't long before Chladek was beating whitewater slalom's elite. In 1988, she won the World Cup, and in 1992, Chladek earned the United States a bronze medal at the Olympics in Barcelona. Four years later at the 1996 Atlanta summer games, Chladek faced her greatest challenge in a difficult Ocoee course coming on the heels of her recent shoulder surgery. With only five months of training behind her, she flipped on the first run, earning herself a last place seed for the decisive second run. Undaunted, Chladek ripped the course on her second run, posting a time that remained unbeaten all day. Unbelievably, Chladek's time was tied to a hundredth of a second by Czech paddler Stepnaka Hilgertova. Chladek says of the bittersweet finish, "It still hurts to think about it." Dana's silver was the United States' best finish for any whitewater event at the games.

"I've always liked racing better than running rivers," she says. Her reason—there's no shuttle required to paddle a race course. In that case, her classic pick makes perfect sense. Grand Canyon offers 18 days of paddling with only a few hours of shuttling. Besides the short shuttle, Dana loves the Canyon for the relaxation factor. "It's eighteen days of great scenery, great people, and no phone calls." If anyone deserves a rest like that, it is Chladek.

Grand Canyon

Running the Colorado River through Grand Canyon is probably the greatest multi-day adventure available to mainstream river runners. Well, sort of available anyway. Currently the wait for a private permit is in the neighborhood of twenty years.

Assuming you finally get a permit to run the river, you will be committed to 226 miles on the Colorado before the first road access is available at Diamond Creek. Covering this distance in a non-motorized boat takes from 11 to 16 days, though many trips take the maximum allowable 18 days to have ample off-river hiking time. The scale of the landscape and colorful scenery are mind-boggling throughout the trip. From the serenity of evening light playing on the flat water, to the roaring hydraulics of Lava Falls, there really is no other river experience like the Grand.

Most of the rapids are found in the middle of the trip between miles 76 and 132, but Grand Canyon saves its biggest rapid as a climax near the end of the run. Lava Falls is located at mile 179. Lava stands out as being an obvious notch above anything else in the Canyon. Between its vicious ledge hole at the top, and its imposing black rock at the bottom, Lava has likely produced more 'no shit, there I was' stories than any other rapid.

Below Lava, the canyon opens significantly, adding to the effect of being past the crux. The scenery is still impressive, but at this point one's senses are dulled from the previous two weeks of awe. Those who explore far from the river will easily appreciate the remoteness of this lower section.

One can only imagine the trepidation felt by John Wesley Powell and his team as they forged their way through this unknown country in 1869. Having no maps, and dwindling supplies, theirs was perhaps the greatest first descent in the history of river running.

The distinguished and talented Powell and nine other hardy adventurers launched from Green River, Wyoming on May 24th, 1869. By the time they reached Lees Ferry (today's Grand Canyon put-in), they had already been on the water for 72 days. The haggard party pushed downstream in their narrow wooden boats, not knowing what they would find around each new bend. Some reports told of the river falling over a giant waterfall deep within the canyon. Although they suspected this not to be true, an air of uncertainty surely gnawed at their resolve. To make matters worse, heavy summer thunderstorms harassed the group as they slowly proceeded through the crux of the gorge. Sockdolager Rapid at mile 79 forced them to run without a proper scout, as the sheer canyon walls prevented landing. Downstream at Bright Angel Creek, they stopped and made new oars out of cottonwood trees.

On August 29th, the party passed the Grand Wash Cliffs, signaling the end of the Canyon. The trip would have been a total success except for the loss of three team members who decided to hike out at what is now known as Separation Canyon. Official reports have the men leaving because they were intimidated by yet another must-run rapid between intimidating canyon walls, but Canyon historians tend to agree that trip politics were involved. Major Powell, as noble and accomplished as he might have been, was apparently not the most likable trip leader.

The Canyon was run by a handful of adventurers over the next several decades, but it wasn't run in a kayak until 1941, when Alexander "Zee" Grant paddled along with a Norm Nevills expedition.

The most intriguing whitewater of Grand Canyon for kayaking is found on the tributary streams of the big river, and the biggest tributary within the Canyon is the Little Colorado. A descent of the "Little C," as locals call it, is the quintessential Southwestern paddling experience.

The gorge of the Little Colorado winds for nearly 50 miles between Cameron, AZ, and Grand Canyon. For sheer narrowness, the Little Colorado Gorge is more impressive than the Grand. It reaches depths over 3,000 feet, and it is never more than a half-mile across. Adding to its appeal for whitewater paddlers, the riverbed is full of rockfall and travertine ledges reminiscent of southern Mexico, creating class IV action throughout the run.

The first complete descent of the Little Colorado was made by Tim Cooper and Brad Dimock in 1978. They survived three frigid days in the wilderness gorge only to run smack into the jaws of bureaucracy. During their 26-mile paddle down the big Colorado to Phantom Ranch, where they planned to hike out, they unfortunately passed a ranger boat. Dimock and Cooper were fined for paddling the Colorado without a permit, and charged additionally for a helicopter evacuation of their boats. It seems the hazards of adventuring in Grand Canyon in this era can sometimes be even greater than in Powell's time.

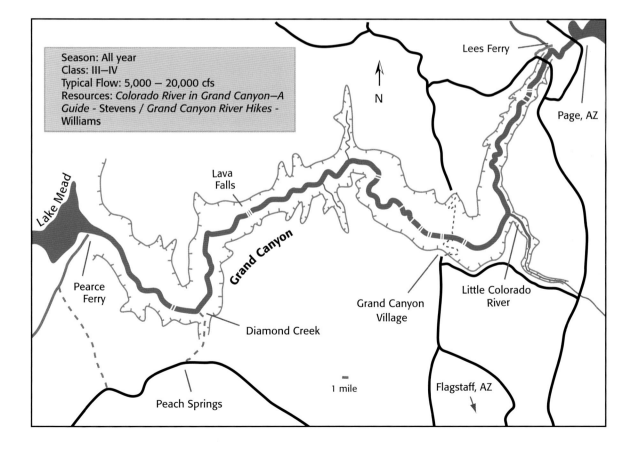

Season: All year
Class: III–IV
Typical Flow: 5,000 – 20,000 cfs
Resources: *Colorado River in Grand Canyon—A Guide* - Stevens / *Grand Canyon River Hikes* - Williams

Emerging from the Embudo Canyon

Gordon Banks

Guidebooks, however maligned they might be, have always been an important tool for river runners. From Randy Carter's 1959 guidebook to Virginia canoeing to the cutting edge guides of today, paddlers have long used guidebooks for essential flow information, shuttle directions, or just vicarious adventuring while waiting for the rivers to rise. The genre has evolved over the years from basic typewritten information packs to full-color collages that tell the story with eye-popping photos and graphics. Setting the standard in the modern era of whitewater guides is *Colorado Rivers & Creeks*, written by Dave Eckardt and Gordon Banks.

Banks saw the need for a new guidebook as increasing numbers of new runs were completed in Colorado in the 1990s. He says of the book, "I believe Dave and I raised the bar for river guides. At the same time, I look forward to the day when CRC provides new schoolers with some good campfire chuckles and some extra toilet paper."

Campfire chuckles have always been a staple of Banks' life. Like many Rocky Mountain adventurers, he gravitated to climbing as a young man, challenging himself on Colorado's steepest rock. It wasn't until after college that Gordon took up kayaking. It was the early '80s, a golden age of western whitewater when several high water years arrived just as plastic boats began to see wider use. Paddling the ubiquitous Perception Dancer, Banks was one of a burgeoning crop of new paddlers that would mold the sport for the next decade.

With boating, Banks discovered a new world of

Debra Banks

mountain adventure, and wilderness creeks became his medium. Clear rivers of snowmelt racing through the mountains continue to be his favorite type of paddling to this day. Whenever rumors of a new run are in the air, Banks is quickly there to sample the goods. "I leave the first descent work to other guys. I'm more interested in boating," says Banks. And boat he has, methodically picking off all the best runs in the western U.S. He has made a habit of following spring runoff, traveling to California, Idaho, and the Northwest as flows dictate. His favorites include California's Clavey and North Fork of the Middle Feather, Washington's Clear Fork of the Cowlitz, Colorado's Big South, and of course, New Mexico's Embudo.

His first run here helped provide some inspiration for a new guidebook, as accurate flow information would've saved Gordo some grief. The river was at the ridiculously high level of 4.3 on the gauge (3.0 to 3.5 is optimal). Gordon recalls, "We put on only knowing that the creek had been run, and we were clueless about water levels." He continues, "The level seemed fine at the put-in, but as the gorge choked down, I had a sinking feeling." As can often be expected in such conditions, the run ended with a firm spanking. Banks swam at the exit of the first gorge, and had to hike out a notch in the canyon rim. Since his inauspicious first run, Banks has returned to the Embudo over fifteen times. The Embudo traditionally offers this region's first class V opportunity each new season. And if the rest of us want to experience the Embudo firsthand, there is a certain guidebook that will help us get there.

Rio Embudo

The tangy scent of sun-baked juniper and sage is a far cry from what we normally associate with a whitewater river, yet tucked in the semi-arid hills of the Southwestern U.S. there is a whitewater gem, a true classic called the Embudo. Embudo means funnel in Spanish, and once you see this river canyon, the translation becomes obvious. This is one little fire hose of a creek.

El Rio Embudo is located in enchanting northern New Mexico, where Spanish is heard as much as English, and newcomers are viewed with guarded suspicion. High mountain peaks rise over small villages with their chili pepper-adorned adobe pueblos, dirt streets, church squares, and small local farm plots.

This scenic and diverse land often finds itself south of the storm track, and the sun shines brightly most of the year. Accordingly, there never seems to be quite enough water. Precious agua is held in such reverence here that the 12,000-foot peaks producing the streams of the region are called the Sangre de Cristos, or Blood of Christ mountains.

The Embudo is a major artery emanating from the Sangre de Cristos. After trickling down from the cool aspen groves of the high slopes, it winds through lowland bean fields before cutting into a granite canyon below the town of Rio Lucio. (Note that the Mexican custom of re-naming a river every time it enters a new valley is in effect here.)

The modest Embudo weaves through hillsides of junipers and pinyon pines until textured walls of granite slowly emerge near the put-in. The little creek splashes past stately ponderosa pines growing in the shade of the canyon, and of course, the ubiquitous New Mexican collection of abandoned furniture. It remains shallow and tame for the first couple of miles below the put-in, nothing more than a low-water float. Then all hell breaks loose.

Intimidating canyon walls pinch down on the creek, and the funnel river suddenly lives up to its name. Continuous class IV whitewater sluices through the gorge, broken only by the steeper class V drops. Eddies are small and somewhat sparse. Action is non-stop.

The rapids build in difficulty to a climax near the end of the canyon called Slots of Fun. Here the already narrow Embudo squeezes down to a flume less than ten feet wide as it jets between solid chunks of granite. If you don't feel like gaining the perspective of a spit watermelon seed, you can make a difficult portage on the right, or an easier portage of the upper rapid on the left, followed by a hairy ferry back to river right at the lip of the final crux slot. This portage-ferry-portage approach can sometimes provide more adrenaline than running the rapid.

On one of the first descents of the river in the early '80s, a drowning occurred at Slots of Fun, and local paddlers avoided the lower canyon based on its macabre reputation. Paddlers always took out above this, hiking out of the canyon via a rugged trail just above the drop. Eric Bader finally ran the class V flume successfully, and the standard run was extended to the mouth of the gorge.

The rapids don't let up until completely beyond the canyon, and class III rapids are found even as the farms of Canoncito line the riverbanks. Although locals can bomb down it in an hour, first timers should expect to scout several times, and maybe make some portages. This will bring most paddlers into the three to six hour range for the entire run.

The paddle out includes two diversion dams and a couple of logs, but steady current delivers you to the highway bridge before things get tedious. Not bad for a funnel in the desert.

The granite canyon of the Embudo

Entering the gorge

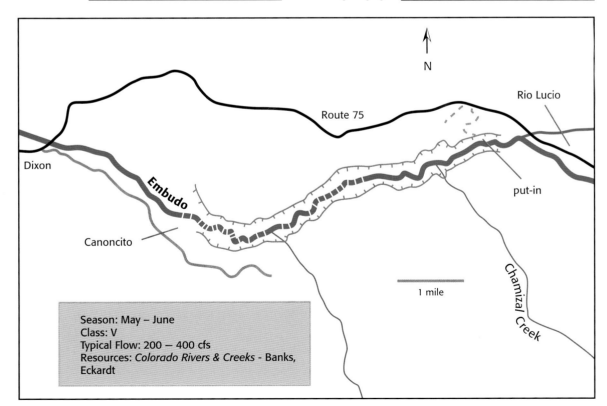

Season: May – June
Class: V
Typical Flow: 200 – 400 cfs
Resources: *Colorado Rivers & Creeks* - Banks, Eckardt

The Roaring Fork

Roger Paris

In the year of 1941, Hitler's German army continued their terrible advance across Europe by invading the Soviet Union, the United States declared war after being attacked at Pearl Harbor, and twelve-year-old Roger Paris (pronounced Roe-zhay Paree) began paddling whitewater.

German bombers had devastated Roger's hometown of Orleans, France, burning the main street into an apocalyptic scene of destruction. In the wake of the demolition, the town bridge over the Loire River was turned into a scattered mess of debris that fell into the streambed, forming a rapid where previously there had been smooth water. Roger took a canoe down to the newly created rapids, and began what would become an illustrious paddling career in the whitewater wreckage.

He used paddling as an escape from the horrors of daily life during German occupation, paddling the river whenever possible. Roger even camped next to the river's soothing flow while just a few feet away lay the war-ravaged French countryside. The river offered a tiny bit of sanity in an insane world. Roger recalls, "Food was scarce. War dangers were always around. Those four years seemed to last forever." American troops liberated the town in the summer of 1944. Roger was 15 years old.

By 1948, Roger was national French junior champion in C-1 and C-2. When he first came to the U.S. five years later, he was firmly established as one of Europe's best paddlers, having run most of that continent's top whitewater, and having won a world championship in C-2 slalom with his teammate Claude Neveau. Along with their coach André Pean, the Frenchmen traveled to Colorado for the Salida downriver race on the Arkansas River in June 1953. It was a seminal moment in the development of American paddling, as Paris and other Europeans who would follow brought with them new boat designs and advanced techniques to share with the enthusiastic but unpolished American paddlers.

After the race, Paris and his companions toured the area. They paddled the Arkansas' Royal Gorge, and made the first descent of Brown's Canyon. It was the start of many annual trips to the Salida race (today's FibARK), and eventually led to Paris' immigration to the U.S. in the early '60s. His explorations throughout the West continued, with several first descents along the way, including California's Kings Canyon.

To support his outdoor lifestyle, Paris taught skiing in the winter, and whitewater paddling in the summer. His "Roger Paris kayak school" along the Roaring Fork gained a reputation as one of the best in the nation, turning out renowned paddlers like David Nutt, Eric Evans, Andy Corra, and Nancy Wiley.

Although his kayak school is no longer active, Roger still is. He ski instructs at Crested Butte, and still paddles extensively, usually by himself. I ran into Roger several years ago on a Green River trip. My group was four days into our float when we saw someone paddling upstream towards us. It was Roger, returning from a week-long hike in the Maze of Canyonlands. He was headed back to the put-in. The moral of this story? If you happen to see a rock-solid septuagenarian paddling down the Roaring Fork, don't try to slow him down. He's seen much more turbulence than what a river could ever provide.

Roaring Fork

The Roaring Fork offers something for everyone. Fisherman pull rainbow trout out of the river, and human populations near and far use Roaring Fork water to make their lives a little more comfortable. For paddlers, the Roaring Fork gives a variety of whitewater challenges. There is a perfect beginner's section on the stream's upper reaches, class II—III runs farther downstream, a class IV piece running through the town of Aspen, and class V—VI water above town. Additionally, there are a variety of runs on Roaring Fork tributaries, like the Crystal and Fryingpan. All this diversity helped make the Roaring Fork a perfect location for Roger Paris' kayak school a quarter century ago, and the river still serves as home to at least two paddling schools today.

Many first lessons take place on a placid stretch of the river just below the headwaters in Colorado's lofty Sawatch Range. These are the same high mountains that loom above the Arkansas River to the east. Unlike the Arkansas, the Roaring Fork is blessed with a location on the slightly wetter west-facing side of the mountains. Ironically, this natural advantage is a curse to the river, as water of the Roaring Fork basin is diverted to the drier Arkansas drainage to supply cities on the east side of the mountains. This means that the Roaring Fork no longer runs with the copious flood of snowmelt that it once did. And when rare water-rich years do come along, paddlers are sometimes caught off guard.

Normally, peak runoff occurs on the Roaring Fork in June. Some years, like 1995, are anything but normal. When mid-July rolled around that season and the river was still running a moderate 1,000 cfs, many of the Aspen area paddlers had given up hope for the high water they were expecting. Theories circulated. Maybe the diversions took it all? Perhaps a slow steady melt

had trickled away the high water? In any case, it was decided that one way to salvage the disappointing season would be with a moonlight run on the Roaring Fork's Slaughterhouse section. If nothing else, the short and familiar class IV run would be especially beautiful in the nighttime luminescence.

Word spread quickly of the plan, and as night fell, the put-in parking lot on the edge of bustling Aspen slowly filled with groups of paddlers. The warm summer evening created a festive atmosphere, and the scene turned into an impromptu party. Varying degrees of mood alteration occurred as boats were unloaded and the surreal chemical glow of luminary sticks were attached to helmets.

Local Charlie Macarthur was a bit more subdued. He had seen the high country snowpack recently, and knew that high water was still on its way. Judging from the sound of the river next to the parking lot, it had arrived. He walked down to the rising water's edge and estimated the flow to be three times what it had been the day before.

Upon returning to the put-in party, Charlie warned the revelers that "It's gonna be big." But as he recalls, "That wasn't very popular advice." Before the last of the night paddlers had launched, there was already one person swimming. The high water became apparent to all when a surf wave appeared at the put-in that hadn't been there all spring. As paddler Paul Teft surfed up the newly-formed wave, an uprooted Engelmann spruce came floating past, narrowly missing him. Between his fixation on the wave and the low light, Teft had never even seen the tree. Charlie did, though, and the near-skewering prompted him to again be the unpopular voice of reason, and suggest pulling off the swollen river. His admonishments were again quickly discarded, and he found himself paddling downstream with the fun-crazed mob to Slaughterhouse Falls. At least this high water nighttime class V rapid induced a scout. As the energetic group stared out at a moonlit river-wide hole, a mature pine tree came ponderously crashing through. Everyone saw it this time. Duly impressed with the power of the spring flood, the group didn't need any more convincing to call off the run. Buzzes now thoroughly killed, they shouldered their boats and humbly walked back to the parking lot.

Night runs didn't provide the only high water excitement that season. A big eddy at the mouth of the Roaring Fork in Glenwood Springs collected wayward boats almost daily, until the snowpack finally tapped out in August. Then the Roaring Fork returned to its more modest self, rippling over gravel bars. Fisherman

returned to the river, beginning paddlers practiced their eddy turns on the gentle current, and new anticipation was sparked for the next big snow year, when Mother Nature will overwhelm the diversions, and the Roaring Fork will roar again.

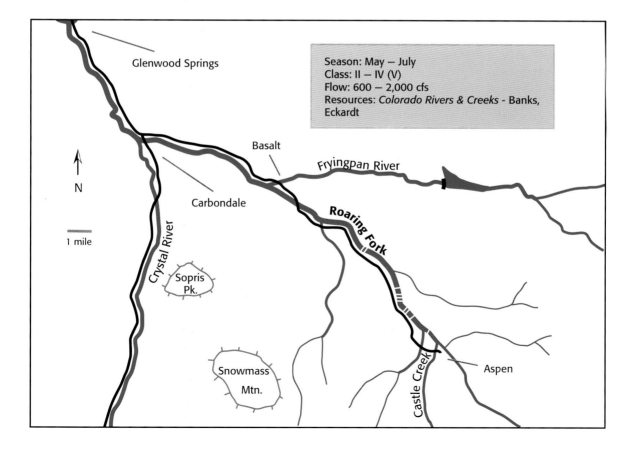

Glenwood Springs

Season: May — July
Class: II — IV (V)
Flow: 600 — 2,000 cfs
Resources: *Colorado Rivers & Creeks* - Banks, Eckardt

Basalt

Fryingpan River

N

Carbondale

Roaring Fork

1 mile

Crystal River

Sopris Pk.

Snowmass Mtn.

Castle Creek

Aspen

Lars Holbek and Tony Miely probe the gorge on Vallecito

Eric Southwick

Anyone who denies that a good attitude will take you far should follow the story of Eric Southwick. Nicknamed "Smiley" for his optimistic persona, "Wick" (his other nickname) has found success in a way that would make an idealist grin—hard work and good karma.

The hard work began at age ten, when Eric started his own lawn mowing business to make money to buy his first kayak. Dad pitched in for the accessories, and soon both father and son were off to terrorize the rivers of their native New Mexico, "How to Kayak" book firmly in hand.

At fourteen, Eric studied slalom racing technique under the tutelage of Nancy Wiley and John Brennan. Wick was hooked, and moved to Durango, Colorado to paddle and race full-time. Though his skills were lagging behind the top junior paddlers, his grit never faltered.

Southwick's tenacity caught the eye of legendary coach Fritz Haller, who invited Eric to the year-round training facilities of North Carolina's Nantahala River. The seed of potential that Haller had seen began to blossom, and at age seventeen Eric earned a spot on the U.S. junior team and a subsequent trip to Norway for international competition.

The Europe trip sparked a travel bug in Southwick. He's barely been in one place for more than two months at a time since. This wanderlust eventually steered Eric out of racing, although financial pressure contributed too. His enthusiastic training resulted in three broken boats a year, and at $1,000 a piece, it added up quickly. Besides, dominance on the American team was unrelenting. Says Wick, "(Scott) Shipley and (Rich) Weiss were a good four seconds ahead of everyone else on the course."

Eric moved back to Durango and took up ice climbing. Then the phone rang. It was Wave Sport (an old race sponsor), and they wanted Wick to paddle their boats again, but this time on the freestyle circuit. Southwick had never even entered a whitewater rodeo, but the offer was too good to pass up.

He flailed through the first half of the tour season before getting his freestyle technique honed. By the end of the season, he narrowly missed a qualifying spot for the World Championships. The missed opportunity only hardened his resolve to make it next time.

New Zealand in 1999 was the next time, and Southwick was going to be ready. He flew to the Southern Hemisphere months ahead to train in the championship hole, only to find the dam-controlled river dry. When the competition date finally arrived, Southwick was battling a nasty international flu virus. He survived the competition by holding his breath while in the hole to keep from vomiting, and came away as world champion.

Though still occasionally competing, Southwick now has his sights on new challenges: learning to speak Thai, and flying ultralight aircraft. The ultralights allow Eric to scout new rivers to run, like Vallecito. He often combines this run with a dash down lower Lime Creek, and South Mineral Creek, completing a one-day Durango area "triple crown." Typical behavior, really, for an optimist called "Smiley."

Vallecito Creek

Vallecito Creek and the Animas River are sister drainages. The streams lie side by side on the map, both flow north to south, and both drain the same 13,000-foot peaks of the western San Juan Mountains. They each contain miles of continuous whitewater in their mountainous upper reaches, and each river plummets through a narrow granite gorge before emptying into the southwestern deserts.

The Animas is the more mature of the two, while Vallecito is the wild and tempestuous little sister. The Animas has been a route of travel for many years, with a mining town and a railroad along its banks, whereas Vallecito runs through wilderness, maintaining its restless nature along its length until it is subdued by Vallecito Reservoir as it exits the mountains.

Just above the reservoir lies Vallecito's lower canyon, where class V paddlers come to test themselves on what the regional guidebook calls "the best mile of boating in the state of Colorado." Clear, fresh Rocky Mountain water cascades through a jumble of fallen boulders in the depths of this narrow granite gorge, making it a true gauntlet of dramatic and committing whitewater.

A run on Vallecito begins with a healthy 1.5-mile, mostly uphill hike. Views of the nearby mountains, and the majestic gorge below the trail make it a worthwhile place to visit, with or without a boat. It is a beautiful and invigorating setting. On the trail, boaters are likely to encounter hikers and fishermen who will question their intentions with stupefied expressions. Paddlers who aren't on top of their class V game will likely share in this amazement after looking into the inescapable gorge. A steep hiking route leads down to a point 30 feet above river level, allowing a pre-scout of the crux of the run.

If you are still psyched to give Vallecito a try after looking at its slimy walls and sharp drops, continue up the trail to above the canyon, and prepare for action. Entry Falls is just hundreds of feet downstream.

Entry, a relatively simple waterfall, was the first drop ever to be run on Vallecito, but the rest of the canyon wasn't paddled until later. Locals Andy Hutchinson and Dennis Williams made an ultra low water canyoneering-with-kayaks descent in the Autumn of 1986.

The same duo ran upper Vallecito the next season, hiking over a mountain pass near the town of Silverton in order to access the stream's headwaters. They put in on a tiny sub-alpine watercourse that was narrower than their boats were long. The creek cascaded continuously at first, forcing Hutchinson and Williams to portage many class VI waterfalls, several of which Hutchinson feels are likely runnable by today's steep creeking standards.

As the stream grew, beautiful sections of class IV were unfortunately interrupted by regular logjams. Late on day two, they arrived at the final gorge, and finished their trip by portaging the high water class V box. Hutchinson recalls 12 to 15 portages on the entire run, mostly due to logs and the class VI cascades at the top.

The Vallecito Gorge remained unvisited by kayaks for several more years until the late adventure boater John Foss organized an attempt with Andy Corra and Aaron Phillips in 1992. The level was a respectable 2.0 feet.

The group had a smooth run until reaching the final drop of the vertically-walled, unportageable section. A large boulder sat in the middle of the riverbed, forcing the water into channels on either side, against the overhanging walls of the canyon. The right side channel was completely blocked by a log, and the left channel was a narrow waterfall dropping out of sight. Portaging, or even exiting their boats was not an option. They were in the classic first descenter's predicament. Even though the rapid had yet to be run, it already had a name—No Way Out.

Foss, being the one whose bright idea it was to go kayaking in this claustrophobic cleft, was voted to take the plunge. His probing didn't help Corra and Phillips much, however, because the big boulder obstructed their view of the river below. They had no idea whether John had made it, or was getting pummeled somewhere. There was only one way to find out, so the two paddled hard off the lip, and happily joined their compadre who was waiting in the pool below the narrows.

Vallecito's narrow canyon makes the gauge readings very sensitive. The difference between 2.1 and 2.4, for example, is huge. If you are feeling polished enough

to give this short but demanding run a try, keep a keen eye on the level before embarking. Paddlers who successfully travel the Vallecito Gorge will find it to be one of the most memorable miles of whitewater anywhere.

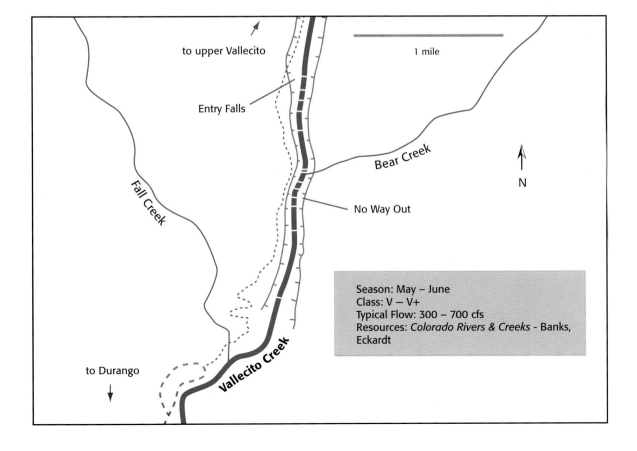

to upper Vallecito

1 mile

Entry Falls

Bear Creek

Fall Creek

No Way Out

N

Season: May – June
Class: V – V+
Typical Flow: 300 – 700 cfs
Resources: *Colorado Rivers & Creeks* - Banks, Eckardt

to Durango

Vallecito Creek

Royal Gorge of the Arkansas

Cathy Hearn

Women have always been a minority in the whitewater paddling scene, but their numbers are growing, due in part to a number of top female boaters who serve as role models for younger athletes. Today women are regularly seen shredding the play spots and steep creeks alike. In the 1970s, however, the persona of "gnarly river chick" had barely been invented. This was a period in American history when women were just beginning to gain a foothold in athletics, and female leaders in sports were more important than ever. In the sport of whitewater paddling, the leader was Cathy Hearn.

Cathy's paddling career had its beginnings with her first swimming lesson at age three. Her parents, being avid canoeists, had her riding in the family canoe just as soon as the toddler could keep herself afloat, and weekend trips were the norm. One of the family's most adventurous outings took them to Montana's Missouri River. The semi-arid landscape of central Montana left an indelible mark on Cathy. It would be that same scent of windblown sagebrush and pinyon pine that made the Arkansas River a favorite of hers as an adult.

By age six, Cathy had paddled a kayak, open canoe, and C-1. Getting on the water was the important thing, regardless of the boat. Eventually she made her mark by paddling a kayak, because that was the only racing class available to women, but she wasn't limited by convention in her early years. She recalls, "We raced every event we could when we were young."

The variety of competition paid off as Hearn took her racing to the international stage. In 1979, she won three gold medals, including the world championship in K-1 slalom. By the time she retired from her 20-plus years of whitewater racing, she had over a dozen world championship medals and seventeen national titles—eight coming in K-1 slalom.

Racing was always just one facet of Hearn's paddling repertoire, however. She reflects on her involvement with racing as "just a way to really push my limits." She pushed her limits by running remote and difficult rivers, too. As a still-learning teenager, she ran West Virginia's New, and Pennsylvania's Youghiogheny at high water, and returned with a new confidence that would propel her to the leading edge of the sport, both in racing and river running. The apex of her class V river exploration came in the early '80s, when Cathy traveled to southern Mexico to participate in first descents of the steep travertine rivers of that politically embroiled region.

Lately, Cathy has re-programmed her paddling expertise to the coaching realm. She is currently technical director of the Italian national slalom team. Her adventure boating has taken a new twist, also. She now races outrigger canoes between the islands of Hawaii in the annual Na wahine o ke kai (women of the sea) event. She says she would "like to do more with that." Given her history, there's little doubt she will.

Arkansas River

There are over 100 miles of runnable whitewater on the Arkansas, this whitewater feast has not gone unnoticed. At last count, 65 different commercial rafting outfitters were operating here, making the Arkansas the most paddled whitewater river in the country.

Besides the natural gradient, boaters on the Arkansas benefit from man's manipulation of the surrounding waterways. Water from the west-draining Roaring Fork basin is diverted and pumped through the mountains into the east-flowing Arkansas, unnaturally boosting the flow in the river. Of course, this audacious engineering project was not undertaken to augment the paddling season; its function is to send water to sprawling Denver, and Colorado Springs. In any case, paddlers enjoy the natural pipeline of the Arkansas late into the season. Adding an ironic twist to the water politics are the raft companies, who have negotiated a minimum flow of 700 cfs throughout the summer—only if there is enough water left after Colorado Springs has sated its thirst, of course.

These reliable flows help produce good whitewater on several different sections of the river. The Royal Gorge is the farthest downstream run, unless you want to paddle the remaining 1,300 miles to the Mississippi—an interesting proposition, but lacking much whitewater. The Gorge contains good class III pool-drop in a canyon that is as spectacular as its name implies.

Just upstream from the Royal Gorge is the easily accessed Pinnacle Rock section, home to more class III. Above this is the river town of Salida, complete with its own downtown surf wave, and home to FibARK—the oldest river race on the continent.

The First Annual Royal Gorge Boat Race (changed later to FibArk, for First in Boating Arkansas River Club) was held in 1949. In true Western style, the first race was born in a Salida tavern, when two bar patrons started talking big about rowing the springtime high water. Word spread of the challenge, and soon a race was organized, running 57 miles from Salida through the Royal Gorge to Canon City. On race day, the river was high, brown, and powerful, scaring off many would-be contestants before the start. Of the five boats that raced, only one finished—a foldboat paddled by touring Europeans Robert Ris and Max Romer. The Europeans collected their $1,000 purse for first place, and a tradition of racing on the Arkansas was begun.

Throughout the 1950s, the Salida race continued to be dominated by Europeans, and served as a catalyst for the growth of whitewater sport in America. The first truly whitewater-designed canoe in America debuted here, along with the revolutionary C-1 a few years later. In 1953, one of America's earliest demonstrations of whitewater slalom occurred at Salida, spurring growth in the sport for years to come.

Besides these landmark events, the race attracted talented paddlers to the Arkansas who in turn pioneered new rivers in the area, and shared their skills with numerous beginners. Roger Paris won several Salida races, and then stayed in the area to teach hundreds how to paddle through his kayak school. Walter Kirschbaum traveled from his native Germany to the Salida race in 1955, bringing the famed Duffek stroke with him. He later became the first to run the Colorado River's Cataract and Grand Canyons without any portages.

In addition to Salida's FibARK races, the Arkansas has hosted many other racing events. Cathy Hearn first came here to train with the national team, and later raced both wildwater and slalom on the Ark. She always wanted to bring the world championships to her beloved Arkansas, though her motivations for the Wild

West venue were admittedly irreverent. With candid competitiveness, she smirks, "The Europeans would've been frying in the sun." Cathy's favorite section of the river is Pine Creek through the Numbers, located above the town of Buena Vista, Colorado.

Along this upper section, the river and its environs change character slightly. Here the small to medium-sized Arkansas flows through a high and dry mountain valley. Stunted pinyon pines grow amidst fields of brown granite boulders that litter the valley floor. Given the arid appearance of the place, newcomers might be surprised to learn that the valley bottom sits at a lofty 8,000 feet. Snow-draped ridges beyond tree-line loom a short distance above the river. These are Colorado's highest mountains, including the champion Mt. Elbert at 14,433 feet.

Below these high peaks is the Arkansas' toughest rapid—Pine Creek. Here the Arkansas is funneled into a continuous and powerful sluice for nearly a half mile. Pine Creek would be a fun class IV+ rapid were it not for a nearly unavoidable hole lurking halfway down the drop. Fortunately, there is an easy portage along a road on river left. Many boaters put in just below the hole for a bouncy ride through the lower part of the rapid.

Below Pine Creek, the Numbers begin, where the rapids are simply titled numerically. There are six of them, number four being the hardest at most levels. This is perfect class IV paddling, with constant action all the way through. The rapids are boulder gardens, and the "pools" between numbered drops are swift sections of class II and III. The only drawback to the Numbers is that the fun is over too soon. But wait, this is the Arkansas. If you haven't had enough, there's 75 more miles of good paddling waiting downstream.

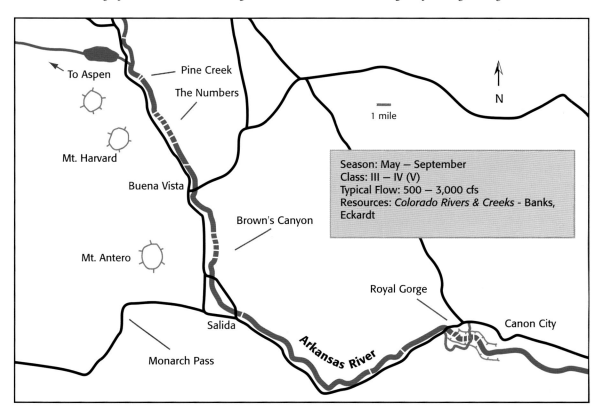

Season: May — September
Class: III — IV (V)
Typical Flow: 500 — 3,000 cfs
Resources: *Colorado Rivers & Creeks* - Banks, Eckardt

The Rockwood Box offers a dramatic change from the mountain scenery of the Upper Animas

Nancy Wiley

Durango, Colorado could be described as the epicenter of Rocky Mountain whitewater. Several cold mountain streams tumble out of the snow-capped peaks that form the backdrop of the city, and a typical summer day will showcase the Animas River running swiftly past downtown, often with slalom gates hung over the rapids. Rafts of fun-seeking tourists bounce downstream, and a line up of play-boaters drift alongside the local wave. There is even a river festival here, complete with races and freestyle events. It is difficult to imagine a more whitewater friendly environment. No wonder a half dozen of the paddlers in this book have at one time called Durango home. The success of this mountain town's paddling history can be summed up in two words—Nancy Wiley.

Nancy started kayaking at age thirteen with her father's encouragement. At that time, there were only four kayakers in Durango, not nearly enough for Nancy's father Milt to have a consistent partner. He needed another boater in the family. Nancy fit the bill. After several failed attempts to teach his daughter the Eskimo roll, Milt sent her to Roger Paris' kayak school near Aspen. This decision proved farsighted. By age nineteen, Nancy was good enough to be sponsored by Hydra, becoming one of the first sponsored athletes in the sport.

The recognition helped propel Wiley into a life of paddling endeavors: instruction, racing, and expeditions. In 1986, she traveled to Peru for a landmark descent of the Paucartambo River. Two years later she was in remote Borneo, safety kayaking for an all women's raft team as part of a documentary film.

Between expeditions, Wiley found time to compete. She finished third nationally in slalom in 1989, and competed in the first two world whitewater rodeo championships. Her overall wilderness skills have always been a strength, illustrated by her winning the 1995 Survival of the Fittest.

Nancy's real legacy, however, is her contribution to the sport of whitewater in her hometown. The whitewater park in downtown Durango owes its existence to Wiley, as does the Animas River Days—one of the best attended festivals in the country. She is also responsible for developing a successful kids paddling program with the City of Durango. For 15 years, she owned and managed Four Corners River Sports, a hub of whitewater activity with a paddling school and whitewater shop perched on the banks of the Animas.

When Nancy was fifteen years old, she was running the class IV-V upper Animas. Though she wasn't the first to paddle the river (that distinction belongs to Roger Paris and company), she can certainly be called one of the run's pioneers. Along with her father and friends, Nancy made the first descent of the Rockwood Box—the sheer-walled gorge at the end of the run that contains the river's best whitewater.

Today Nancy is once again turning her energies back toward her Durango home, building an adobe brick house made from the earth on which it stands. No doubt the southwestern hacienda is near the cold running Animas.

Animas River

The Rocky Mountains are the source of many of North America's greatest rivers: the Fraser, Columbia, Missouri, Rio Grande. The Animas, though not in the league of these giants, is in many ways the quintessential Rocky Mountain river. Like the other Rocky Mountain greats, it has its origins in high snowfields, cuts a wild canyon through the mountains, and runs far into the lowlands, providing essential water to an arid region.

The Animas drains the majestic San Juan range of Colorado, arguably the most spectacular portion of the Rockies south of Montana's Glacier Park. The steep snowcapped San Juans perch on the edge of the southwestern deserts, taunting the vast expanses of redrock below with the promise of fresh cold snowmelt. Although weather patterns can be fickle this far south, the 14,000-foot peaks of the San Juans usually catch enough snow to make the high mountain valleys echo with the roar of falling water in the spring.

The historic mining town of Silverton sits in one of these picturesque valleys, with the Animas River at its doorstep. This is the put in for the upper Animas, as the river slices through a narrow V-gap in the peaks just below town.

Continuous is the operative word here, because there are no pools on this stretch of the Animas. The river is on a mission to get out of the mountains, and the waves hardly stop for the entire twenty-seven mile run. At high water, it is a romping fast roller coaster ride, while at lower flows it can be splashy and tedious. Whatever the water level, the scenery is fantastic, with dramatic peaks looming over the river in the upper section, and craggy granite slabs in the lower reaches.

Even with the fast moving current, twenty-seven miles is a long day, so two-day trips are a nice option here. If you're opposed to hauling camping gear on the river, a riverside train can deliver it to you. The narrow gauge Durango to Silverton line runs along almost the entire length of the upper Animas. A century ago, it hauled silver down out of the mountains. Today it hauls tourists, and for a fee, your camping gear.

The biggest rapids on this swift section are Garfield Slide, Broken Bridge, and No Name, a class V at most levels. This is where bad things tend to happen, just ask Nancy Wiley. On one of her earliest upper Animas runs, at age fifteen, she swam out of her kayak near the top of No Name, and made it to shore to find the rapid had stolen her shoes! Soaking wet, cold, and demoralized, the shoeless teenage girl trudged down the tracks to where her companions had gathered her gear, and sullenly paddled the remaining thirteen miles to the take-out.

Most parties take out at a railroad stop called Tacoma, but class V paddlers will want to continue downstream into the narrow Rockwood Box. Here the Animas changes character from a swift mountain river to a constricted canyon run. This box canyon was avoided for years until the Wileys pushed through in the late '70s. Nancy describes that first run as "magical." Even after hundreds of descents, the confined Rockwood Box still retains a mystical quality, especially when juxtaposed with the open upper river. Sounds reverberate between the narrow walls, and the special feeling of isolation that only a canyon can bring is evident. There is a river-wide ledge in the first part of the Box that is the greatest cause for concern, as vertical walls prevent portaging, and even a good scout is difficult to come by. Visiting paddlers are advised to consult with a local about this drop before committing to the gorge, but it usually has a clean line on the right. Below here there are a few not-too-difficult, but intimidating rapids as the river stays confined to the canyon. One of the best rapids in the Box comes after the canyon has opened somewhat. Don't swim here, because the take-out trail is just below. Despite all the fun you might be having at this point, don't be seduced downstream into the lower box, because class VI falls riddled with logs await. For you curious types: Yes, it has been run at very low water, and no, it wasn't worth it.

Remember the famous jump scene in *Butch Cassidy and the Sundance Kid*? "Swim!? Hell, the fall will kill ya." This was shot on the Animas just below the lower box, just before the river trades its granite environs for the open farmland on the outskirts of Durango.

In town, the whitewater picks up again with class III Smelter Rapid, a slalom course, and several good play spots. Below town it is still a nice runnable river, but slowly turns more utilitarian as farms and ranches siphon off its water for their green desert fields. The most recent insult to the Animas, known as the Animas-La Plata project, will take water out of the river in Durango, and pump it to the Ute Indian Reservation many miles to the west. The Animas gives itself up, ultimately, for the convenience of man, just as any Rocky Mountain river is destined to do.

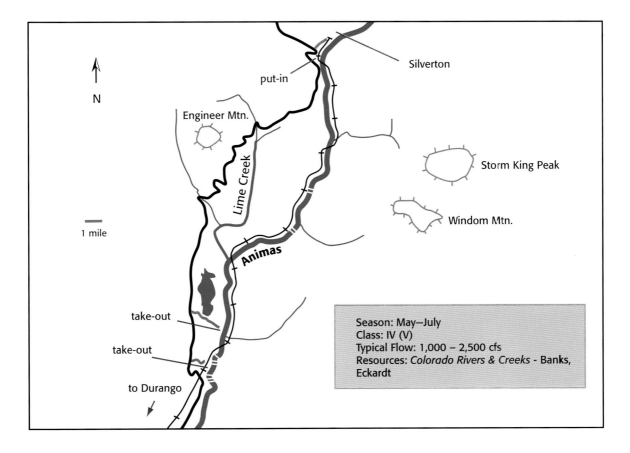

Season: May–July
Class: IV (V)
Typical Flow: 1,000 – 2,500 cfs
Resources: *Colorado Rivers & Creeks* - Banks, Eckardt

Gore Canyon's Tunnel Rapid: Clear the hole, but miss the rock

Buffy Burge

There was a popular television program in the late '90s that portrayed a beautiful young woman who, despite her unpretentious appearance, had a unique ability to out-smart and out-battle threatening characters. The name of the TV show was *Buffy the Vampire Slayer*.

The whitewater world has its own incarnation of this modest superhero. Her name is Buffy Burge (formerly Buffy Bailey), and anyone who has seen her paddle knows that comparisons between Buffy the paddler and Buffy the heroine are justified by more than just their shared name.

Buffy calmly dissects some of the planet's hardest whitewater with the nonchalance most of us could only feign in a familiar class III rapid. Many a macho whitewater warrior has reacted with astonishment when learning that the boater who just shredded the *big* rapid "was a girl, dude, and her name is Buffy."

Buffy's first river running occurred in a canoe at summer camp on North Carolina's Green, just downstream from the class V narrows—a section she has now run dozens of times. The canoeing planted a seed, but at the time volleyball and basketball occupied Buffy's athletic energy. Paddling remained a distant pastime.

With her team sports days behind her as she attended the University of Richmond, Buffy needed something new to satisfy her athleticism. Kayaking on the nearby James River seemed to fit the bill. She took a kayak class at Nantahala Outdoor Center and was soon teaching a class of her own back at the summer camp that started it all, even though she insists that she "still had no real skills.'

A raft guiding job in Colorado gave Buffy the opportunity to improve on those rudimentary paddling skills. She admits, "I wasn't a very good employee," mainly because she spent more time paddling than guiding rafts. Buffy tagged along with the other guides on many runs that were clearly over her head, but her persistent and reliable roll kept her swims to a minimum, so she was always allowed to join the group for the next trip. Her first true class V run was the reputable Gore Canyon.

She flipped and gave herself a black eye in the first big rapid, but with standard Buffy grit, she toughed it out through the rest of the day, and notched her first Gore run. Since then, she has made over one hundred trips on Gore, and won the downriver race there six times.

Besides her extensive Colorado paddling forays, Buffy has kayaked in Chile, Ecuador, Africa, and Nepal, where she regards her descents of the upper Marsyandi and upper Bhote Kosi as two of her stoutest foreign tests. Back in the homeland, she has paddled throughout the Eastern U.S., and logged several trips to the California classics. The Middle Fork of the Kings remains her most memorable Sierra Nevada descent. Thus far, she is one of only three females to have made the grueling wilderness trip. I wonder if the Vampire Slayer could do *that!*

Gore Canyon

The Colorado River originates in the 12,000 to 14,000-foot-high peaks of the Continental Divide in northern Colorado. After meandering through high sagebrush valleys below the mountains, the river slices directly through a spruce-covered escarpment known as the Gore Range. The resulting chasm is known as Gore Canyon—a 2,000-foot-deep gorge of metamorphic rock that contains the most difficult whitewater on the entire 1,400-mile length of the Colorado River.

Gore is named after a great white hunter by the name of "Sir St. George Gore" who came to North America to slaughter wildlife in the 1850s. Mountain man Jim Bridger led Gore and his pack of Anglo-Irish good ol' boys on a route near the canyon, and settlers subsequently coined the mountains and canyon "Gore." During their three-year tour of the American West, Gore and his men killed over 2,000 buffalo, 1,600 elk, and 100 bears. The canyon's splendor is much too great to be named after such a butcher.

Following Gore's time, white men avoided the dramatic canyon until 1905, when a railroad was pushed through. The tracks are still in use today, and offer convenient scouting and portaging if the squealing brakes of the train aren't bearing down. As usual, the debris from the railroad construction has altered many of the rapids.

Altered or not, Gore contains several great rapids. The second major drop of the run is one of them, and is simply titled Gore Rapid. This is the most complex class V on the river, where a myriad of rocks create enough turbulent channels to thoroughly confuse most paddlers with too many options. A large boulder in the middle of the rapid has contributed to many interesting runs. On one of the early commercial raft descents of Gore, an entire crew of paddlers diligently followed their guide's instructions and climbed onto the rock as

their boat threatened to wrap. When the last person exited, the current grabbed the suddenly lightened raft, and quickly sent it downstream, stranding its former passengers on the mid-stream boulder. They were truly marooned, and the isolated black rock that was their refuge instantly had a new title—Gilligan's Island.

Below Gore Rapid, there is plenty of busy water and a few named drops before arriving at Tunnel. A large table rock in this drop seems to continue its steady creep toward the middle of the river as it shifts farther down the talus slope on river left every few years. Currently it sits uncomfortably close to the landing zone of Tunnel's launch-pad boof. Nature's constant change promises ever more interesting rock placements in the future.

Although many paddlers breathe a sigh of relief once past Tunnel, letting your guard down too soon often results in a thorough spanking just downstream at the infamous Toilet Bowl. This author can attest that this hole is sticky, deep, and dark, and generally only releases its prey after swimming a cycle or two.

The remaining named rapid below Toilet Bowl is Kirschbaum's, named after whitewater pioneer Walter Kirschbaum, who was the first to paddle Gore Canyon.

Kirschbaum began kayaking as early as the 1930s in his native Bavaria. Like many of his generation, the second world war altered the course of Walter's life, forcing him into service with the German army at age sixteen. He fought on the Russian front, and spent time captive in a POW camp. The terrible scars of war stayed with Kirschbaum long after the fighting had ended, and running wild rivers became his escape from the haunting memories of his youth.

After winning the world slalom championship, Kirschbaum came to Colorado for the Salida race (today's FibARK) in 1955. He was captivated by the wilderness rivers of the American West, and it became his goal to explore every major tributary of the Colorado River. His quest led to many firsts, including the first no-portage kayak runs through Cataract and Grand Canyons, as well as the Yampa's Cross Mountain Gorge. He also ran Pine Creek Rapid on the Arkansas in 1957. As with most of his runs, this one was completed solo.

There were few, if any, who could paddle with the precision of Kirschbaum. Even in his skilled hands, however, the equipment of the day was still barely capable of handling rapids like those found in Gore. So when he set his sights on Gore Canyon in 1962, he began by making a special kayak specifically designed for the abusive rocks in Gore. Despite his heavy duty kayak, a jolting collision with a rock halfway through the canyon crushed the nose of the fiberglass boat. He could have aborted the descent and hiked out of the canyon along the railroad tracks, but the determined Kirschbaum elected to improvise a patch instead. He stuffed the damaged nose of the kayak with a root ball of driftwood, then taped his paddling jacket over the entire mess. With this jury-rigged boat, he finished the run, and became the first to paddle the now classic Gore.

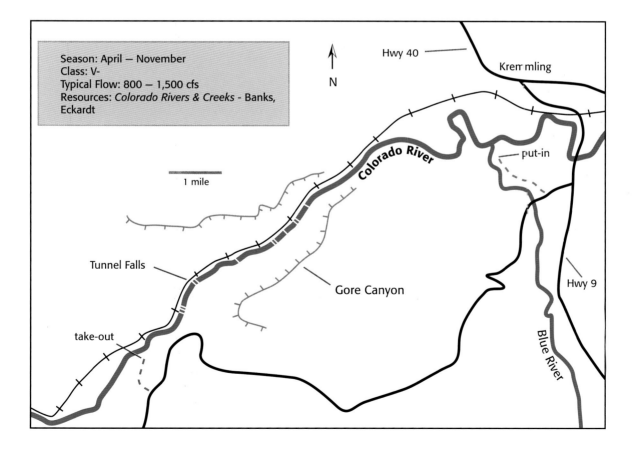

Season: April — November
Class: V-
Typical Flow: 800 — 1,500 cfs
Resources: *Colorado Rivers & Creeks* - Banks, Eckardt

N

Hwy 40

Kremmling

Colorado River

put-in

1 mile

Tunnel Falls

Gore Canyon

Hwy 9

take-out

Blue River

Charlie Munsey

In deep—the Clarks Fork of the Yellowstone

Charlie Munsey

Isaac Newton said, "If I have seen further it is by standing on the shoulders of giants." What he meant by this, of course, is that current achievements are only possible because our predecessors laid the necessary groundwork for future generations' successes. Few paddlers are as keenly aware of this connection to the past as Charlie Munsey. Charlie has retraced the paths of some of the greatest whitewater expeditions in our time, and, being a true adventurer himself, has expanded on those pioneering runs, taking expedition paddling to a new level in his own time.

His first significant paddling influence was schoolmate Bryan Tooley—a fellow Oregonian who was a national champion wildwater racer. With the exposure Tooley provided, the athletic Munsey sought out paddling opportunities. His first river running came in a tandem canoe on the nearby McKenzie River with a partner who Charlie says, "liked to surf holes." Charlie figured a kayak was better to surf holes with than a tandem canoe, so he made the switch. With classmate Eric Evans (the photographer, not the slalom racer), Charlie turned into a kayaking weekend warrior.

After high school, ski bumming in Sun Valley brought Charlie to Idaho, and the prime paddling of Idaho's Payette Rivers kept him there. He paddled the Payette's South Fork religiously, and by the end of the summer he was ready, so he thought, for the infamous North Fork.

Sporting a recklessly brazen bumper sticker that said "why scout?," Charlie and two other intermediate paddlers drove straight to the top of the notorious run and put in. A half mile into the run, they were making a mad scramble into the last possible eddy above the first major drop, called Steepness. Already somewhat rattled, the trio got out to re-think their plans just as famous German paddler Markus Schmidt suddenly appeared out of the bushes. Sensing their apprehension, the veteran offered to take them to an easier part of the run, where he would lead them downstream. With Schmidt leading, they ran the slightly easier lower seven miles of the North Fork without mishap. Charlie recalls, "After that, I was hooked." He has since run the North Fork hundreds of times, often without a paddle.

Munsey met fabled big water paddler Rob Lesser while in Idaho, and gained inspiration for his own expedition agenda which took him across both North America and Asia. He completed first descents on Nepal's Upper Karnali and Thule Beri, and joined Scott Lindgren for the first attempt at Tibet's Tsangpo, where the duo made a first descent on the huge water of the Po Tsangpo before walking away from the much too high main Tsangpo. Charlie considers the pinnacle of his paddling adventures to be his three descents of the Stikine. One of those runs was part of a month long blitz with long time paddling partner Gerry Moffat and others to complete the triple crown of big water—Susitna, Alsek, and Stikine.

Charlie's focus lately has turned to whitewater photography, a field in which he is undeniably a leader. His work can be seen here featuring the Clarks Fork of the Yellowstone—a place he regards as "the most beautiful in the states." It was also where Charlie got his first real taste of expedition paddling.

Clarks Fork of the Yellowstone

The Yellowstone Plateau is the roof of the continent. Three of North America's largest river systems—the Snake/Columbia, Yellowstone/Missouri, and Green/Colorado—all have their origins here. Draining the high alpine plateaus on the northern flank of this uplift are the forks of the Yellowstone River. The main stem of the Yellowstone runs north through Grand and Black Canyons, two spectacular chasms that are classic whitewater runs, but to paddle either gorge is strictly illegal. Your Yellowstone National Park is diligently working to keep kayakers and other undesirable types off these rivers. After all, Yellowstone is made for snowmobiles, not boats. Paddling either canyon of the main Yellowstone will result in hefty fines, or imprisonment. Fortunately, there is a fork of the Yellowstone that lies outside the Park boundary. This, of course, is the Clarks Fork, so named after the great explorer William Clark, who canoed past the mouth of the great river on his return from the Pacific in 1803.

There are three excellent one-day whitewater runs on the upper portions of the Clarks Fork, but the most notable section of the river is the dramatic lower gorge, sometimes known as The Box. Here the Clarks Fork tumbles through a 1,000-foot-deep granite canyon as it exits the high country toward the Great Plains of eastern Wyoming and Montana. The Box of the Clarks Fork is only 20 miles long, but it takes two to three days to complete, giving some indication of the challenging and rugged nature of the gorge. Early descents of the canyon were epic self-supported affairs that involved lengthy and exposed portages around the gorge's many sieve rapids. Over the years, new portage routes and techniques have been discovered, making the run slightly easier and less epic, but it is still a formidable undertaking. The most notable difference in river running style on the Clarks Fork has come with a canyon

escape route that conveniently comes about halfway through the run. Rick Alexander, Guy Erb, and John Gangemi were the first paddlers to discover this route when they paddled around a corner in the seemingly isolated canyon to see a family casually fishing along the bank. Following the trip, Erb and Alexander returned to find the rugged fisherman's trail from the rim. Most paddlers now use this route to hike to the rim for a night of car camping in between their two days in the gorge, allowing them to make the portage-intensive run with relatively empty boats.

Whether the canyon is done in traditional self-support style, or with a hike out, the boulder-choked gorge must be approached with attentive caution. Undercuts and trapping canyon walls are both signature hazards of the run.

The sievey nature of the Clarks Fork was apparent even before its first descent, when kayaker/pilot Kay Swanson flew over the canyon and reported to his paddling buddies that "It looked like it went underground." Despite this ominous report, Swanson's description of the beautiful canyon was enough to entice Ron Frye, Roger Hazelwood, and John Lightner to join him for a run of the canyon on Labor Day weekend of 1976.

They thought the 20-mile run would take a full day to complete, so when they arrived at the put-in at 3 P.M., they all wisely saw the potential for a night on the river, and packed accordingly. Everyone threw in a sleeping bag, and enough food for the night. Hazelwood, a typically well-provisioned member of the group, remembers packing "A dinner, a breakfast roll, and a bunch of hot chocolate powder."

Following an afternoon of technical paddling and some rugged portaging, the foursome made camp deep within the canyon and hungrily gobbled up their food. They were largely unconcerned with their slow progress through the gorge. Ron Frye recalls, "We were pretty sure we'd get out the next day."

As the next day dragged on into a blur of must-make eddies, horizon lines, and sketchy portages over polished granite, the prospects of getting off the river that day steadily ebbed away. Frye, a technically proficient C-1 paddler from back East, led most of the drops and pushed downstream as far as possible without leading the group into a point of no return. At one rapid, he nearly probed too far, and had to be roped back upstream from an eddy that lay at the lip of an unrunnable cascade, and next to a sheer cliff wall.

As night fell on their second day in the canyon, the weary paddlers hunkered down to a gourmet meal of hot chocolate and hard candy. A plane had previously been arranged to fly over the gorge and look for them if they weren't out by day three, and girlfriends and shuttle drivers would obviously be worried if they didn't

show up soon. With another long and daunting portage below them, and fearing another slow, hungry, and committing day in the canyon, they planned to hike out the next morning.

Leaving their battered fiberglass boats by the river, the group clawed their way up the steep gullies and granite slabs on river left. Subsisting on the last of Swanson's sugar candy, they reached a jeep trail after a couple hours of scrambling, and followed it downstream to the take-out. Upon studying maps of the area afterward, they found that the portage below their last camp was likely the last major hurdle of the canyon. Their hike out was only slightly faster than continuing through the gorge would have been. None of the group regretted of their decision, however. That is the price to pay when exploring a place as dramatic and wild as the Clarks Fork of the Yellowstone.

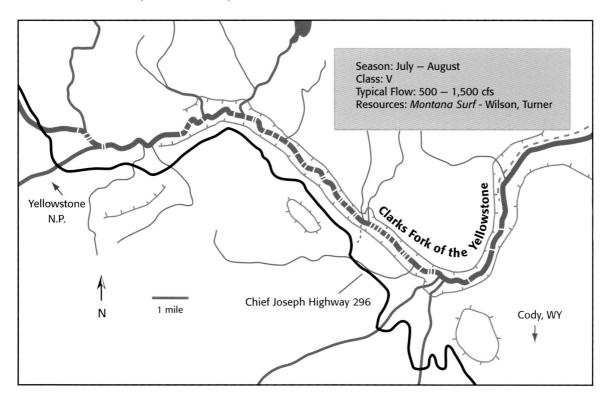

Season: July — August
Class: V
Typical Flow: 500 — 1,500 cfs
Resources: *Montana Surf* - Wilson, Turner

Yellowstone N.P.

N
1 mile

Chief Joseph Highway 296

Clarks Fork of the Yellowstone

Cody, WY

Classic old school paddling on the classic South Fork of the Salmon

John Wasson

In 1993, Hollywood took on the world of whitewater with the making of a movie called *The River Wild*. A high-powered team of professionals was assembled for the $70 million production, including renowned adventure filmmaker Mike Hoover, and academy award winners Meryl Streep and director Curtis Hansen. An all-star team of whitewater pros were brought in to oversee river operations for the whitewater-themed film. Paddlers are an independent breed, however, and a respected leader was needed for these river all-stars so that their skills could form a cohesive unit that would serve the needs of the film.

John Wasson's quiet demeanor may have seemed an odd fit to lead such an ego-driven group, but the respect for him among his peers was unequaled, and he was clearly the man for the job.

Wasson's career with whitewater began in 1964, when young John went on his first river trip to the Yampa River in Colorado. By the time he was out of high school, he was guiding there, and exploring the West's other desert rivers by raft. It was the debut of whitewater kayaking at the 1972 Olympics that turned Wasson's sights from rafting to kayaking. He built a fiberglass kayak, and started re-examining all his favorite raft runs from the seat of his new decked boat. He soon developed a smooth, seemingly effortless paddling style that is unforgettable to anyone who has paddled with him since.

By 1978 he was back on the Yampa, but this time it was for a high-profile high water descent of Cross Mountain Gorge. It was here that Wasson met Idaho paddler Rob Lesser. Lesser invited John north later that summer. Says John "That's when I saw the Payettes and the South Salmon. I immediately moved there."

Numerous films and first descents followed, both at home and abroad. There was Mexico's Jataté, Nepal's Arun, and British Columbia's Stikine. Besides the Stikine, Wasson also ran the other big northern classics including the Susitna and Turnback Canyon of the Alsek. Closer to home, standard Wasson haunts included the Snake River's Milner and Murtaugh sections, and the North Fork of the Payette. Several of these runs were filmed endeavors, firing the imagination of aspiring adventurers across America as they aired on ABC's American Sportsman. In the early '90s, Wasson spearheaded trips to Ecuador, exploring many new rivers that are now a staple of the winter paddling vacation there.

Despite his globe-trotting career with whitewater, Wasson never forgot to keep enjoying his backyard. This is where we find John's classic pick—the South Fork of the Salmon. John is especially fond of the South Salmon when combined with a run on its tributary Secesh River. "The two are rarely done together as a self support," he says. Nevertheless, he continues, "It makes a cool run, 2000 vertical feet the first day if you go down the South Salmon a few miles." Wasson's is one of the most respected opinions in river running. If he says it's a cool run, rest assured—it's a cool run.

South Fork Salmon

In many ways, the South Fork of the Salmon is the quintessential Idaho river. Collecting snowmelt on its upper reaches from mountains covered in thick stands of subalpine fir, the river runs north to the Main Salmon, cutting canyons through the jagged gray granite of the Idaho batholith along the way. The rapids of the South Fork are typical of your standard Idaho boulder garden—a terrifying maze of holes when high, and a bony obstacle course late in the season. The scenery is classic central Idaho, too. Sheltered draws hold dense forest cover, while many slopes are a mosaic of open grassland mixed with the silvery snags of burned-over forest. If you could pick only a single river to run in this whitewater state, the South Salmon might just be the one.

The multi-day canyon section starts at the end of a dirt road several miles below the confluence of the Secesh River. Here the South Salmon is a medium-sized clear mountain river, having gathered all its significant tributaries before making its final run to the Main Salmon 52 miles distant.

The first major class IV rapid comes about an hour below the put-in at medium flows (2.5 to 4.5 feet). Devil Creek Rapid has some big holes to avoid, but also plenty of clean lines. This is indicative of many of the South Salmon's rapids. They are solid class IV—just manageable enough to run without extensive scouting, yet hard enough that you can't simply drift through with impunity.

At high water, many of the rapids wash out completely, and paddlers can make the two-day run in a matter of hours. The few rapids and isolated holes that remain are huge and located at random places along the river.

Rob Lesser discovered this new face of the South Salmon while running the river with Bo Shelby at 8.5 feet. The river was so fast, the duo camped after only two hours on the water their first day, because otherwise they'd have been to the take-out by dark. "We were totally bored," Lesser recalls.

On day two, they continued the high-speed drifting and carried on a conversation as they floated. Then their chat was rudely interrupted by the roar of an approaching hole. By the time they recognized what was causing the noise, it was too late for evasive maneuvers, and they both dropped in.

After a few bounces in the froth together, Rob surfed out the left side of the hole, and turned to see where his friend was. On cue, Bo came launching out of the depths of the hydraulic in a dramatic front ender. As Lesser breathed a sigh of relief that they were both out, he felt himself sliding into another trough. He spun around and back-surfed across the face of this second hole, and again exited out the side. Bo, however, was perfectly lined-up for the middle, and plunged directly through the heart of the monster, where he disappeared before surfacing just downstream of the pile. The suddenly wide-eyed paddlers continued to the take-out in record time, and decided to save their conversations for camp.

The camping along the South Salmon is pleasant. Several beaches are adjacent to sparkling clear eddies, and large ponderosa pines loom over many of the camps. There is even a developed campground along the river, at the South Fork Guard Station where a road bridge crosses the river. There are also a couple airstrips along the river. No, this is not a total wilderness run, but you are still pretty much in the middle of nowhere most of the time.

After emptying into the Main Salmon, twenty miles of mostly flat water lies between you and the take-out. There are definite highlights on this paddle out, however. Lower levels create a few nice surf waves, and at high water there is a big powerful rapid called Chittam just above the take-out. The scenery is nice, too, featuring a surreal maze of granite on river right just below the Main Salmon confluence. Another popular take-out option is to fly out of the river canyon from Mackay Bar, located at the confluence of the South and Main forks of the Salmon. A backcountry flight is a purely Idaho way to end a trip on the South Salmon, Idaho's quintessential river.

Idaho backcountry along the South Salmon

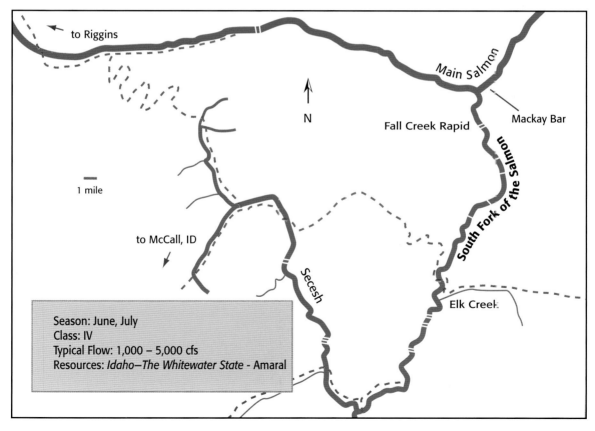

Season: June, July
Class: IV
Typical Flow: 1,000 – 5,000 cfs
Resources: *Idaho—The Whitewater State* - Amaral

Salmon River country

Josh Lowry

Josh Lowry is the embodiment of the dedicated-to-the-core kayaker. To call Lowry a character is an understatement. His square frame, full beard, mumbled speaking style, and unique and genuine laugh seem to be something out of a novelist's creation. His needs are few. His spirit of adventure is unwavering. His lifestyle is driven by a desire to live simply, stay out of the trappings of mainstream society, and above all else, paddle.

Lowry didn't start his paddling life until the age of twenty-five, and even then it was on a lark. When a friend who had just purchased a new canoe asked Josh to join him for some river paddling, the always game Lowry accepted. The only problem was, as Lowry recounts, "You couldn't hitchhike with a canoe." The vagabond Lowry didn't own a car. Not to be discouraged, Josh bought an inflatable kayak, took a canoeing course, and applied what he had learned about canoeing to his inflatable boat. Soon he was hitchhiking to rivers, inflatable "ducky" in tow.

With fifteen days of paddling under his belt, Lowry took the next logical step in whitewater progression—a trip through Grand Canyon. By the end of the 18-day trip, Josh was ready to try a hard boat.

His first rolling lessons were in classic old school style—from a book, and on a lake. His roll and other skills improved as he traveled to Colorado to visit his brother and run new rivers. In 1984, Josh took a job guiding in Grand Canyon, and his river junkie's lifestyle was in full swing. His guiding and kayaking took him to Costa Rica, southern Mexico, and Chile, where he first traveled in 1986 with the last of his savings.

Chile's visiting paddlers from around the world know Lowry for his recognizable ambulance shuttle rig. Lowry was one of the first to make a complete run on Chile's Baker River, and also led the first descent of the Rio Pascua—a multi-day epic in the far south that is so remote, an eight-hour motorized skiff ride is required to reach the nearest settlement from the take-out.

Lowry has many Chilean favorite rivers, but back in North America, his classic pick turned out to be the Middle Fork of the Salmon, a river he guided and paddled on for ten straight seasons. What makes the Middle Fork special to a kayaker like Lowry is the number of runnable tributary creeks that feed the river. Loon and Big Creeks are the standard kayak runs, while Marsh and Bear Valley Creeks serve as headwater access, and Camas Creek fills the class V niche. Josh once ran Loon and Big Creeks on one trip with the help of an airplane shuttle, and the kindness of the river's many raft trips. "We stopped at every camp we saw and got coffee," Lowry recalls. That sort of thing is just part of a day's work for Lowry, the penultimate whitewater man.

Middle Fork Salmon

Idaho's Salmon River is the longest free-flowing whitewater river in the United States. From its origins in the craggy Sawtooth Mountains until it joins the dam riddled Snake River 400 miles downstream, the Salmon runs unimpeded through the heart of Idaho. Much of the river's course lies within the Frank Church River of No Return Wilderness, a rugged land of granite crags, alpine lakes, huge yellow pines, stark grassy slopes, and steaming hot springs. Nearly the entire landscape is carved into a steep maze of ridges, all of which lead precipitously down to the many fingered tributaries of the Salmon.

Each of the Salmon's major forks offers something unique to river runners. If you want quality whitewater, the South Fork is the arm to explore. For picture perfect campsites and abundant wildlife, the Main Salmon is best. For a combination of these features set in a dramatic granite canyon with crystalline water, there is no place like the Middle Fork.

The Middle Fork officially begins where Bear Valley and Marsh Creeks join. This is nearly in the center of Idaho, and exactly in the middle of nowhere. Several miles below this confluence, the river tumbles over dynamite-altered Dagger Falls. Located here is a forest service ranger cabin, and a wooden boat ramp that serves as the standard put-in. The river is no more than a shallow mountain stream at this point. When it empties into the Main Salmon nearly 100 miles downstream, it will have grown into a big river.

The first documented full descent of the Middle Fork took place when Bus Hatch's group of eight adventurers rowed down in the 1930s. Although legendary Salmon boatman Harry Guleke reportedly made a Middle Fork run in a raft as early as 1925, Hatch's descent a decade later ushered in the modern era of boating here.

Bus and his brother Alton Hatch, along with friends "Doc" Frazier, "Cap" Mowrey, and Frank Swain, tried to make a Middle Fork run in July of 1935, but they were stymied by low water. The group of Utah-based boatmen had experience on low water from their descent of Arizona's Grand Canyon during the record low flows (1,600 cfs) of 1934, so they knew how low was *too* low. After four days of scraping down Bear Valley Creek and the upper Middle Fork, they ditched their battered wooden row boats in the woods near Dagger Falls, and resolved to come back the next year.

In 1936, the resolute boatmen returned with three more team members, finished their portage around Dagger Falls, and continued down the Middle Fork. They undoubtedly marveled at the river canyon's abundant hot springs, bighorn sheep, and rainbow trout as they made their way through this rich wilderness.

The Hatch group negotiated the Middle Fork's biggest rapids—Velvet, Weber, Rubber—without major mishap. The trip's worst run occurred downstream on the Main Salmon, and could be attributed to bad karma.

Rounding a corner above one of the Salmon's biggest rapids, Big Mallard, Swain's lead boat spotted a mama bear and cub on the bank, and tried to separate the pair in an effort to capture the frightened juvenile. As the boatman diverted his focus from the river in favor of tormenting the wildlife, he drifted into the biggest hole in the rapid, and flipped. The next two boats followed suit, and when the yard sale was sorted out below, it was discovered that Cap Mowrey had broken his leg. The trip was forced to rush downstream for medical attention, and arrived at the take-out in Riggins, Idaho two days later.

Like the original Hatch expedition, many Middle Fork trips today continue down the Main Salmon after emerging from the Middle Fork canyon, making a wilderness journey of nearly 200 miles. Of course, permit logistics can make this Middle-Main trip difficult to arrange during peak season, as separate permits are needed for each river. Lottery permit season begins on the Middle Fork May 15th. Some parties launch before this date, but this usually means putting in upstream on Marsh Creek beneath banks of snow, as the road to Dagger Falls is still often snowed in at this time. Even in the month of June, snow storms occasionally blanket the river's upper reaches. Snowfall and river running is usually a miserable combination. On the Middle Fork, however, it simply means that it's time to find a hot spring, have a soak, and gaze out at the Idaho wilderness.

Storm light on the Salmon

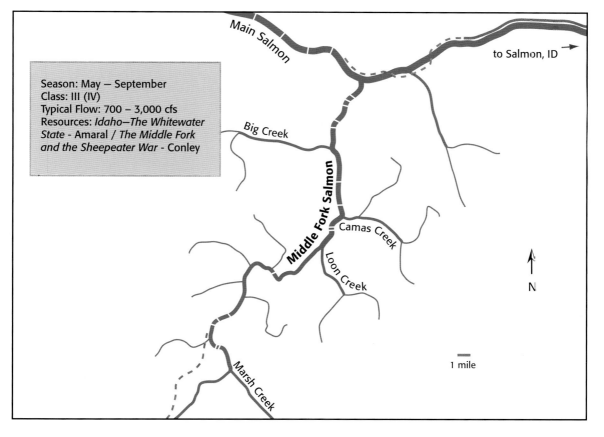

Season: May — September
Class: III (IV)
Typical Flow: 700 – 3,000 cfs
Resources: *Idaho—The Whitewater State* - Amaral / *The Middle Fork and the Sheepeater War* - Conley

The North Fork of the Payette is the definition of whitewater

Doug Ammons

As with all high-performance athletic pursuits, mental outlook is critically important in whitewater paddling. An overabundance of fear is a recipe for disaster, yet underestimating a river's power can be equally bad. A measured mixture of confidence and respect is necessary to paddle challenging whitewater. Few who have ever paddled whitewater have this mental concoction as finely honed as Doug Ammons.

His natural abilities in kayaking stem from an upbringing with water. Doug remembers playing underwater charades as a kid in the local pool. The hours of pool time helped him develop into a competitive swimmer and earned him a scholarship to his hometown University of Montana, where he had his first significant exposure to kayaking.

After swim practice, Doug and his teammates would take kayaks to the high dive and launch themselves off in dramatic fashion. It was hardly river running, but it was a start.

Doug continued to dabble in the sport when his older brother took it up, but then his interest waned. It wasn't until a friend asked him for roll lessons that Ammons really fixed his focus on kayaking. Within a year, he was paddling the North Fork.

From beginner to expert in one year is an extremely rapid ascent in skills, and serves as testament to Ammons' mental strength. When Doug Ammons devotes himself to something, he runs on an obsessive, nearly fanatical course. As an example of his devotion, he has practiced guitar for twenty hours in a day. This intensely-cerebral Ph.D. in psychology looks at whitewater paddling in a highly esoteric way, always looking

for deeper understanding through his intimate interactions with the water. To him, "Running rivers is like playing long, intricate pieces of music, improvising, linking, and joining."

His first top-to-bottom run on the North Fork was in 1983. For most, a North Fork top-to-bottom is a pinnacle reached, something to look back on with pride. For Ammons, it was a portal to new possibilities.

After making a run with Tony Brennan and Greg Moore at the highest ever level of 7,000 cfs, Ammons says, "We felt we had reached into another world and touched the limits of what was possible." Ammons would continue to seek new limits. Later that summer he completed five top-to-bottoms in one day, totaling 8,500 vertical feet of whitewater. Following this almost surreal experience, Ammons says he "dreamed wildly of the North Fork for the next week."

The North Fork is Ammons' special river close to home, but he has also sought challenge on major descents in Bolivia, Nepal, and most notably, British Columbia's Stikine. The "American Sportsman" episode of the first descent there made an impression on Ammons early in his kayaking career, and he later soloed the infamous three-day run.

Surreal experiences like this one are more of a mental challenge than physical, something Doug Ammons is perfectly suited for. It is just another part of the puzzle on his life-long journey of learning from the river.

North Fork Payette

Most rivers, even the biggest and fiercest, appear relatively tame when viewed from the comfort of a passing vehicle. Not so with Idaho's North Fork of the Payette. This river looks fearsome and powerful even from the road. It roars alongside Highway 55 in a continuously spitting, snapping, roiling, crashing, pulsing torrent of white, projecting an obviously wild character even to non-boaters. The reason it appears to be so ragingly powerful? Because it is.

The final sixteen miles of the North Fork contains very continuous whitewater with only a few pools. For reference, the river is split into three different sections. The top section is home to a few standout rapids, including Disneyland and Nutcracker. Nutcracker is one of the most intimidating rapids on the entire run, second only to Jacob's Ladder.

Found in the meaty middle section, Jacob's is ridiculously fast and constricted. North Fork veteran Rob Lesser estimates the speed of the water in Jacob's at 25 miles per hour at higher flows. Even at moderate flows, hitting the rock drop—the key boof of the rapid—is one of the all-time greatest moves in whitewater.

Hounds Tooth marks the start of the North Fork's lower five miles. This is the easiest section, where things moderate to IV+ and "easy" class V. Juicer and Crunch are the big drops down here.

Naturally, the bottom five miles was the first part of the North Fork to be run. Idaho whitewater pioneers Tulio Celano and Walt Blackadar attempted this stretch as early as 1970.

Neither Blackadar nor Celano had much paddling experience at the time, but Blackadar was hell-bent on giving the dynamic roadside run a try. In preparation for the upcoming attempt, Celano put on the river by himself in the relative slack water (class III-IV) below Hounds Tooth Rapid a few days before Blackadar's

visit. A rolling frenzy began almost immediately, and it wasn't long before Celano was swimming. He recovered portions of his broken fiberglass boat later in the day, and called Blackadar to explain that their North Fork run would have to wait, because he was now boat-less. In true Blackadar style, Walt responded with, "I'll bring you another one." The trip was back on.

Celano, though slightly humbled from his solo experience, figured that the unflappable Blackadar would get him through this time. The two put on at the base of Hounds Tooth, and Blackadar immediately joined the North Fork swim team. Celano, suddenly feeling quite alone with his charismatic leader swimming, drifted into a hole and, in his understated words, "had a bad swim."

Following these initial thrashings, it is no wonder that the North Fork remained unrun for another four years. Then, Boise paddlers Roger Hazelwood, Tom Murphy, and Keith Taylor began pecking away at the challenge of the North Fork. Throughout the summer of 1974, they ran progressively harder sections of the river, starting with the lower three miles, and then the lower five. They finished the season with a descent of the demanding upper section, taking out at Big Eddy.

The steeper middle section of the North Fork remained unrun until 1977, when a trio of Eastern paddlers called "the crunch bunch" (because they were always "crunching" their fiberglass boats) came through on an Idaho paddling safari. The group joined forces with fellow Louisville, Kentucky boater Bob Walker (ironically, they had never met previously), and they ran the lower and upper runs together. After honing in on the river's pace, Walker and crunch buncher Dennis Whitehouse set their sights on the unrun middle section. The level was a medium-low 950 cfs, and Walker and Whitehouse were on the top of their games. Conditions were ripe for a first descent.

The run went smoothly until reaching the then unnamed Jacob's Ladder. Whitehouse flipped near the top of the rapid. Upon rolling up, he found himself backwards, and heading for the crux rock drop. Fighting to stay upright, he had no chance at making the boof, and was soon surfing a big hole. Things went from bad to worse when his sprayskirt blew. He swam through the dreaded Taffy Puller immediately below, and fortunately made it to shore quickly. Badly bruised from his swim, Whitehouse called it a day, and Bob Ladder came in to finish the run with Walker.

With a river as alluring and accessible as the North Fork, firsts don't end with the first descent. The first to make a complete top-to-bottom run were Rob Lesser and Don Banducci in 1978. Banducci was so inspired by their accomplishment that he started Yakima Rack Company the next day, and boat racks were never quite the same.

A decade later, when top to bottoms became commonplace for the North Fork's elite, Bob McDougall linked three in a row to make a vertical mile of whitewater in one day. The year 1993 saw Doug Ammons complete the first hand paddling run.

With all these different firsts completed, one might think the North Fork is passé. Not so. In fact the North Fork has stood the test of time more than most difficult rivers. Today's shorter boats do little to make the big, powerful water of the North Fork more manageable. In order to run the North Fork, one must get into rhythm with the river's staccato pace, and react to the water's wishes. Using the river as a platform for metaphor, we are taught a great lesson by paddling here. Overpowering the river will not work—only by working with the overwhelming currents will a paddler find success.

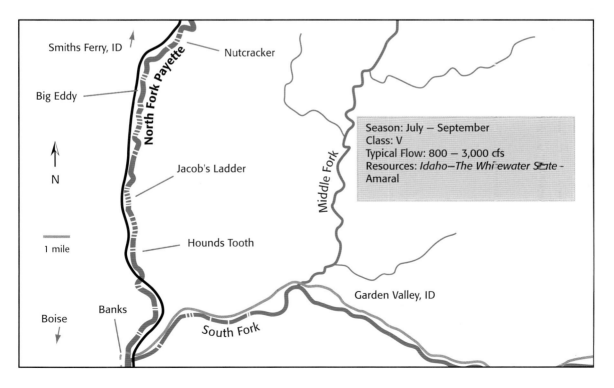

Smiths Ferry, ID

North Fork Payette

Nutcracker

Big Eddy

N

1 mile

Jacob's Ladder

Hounds Tooth

Middle Fork

Season: July — September
Class: V
Typical Flow: 800 — 3,000 cfs
Resources: *Idaho—The Whitewater State* - Amaral

Garden Valley, ID

Boise

Banks

South Fork

Willie Kern leads paddlers down the Lochsa

Dan Gavere

The 1990s saw big changes in the world of whitewater. Recognition of the sport by mainstream media grew during the period as radical new videos and freestyle boating drew in a larger and younger audience than ever before. "New School" was suddenly part of the whitewater vernacular. A host of young paddlers helped initiate this time of change, and one of them was Dan Gavere.

As a child, Dan's playful energy was a tough fit for the conservative culture of Utah where he grew up. His escape from this structured society was skateboarding, and Dan recalls much of his youth spent "skating with my posse of defiant friends." Dan's father Alan had his own outlet, and it was canoeing.

Alan took his son on numerous multi-day canoe trips on the desert rivers of the Southwest. Although the trips were generally successful, Dan never quite took to tandem canoeing. His typical reaction to whitewater was to drop his paddle, grab the gunnels, and cower from the passing rocks for fear that they would smash into the canoe. "I didn't get the pillow thing," he humbly admits.

When Dan got a kayak at age eleven, his outlook on whitewater improved, and weekend trips to Idaho's Payette and Wyoming's Snake were anticipated events. By the time Gavere went away to attend the University of Montana, he was paddling his kayak with the same playfulness he once shredded the streets of Salt Lake City with on his skateboard.

His skating background made him a natural fit for the world of freestyle kayaking. At one of the first rodeos he entered, Gavere saw Teva's Adam Druckman promoting footwear at the event, and he thought, "That guy has

my dream job." Gavere boldly approached Druckman, and lobbed for some sandals and a job, telling Druckman that, "I'm gonna be a great ambassador for your company when I become famous." Druckman was humored by Gavere's prediction, if not convinced. Dan went on to win the event, and it was the start of Gavere's long tenure as a Teva-sponsored athlete.

At the 1993 world championships, Gavere finished a strong second place in the hole ride, giving him a respected voice that he used to contribute essential rule modifications to the sport. When freestyle events essentially became cartwheeling contests in the late '90s, Gavere helped establish a new scoring system that awarded more variety. He remembers, "We realized, 'we've gotta do something, or everyone will fall asleep and leave'."

Dan has always kept variety in his athletic pursuits too. He is an avid snowboarder, and since moving to the wind sail Mecca of Hood River, Oregon, he has taken up kite boarding. Still, paddling has remained his foremost activity. He lists his most intensive month of whitewater as a 28-day stint in Chile for the filming of *Paddlequest*. This groundbreaking film starring Gavere was the foundation for the wave of kayak videos that followed.

Gavere remembers runs on the North Fork of the Payette and Vallecito Creek as landmarks in his development, but the Lochsa was his regular stomping ground during his highly developmental college years. The Lochsa was a catalyst in Gavere's growth as a paddler, and Gavere has in turn been a catalyst in the growth of whitewater paddling.

Lochsa River

The Lochsa (pronounced lock-saw) River cuts through one of the most uninhabited regions in the United States—Idaho's Bitteroot and Clearwater Mountains. Covered in a mosaic of forest green hues, Lochsa country is a beautifully rugged region of steep mountains, clear cold raging streams, and steaming hot springs. To the south of the river lies the largest roadless tract in the lower forty-eight states. To the north there are some dirt roads, and logging has made some impacts, but it is still a big, unpeopled land.

The highest peaks in the area barely manage to poke above treeline at 8,000 feet, but the area receives copious rain and snowfall, which produces dense forests of cedar, white pine, and a diverse mix of other moisture-loving species. Carving this verdant landscape are a multitude of small creeks that join to form the Lochsa.

The Lochsa officially starts when Crooked Fork and White Sands Creek (a.k.a. Colt Killed Creek, as named by Lewis and Clark) join forces near the Powell Ranger Station. It is wide and gravelly here, perfect for the migrating steelhead that call the Lochsa home.

The river imperceptibly grows as it moves along, gaining flow from a number of small feeder creeks. By the time the first significant whitewater is encountered 25 miles downstream, the river has grown large, especially in snowmelt season when it is most popular for paddling.

The Lochsa at high water resembles Grand Canyon style rapids—straightforward but big. Unlike the Canyon, however, the Lochsa offers little recovery time between rapids. This is especially true on the less-traveled upper run above the popular Fish Creek put-in.

The section below Fish Creek is known as the Goat Range. The pools are a bit bigger down here, but so are the drops. House Wave and Grim Reaper are standout rapids. For first timers, the Lochsa will be remembered as a big water blur, except for the notable Lochsa Falls and the surf wave. Lochsa Falls flips lots of rafts at high water, and its large flushy hole can be intimidating to kayakers. The surf wave, sometimes called Pipeline, is one of the best waves in the West. At most levels, the eddy next to the wave doesn't quite auto-load, but a well-placed rope can assist the attainment for another ride. Surfing opportunities abound on the rest of the run too, but eddies are scarce, so the waves are nearly all one-shot affairs.

Today, we tend to get so focused on the surfing that the difficulty of the surrounding terrain slips by us. After all, the Lochsa is easily accessed, with Highway 12 running along river right for its entire length. Before the 1960s, however, Route 12 was not even paved, and a generation before that, there was no road at all. Today's popular Goat Range run was once considered the inaccessible Black Canyon, a dreaded wilderness trap to be avoided if at all possible.

The first non-natives to attempt boating through the gorge were forced to do so in order to evacuate an ill member of their hunting party.

The year was 1893. The five-man team built two well-constructed log boats while snowed in at their hunting camp on the class I-II upper Lochsa, and started downstream on a cold and rainy November 3rd. The river was moderately high due to the stormy weather, making the descent especially treacherous. They struggled downstream, running the small rapids and lining the bigger ones, continually getting soaked from wading in the freezing river, and pinning the rafts on midstream rocks more than once. After nine days of miserably slow progress, the hunters encountered the rapids of today's upper Lochsa run, and decided to hike the rest of the way out, leaving the nearly comatose evacuee behind, where he died. It took another ten days of survival hiking before the famished group encountered a rescue party several miles above the Selway River.

Somewhat more successful runs on the Lochsa began in the early 1970s, when boaters began realizing that the innocuous looking Lochsa was actually quite a challenge. Missoulan boater Lynn McAdams recalls the local paddling community virtually ignoring the Lochsa in the '60s, owing partly to the fact that "it didn't look that spectacular from the road." It was a classic case of N.P.R. syndrome—No Problem from the Road. As reports of the river circulated, however, paddlers soon realized that the Lochsa was "wilder than the Selway," says McAdams. After all, Lochsa is a Flathead Indian word meaning rough water. The natives avoided it.

Historically, travel through the mountains took place on the Lolo Trail, which followed ridge lines to the north of the Lochsa, well above the river canyon. This is the route Lewis and Clark followed on their journey to the Pacific. It also happened to be the most harrowing and desperate part of their entire continental traverse.

Classically inclement north Idaho weather hammered the explorers with several inches of snow on September 16th, prompting the hardy Clark to write, "I have been wet and as cold in every part as I ever was in my life." They continued their miserable march, slogging through wet snow and surviving on inadequate amounts of horse meat and grouse. Finally, the Corps of Discovery reached the accommodating villages of the Nez Perce Indians, and the rest is history. It had taken the explorers nine long days and all their resolve to get through Lochsa country.

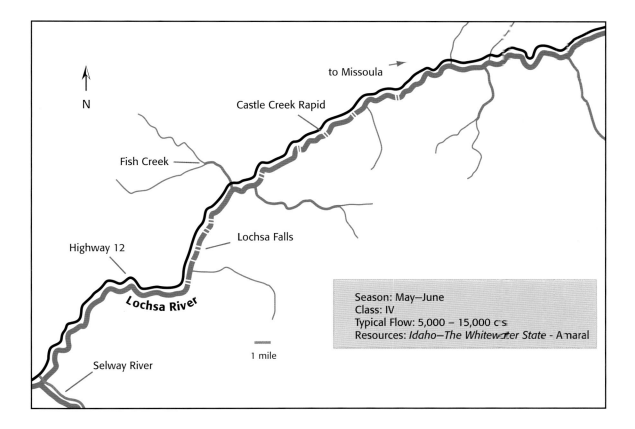

Season: May–June
Class: IV
Typical Flow: 5,000 – 15,000 cfs
Resources: *Idaho—The Whitewater State - Amaral*

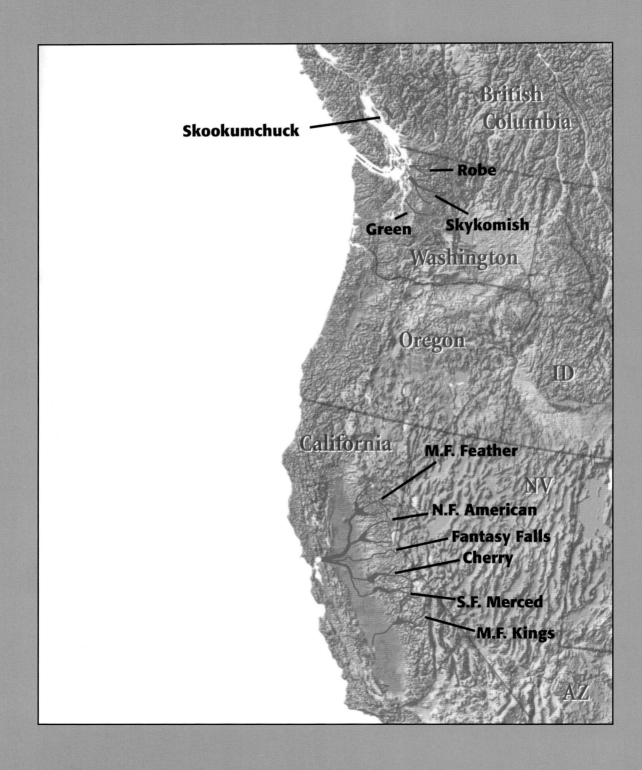

Skookumchuck

Robe

Green   Skykomish

British Columbia

Washington

Oregon

ID

California

M.F. Feather

NV

N.F. American

Fantasy Falls

Cherry

S.F. Merced

M.F. Kings

AZ

West Coast

> "Noble walls—sculpted into endless variety of domes and gables, spires and battlements and plain mural precipices—all a-tremble with the thunder tones of the falling water."
>
> *John Muir*

Plentiful precipitation, big mountains, and corridors of wilderness make the West Coast an optimal paddling destination. This is the leading edge of the continent, where the Pacific storms that shape North America's weather first make landfall.

Throughout the region, winter is the rainy season. This season lasts longer in the north, where unsettled weather can persist even in mid-summer. In contrast, rain almost never falls during July and August farther south in California, where 80 percent of the yearly precipitation comes between October and March.

The rivers profiled in *Whitewater Classics* drain the two major mountain ranges of the region: the Cascades and the Sierra Nevadas. California's Sierras are a whitewater paradise, considered by many to be the best paddling locale in the world. Glacially-worn granite bedrock is the area's most striking feature, but the steep mountains, saturated snowpacks, and sunny warm weather during paddling season also earns the Sierras their world class reputation.

Farther north in Oregon and Washington's Cascades, there is a tremendous variety of rivers, and a nearly year-round paddling season. In fall and winter, seasonal rains bring high water to the rivers and creeks. With springtime comes snowmelt from higher elevations. The warm, long days of summer melt the glaciers of the big mountains, making certain rivers runnable even in the dry season.

Besides the Sierras and Cascades, coast ranges hold an array of lesser-known but nonetheless fantastic rivers. British Columbia's Vancouver Island is home to numerous rain-fed creeks. Washington's Olympic Peninsula contains several known classics, and a few more that still await a first descent. Oregon's coastal mountains contain several hidden gems, and Northern California holds a lifetime of paddling options.

For an extensive season, and unlimited variety, the West Coast is the jewel of the continent.

Johnnie Kern

One of hundreds of drops on the Middle Fork of the Kings

Scott Lindgren

California has produced many eminent paddlers over the years who have led the way in exploring rivers both in their native state, and abroad. Like his predecessors, Scott Lindgren has raised the bar for runnable whitewater both in California and in distant foreign lands. He is one of the leading expedition paddlers of his time.

Throughout high school, he was an admitted sports junkie, participating in soccer, football, tennis, track, skateboarding, skiing, and surfing. It was in kayaking, however, that he found his true calling.

After graduation, Lindgren quickly adopted the lifestyle of itinerant raft guide, freelancing throughout his native California, and working Grand Canyon trips when he could. Guiding eventually led to Idaho, where he lived alongside the North Fork of the Payette. Here, he honed his paddling skills, running his class V backyard almost daily after work. Two of Scott's paddling partners at the time were Gerry Moffatt and Charlie Munsey—North Fork regulars who shared Lindgren's thirst for adventure. Like Payette paddlers Rob Lesser and John Wasson had done a decade earlier, the Lindgren, Moffatt, Munsey trio used their North Fork runs as a launchpad for significant first descents in Asia's Himalayas.

It was in the Himalaya, on an exploratory run of Nepal's Thule Beri, when Scott got his introduction to filmmaking. When accomplished filmmaker Roger Brown had difficulty capturing the descent from shore, Scott began shooting from the river. His footage was well received, and an apprenticeship under Brown followed. It wasn't long before Lindgren won an Emmy award for his cinematography in the adventure film *Amazon to Andes*.

Back in California, Lindgren joined forces with paddlers Mark Hayden and the Knapp brothers to produce his first purely whitewater movie. *Good 2 the Last Drop* rocked the whitewater film industry, and it was apparent that Scott had found his niche—running the world's most difficult whitewater, and capturing it on film.

It is generally recognized that Tibet's Tsangpo is the greatest whitewater challenge in the world, so it was no surprise that February of 2002 found Lindgren there, leading and filming the first descent of the Tsangpo's upper gorges. Even for the world's best kayakers, this supreme accomplishment would serve as a crowning achievement, but it is just one piece of the puzzle in Lindgren's quest to run all four rivers emanating from sacred Mt. Kailas in western Tibet.

While his Asian exploits could be considered his greatest, Lindgren has completed most of North America's toughest wilderness runs too. He has made the highest water level descent of British Columbia's Stikine, and is a leading authority on the big adventure runs of California's Sierras, where he made first descents on the Royal Gorge of the American, and Upper Cherry Creek. It is one of his local Sierra Nevada rivers that he picked as his classic—the Middle Fork of the Kings. Lindgren says of the nearly 8,000-foot descent, "It's action-packed for six days straight. There's not another run like it in the world." He ought to know.

Middle Fork Kings

Running the Middle Fork of the Kings is the ultimate whitewater adventure in the Sierra Nevadas. A trip down the Middle Kings crosses the breadth of the mountain range, and finishes in the foothills 50 miles downstream. En route, the river drops nearly 8,000 feet in elevation. The journey requires one to two days of hiking to reach the put-in, followed by five to seven days of paddling. There are class V rapids every day of the trip, and a handful of class VI drops. One could hardly create a more perfect setting for cutting-edge wilderness whitewater than the Middle Fork of the Kings.

The first exploration of this river was just one piece of an audacious plan to run all three rivers that bisect the southern Sierra Nevada. The rivers are the San Joaquin, the Kern, and the Kings. The adventurers who made it their mission to descend all three in kayaks were Reg Lake, Royal Robbins, and Doug Tompkins. Reg Lake was the most skilled paddler of the trio, while Robbins and Tompkins were more renowned for their climbing exploits, and their successful business acumen. Robbins was the first to climb Yosemite's Half Dome, and his self-named clothing line gained reknown worldwide. Tompkins started the outdoor giant The North Face, and later became well known for spending his millions to preserve massive tracts of wildlands in Chile. The original thinking and drive that brought these funhogs their business success was also likely at work in their kayaking plans. They systematically ran the three major trans-Sierra rivers in consecutive seasons, starting with the Middle Fork of the San Joaquin in 1980. This descent is considered the most impressive of the three, as the group had to employ a great deal of problem solving technique gained through their climbing experience to portage their way through the San Joaquin's sheer-walled gorges. It was the Middle Fork of the Kings,

however, that Royal Robbins remembers as the "toughest of the three."

Joining Robbins, Lake, and Tompkins for the Kings was Newsome Holmes, an aggressive paddler whom they had met in Chile. The approach to the river began high on the eastern slope of the Sierras at scenic South Lake. Several friends helped the boater's carry their gear over the nearly 12,000-foot Bishop Pass. After the two days of hiking with their friends, the paddlers set off down the normally shallow headwaters of the Middle Fork. This year, however, things weren't so shallow. Despite waiting until late August for the water to drop, the Kings was still flush with snowmelt following the above-average winter of '82, and snow bridges occasionally blocked the entire river. The snowy undercuts obviously forced the group into multiple portages, and so did the 200 to 400 foot-per-mile gradient. With no committing gorges along the river, however, they smoothly paddled and portaged their way downstream for five days, negotiating 2,400 cfs on the main Kings as a grand finale.

The descent was certainly a triumph in exploration, but reports of the run's whitewater were less glorious. The California whitewater guidebook summed up the Middle Fork's first descent in one poignant sentence: "Be prepared for extensive portaging." Boaters stayed away from the Middle Kings for the next 13 years, the only exception being one rafting attempt on the lower half of the run that turned into a survival epic. Then Scott Lindgren set his sights on it.

Lindgren assembled an all-star team for the second full Middle Kings descent: Buffy Burge, Mark Hayden, Chuck, Johnnie, and Willie Kern, Brandon and Dustin Knapp, and BJ Johnson. This elite group of paddlers ran most of the rapids that had been too much for Robbins and company, and came away calling the run "wonderful." Johnnie Kern remembers being "surprised by how much we could run," but also called the Kings, "As far as effort, the hardest thing I'd done to that point."

The heavy lifting started at the South Lake trailhead when the mules that were scheduled to carry the kayaks instantly spooked at the sight of the boats. The paddlers stuffed their gear into the mule's saddlebags, and schlepped the plastic themselves.

Once at the river, they found a series of runnable slides dropping into deep pools, all surrounded by the granite moonscape of the high Sierras. Le Conte Canyon provided several dramatic drops early in the trip, but the steepest continuous gradient came in the ominously named Devils Washbowl. Here, a four-mile sequence of stomping gradient read like this: 340, 440, 380, 340. After this crux section, the team had another 24 miles to look forward to, with an average gradient of almost 200 feet-per-mile. By the time they passed the granite monolith of Tehipite Dome, the river had grown from 100 cfs at the put-in to several hundred cfs. The riverbed was more continuous, and the gradient was still impressive. Kern says. "That's the part where people start to melt down a little bit." The dream team avoided any major mishaps, however. Chuck Kern even cleaned the run without so much as a flip. At the confluence with the South Fork of the Kings, the group took out via the Yucca Point trail. Lindgren, however, normally prefers to continue downstream through the main Kings' Garlic Falls and Banzai sections. The Garlic Falls run is a fantastic class V run in its own right, and the class III Banzai run is a perfect way to wind down from the most action-packed run in California's Sierras.

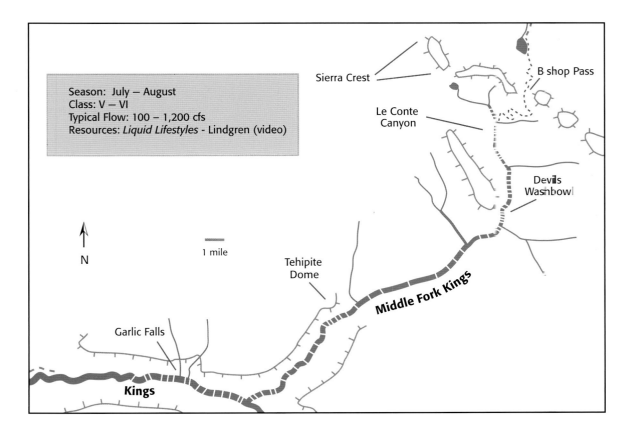

Season: July — August
Class: V — VI
Typical Flow: 100 – 1,200 cfs
Resources: *Liquid Lifestyles* - Lindgren (video)

N

1 mile

Sierra Crest

B shop Pass

Le Conte
Canyon

Devils
Washbowl

Tehipite
Dome

Middle Fork Kings

Garlic Falls

Kings

"I can't remember, was it left or right at this rock?" Threading a boulder maze on the South Merced

Lars Holbek

Lars Holbek has logged more first descents than anyone else on the planet. This is certainly a bold statement to make, but tough to argue with nonetheless. Just a sampling of his exploratories reads like a tick list of California classics: Golden Gate and Lover's Leap (S.F. American), Bald Rock Canyon (M.F. Feather), Generation Gap (N.F. American), Fantasy Falls (N.F. Mokelumne), and the Little North Fork of the Middle Feather name only a few. Though he is primarily known for his Californian exploits, Holbek has also been involved in landmark first descents outside of his native state, most notably Peru's Paucartambo, British Columbia's Grand Canyon of the Stikine, and Chile's Futaleufu.

All this exploration started for Holbek as a senior in high school in Santa Rosa, California, where he was introduced to kayaking by his older climbing partners. It was the classic school-of-hard-knocks learning program, complete with macho-man advice such as "Lars, you've got to paddle like a predator."

One year after starting, Holbek met Chuck Stanley and Richard Montgomery, childhood friends who had received slalom training. Their tips quickly polished Holbek's technique, and there was no looking back. His recollections of his early kayaking years resonate with the wonderment that many of us feel toward the sport. "Simply, kayaking in those days is what fired my imagination and curiosity, got me out of bed, and filled my life with the adventure, excitement, and energy that made life worth living."

Holbek paddled 200 days a year, primarily with Stanley and Montgomery. Between 1978 and 1986, the trio tore through the whitewater wonderland of the Sierra Nevada like kids (or perhaps, predators) in a candy store. Holbek says of the period, "We were possessed." The by-product of his obsessive kayak exploration is *The Best Whitewater in California*, an information packed guidebook that Holbek co-wrote with Stanley. Now in its third edition, it is essential reading for anyone with an interest in the whitewater of the Golden state. The book is held in such esteem by locals that it is referred to as "the New Testament." The back of the book contains a listing of California's first descents (prior to 1998), 22 of which were made by Holbek.

Interestingly, when Lars was asked what his classic pick was, he responded without hesitation, "South Merced"—not a first descent of his. That honor goes to Ron Thompson, who ran it solo in a hollowform in 1979! Holbek didn't get to the South Fork of the Merced until the late '80s, after being put off by tales of unavoidable poison oak. When he finally did arrive, he found, in his words, "one of the best multi-day, super high quality and difficult runnable class V runs in the world."

Though perhaps no longer possessed, Holbek continues to explore some of the steepest river canyons on the continent. Even after thirty or more descents, he still returns to the South Merced regularly—a testament to his continuing high level of dedication to the sport.

South Fork Merced

A trip down the South Merced infiltrates your mind. Even days after getting off the run, your mind's eye is constantly filled with the image of the South Merced's fluffy white holes and big round boulders. For those who have run it, the South Merced is a river hard to forget.

The river gathers snowmelt from the 11,000-foot peaks of the central Sierras. Much of its watershed falls within the southern portion of Yosemite National Park, so its waters are clear and pure, the type of flow that is transparent enough to watch river cobbles under the water race by as the current accelerates down a riffle. Uncut forests full of huge ponderosa pines and incense cedars line the river's banks, not that you'll have many chances to bask in the splendor of the South Merced's scenery.

This is a Sierra Nevada river, and one of Lars Holbek's favorites. Those two factors alone should tell you that this run has mega whitewater. Domed gray rocks congest the river channel for much of the run, forming long boulder-strewn rapids. Although these boulder mazes are the most common rapid type, there is also a marbled red and brown bedrock that surfaces periodically throughout the run. As might be expected, the bedrock creates some of the most exciting, runnable, and memorable whitewater of the trip. One of the last big bedrock rapids is a noticeable notch above anything else on the run, and serves as one of the South Merced's few standard portages.

This is certainly a memorable spot, especially for long time California paddler Lee Wilhelm. Lee once launched solo on the South Merced in hopes of catching his buddies Holbek and company who were already on the river. Racing downstream, Lee mistakenly paddled one drop too many as he entered the normally portaged four-tiered falls. Although he knew where he was, the polished sloping bedrock next to his tiny eddy offered little chance for an exit. Wilhelm says, "Before I had a chance to freak, knowing there was no other option, I peeled out into the current and breathed deeply. I rolled twice, presumably in each of the diagonals, and emerged at the bottom unscathed."

The following day, Holbek convinced Wilhelm to join him for a speed run down the South Merced. The duo bombed the 23-mile run in a record 4 hours and 14 minutes! Besides having run it the previous day, they had paddled the river many times before, so they remembered almost all of the lines. Still, a four hour run of the South Fork of the Merced is mind-boggling, considering that most parties require two long days. If you plan on scouting thoroughly or portaging much, plan on three days.

The sustained high quality of this run is what attracts the top paddlers. The fact that nearly every rapid has a line makes the down river racing antics feasible. Few other places in the world have this many class V rapids with so few portages. At optimal levels, everything is runnable, although even gurus like Holbek usually elect to carry a couple drops each run.

Water level is key here. Low water (less than 800 cfs at the take-out) turns some of the boulder rapids into sievey rock piles, requiring more portaging. A run on high water (over 1,200 cfs at the take-out) has been described as "being scared to death for six hours at a time." An optimal flow of 1,000 cfs means there's plenty of cushion to the holes, and some of the broad bouldery rapids contain side channel creek lines.

There are no working gauges on the South Merced, so estimates must be made based on the main Merced's flow. If you are there in person, it's the ol' "Looks good from the bridge" technique. Optimal flows on the South Fork can be elusive, adding even more mystique to this gem.

The lower seven miles of the South Merced are much easier than the sixteen miles above. This lower section is viewed as merely the paddle out by those who have survived the chaos upstream. It is a nice break from the constant action above, a time to again enjoy the subtleties of a river, like an eddyline's aerated bubbles slicing into the clear green water beneath the surface. The lower seven miles would be a great run for an adventuresome class III boater willing to portage some, or a class IV boater who doesn't mind a hike to the put-in.

Clear mountain water, boulder gardens, bedrock slides, scenery, remoteness. In more than one way, the South Fork of the Merced qualifies as a true whitewater classic.

A rare relaxing moment on the South Merced

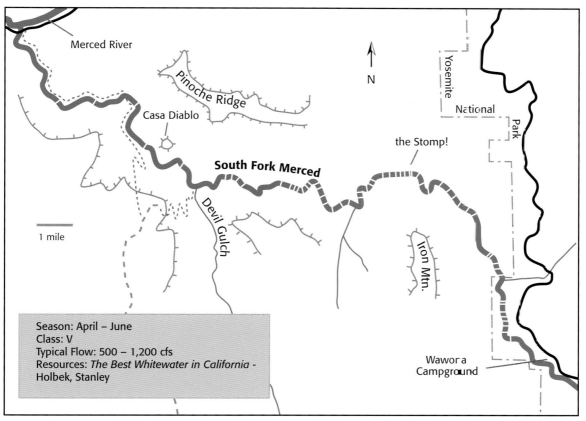

Season: April – June
Class: V
Typical Flow: 500 – 1,200 cfs
Resources: *The Best Whitewater in California -* Holbek, Stanley

Jed Weingarten

Going big in Royal Gorge

Shannon Carroll

Athletic pursuits are generally dominated by men, yet many of those pursuits have also seen a female participant that is so strong and skilled, she is not thought of as a "female athlete," but simply one of the best athletes, period. Tennis' Williams sisters come to mind as examples of this, as does golf's Annika Sorenstam, or track and field's late Florence Griffith Joyner. In whitewater paddling, today's boldest female athlete is Shannon Carroll.

Colleen Laffey

Shannon's aggressive style on the water can be traced to her competitive background in team sports, and her independence. Her determined nature was evident early in her kayaking career when the eleven-year-old Shannon would set out on the upper New River without a roll. Swimming the big river was of little concern to her, however. She was accustomed to it from a childhood of canoe trips with her dad. Her parents ran a summer camp in the heart of West Virginia's New River Gorge, so Shannon formed an early bond with the river there.

Back home in Virginia, Shannon's energies were occupied with basketball, volleyball, and softball through high school. The call of the river was in her blood, however. When she missed volleyball practice to run the narrows of the Green, a chain reaction was begun that eventually led to her position as a world class kayaker. Her run on the Green promptly got Carroll kicked off the volleyball team, which opened the door for her to work as a video boater that Gauley season. Her paddling skills blossomed, and a scholarship to Liberty University was traded for a kayaking trip in Costa Rica.

Since then, Carroll has been featured in several paddling films, made a spot on the U.S. freestyle team, won a world championship in surf kayaking, and earned a reputation for running the beefest lines in whitewater. Her descent of 78-foot Sahalie Falls in Oregon was a world record until waterfall hucking came into vogue in the months following her run.

With her pursuit of class VI, and busy filming schedule, Carroll has been on paddling forays to New Zealand, Norway, Europe's Alps and Pyrennees, and across North America. Lately she bases her travels from Truckee, California, close to the North Fork of the American's Royal Gorge. Shannon was drawn to this newly-probed classic from the first time she saw it on a Scott Lindgren film. When Carroll arrived there in person, she became the first to clean the entire Heath Springs Gorge—the most committing set of big drops on the run. Descents like this are something any of whitewater's best paddlers would be proud of—man or woman.

North Fork American

The North Fork of the American River is a perfect platform for illustrating the development of whitewater paddling in California. The river gets progressively more difficult as it runs from the lower foothills to the crest of the Sierras. Consequently, exploration of the North Fork has steadily moved upstream over the years.

In the 1950s, only the lower portions of the river were run. By the '60s, Carl Trost and company were running the class IV Chamberlain Falls section just upstream. The '70s saw the first attempts at the infamous Giant Gap canyon. In the '80s, the appropriately named Generation Gap was probed as a new generation of boats and boaters pushed the class V level. The '90s again raised the standard of runnable whitewater, and the North Fork of the American River's uppermost canyon—Royal Gorge—was finally descended.

Scott and Dustin Lindgren had grown up skiing at Sugar Bowl ski area near the river's headwaters, so it was natural that they led the first descent of the Royal Gorge in 1997. The trip got off to a rough start when residents of the trophy homes lining the put-in road stopped the group of kayakers, and threatened to call the sheriff if the paddlers didn't leave immediately. Although they had done nothing illegal, the boaters figured that a meeting with Johnny Law wasn't the best way to start a first descent on class V—VI whitewater. They bailed on the brewing confrontation, returned in the middle of the night, and put in at a hidden location the next morning.

The kayakers thought their access problems were behind them until Clay Wright was approached by a security guard while he was shooting video. Clay talked with the oddly curious employee of the homeowners development, and they were soon discussing the feasibility of running the 50-foot waterfall below them. The guard insisted that the fall was unrunnable, but Clay

swiftly ended the conversation by saying, "Just watch this." Tao Berman launched the drop on cue, and came paddling out of the foam below. After seeing this, the guard's attitude lightened. Clay recalls. "After that, he cheered." Soon the paddlers were on their way downstream, beyond the reach of the hostile natives.

Access remains an issue on Royal Gorge. And if that doesn't deter you, the short season might. This tight upper canyon only has about a week-long window of runnable flow in most years, just as the snowmelt tails off. If Royal Gorge has an optimal water level, then Generation and Giant Gaps will be on the low side, and the only way out is through the Generation and Giant Gap runs.

Generation Gap was first run by the Holbek, Montgomery, Stanley group, along with Mike Schlax, in 1980. Earlier that spring, the Holbek trio had already made exploratory runs on the Feather's Bald Rock Canyon, and the South Fork of the American's Golden Gate run. When they made it to Generation Gap, they had the routine down. They made the run without mishap, and continued into the more familiar territory of Giant Gap. Montgomery and Stanley had made the first no-portage run on this section several years earlier.

The two were plenty pumped for the run after years of reading the ominous reports of the canyon in the original California guidebook—*Sierra Whitewater*. They cautiously arrived at the trailhead the day before their planned launch, and carried one boat down the trail that afternoon before returning to the trailhead to camp. Hiking the steep trail in and out of the canyon proved one of the toughest parts of the trip. Montgomery recalls, "Our thighs were seized up the next day." The following morning, they got an early start in anticipation of the many arduous scouts and portages ahead. "We figured we'd portage down the whole thing," Montgomery recalls. A couple dozen rapids later, Montgomery wasn't sure they would have to portage at all. He suggested that they might be past the crux of the run, but Stanley was unwilling to let down his guard. He insisted that they hadn't reached the big stuff yet, and they continued eddy-hopping downstream looking for that constricted mist-shrouded horizon. When the canyon opened more and they still hadn't reached "the big stuff," it was obvious they had made it through Giant Gap. They had yet to portage a single drop.

The first attempt at the canyon didn't have it so easy. John Googins, Charlie Martin (author of *Sierra Whitewater*), and John Ramirez first paddled Giant Gap in 1971, but the flow was much too high (1,800 cfs) for a first descent, and they abandoned their boats and hiked out while they still could. Ramirez returned a few weeks later when the flow had dropped by half, and became the first to run Giant Gap when he finished the run solo. Googins and Martin waited for ultra-low water later in the summer before scraping out of the canyon in their boats.

Regardless of water level, the North Fork of the American cuts a beautiful canyon for its entire length. The crystal clear green-hued water is enough to enjoy even without the whitewater. Paddlers, however, get the added bonus of exhilarating rapids. From the class IV of Chamberlain Falls to the class VI of Royal Gorge, the North Fork of the American has classic written all over it.

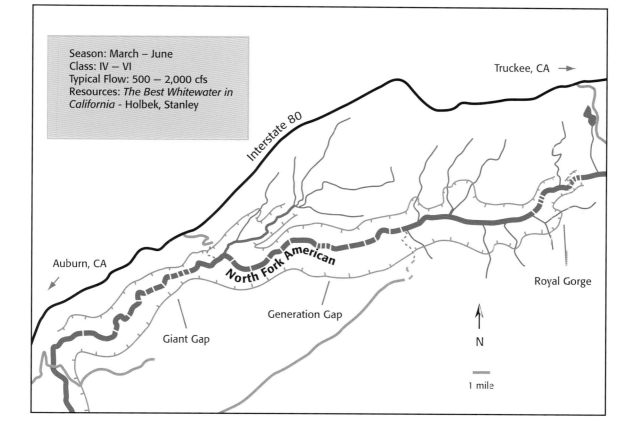

Season: March – June
Class: IV – VI
Typical Flow: 500 – 2,000 cfs
Resources: *The Best Whitewater in California* - Holbek, Stanley

Truckee, CA →

Interstate 80

Auburn, CA

North Fork American

Giant Gap

Generation Gap

Royal Gorge

N

1 mile

Taylor Robertson

Dan Gavere enters Lumsden Falls on a high water Cherry Creek run

Beth Rypins

Whitewater may have saved Beth Rypin's life.

Her childhood was not an easy one. After struggling through recovery from a stroke she suffered at the tender age of seven, Beth's next challenge lay in negotiating the many temptations of San Francisco's Haight-Ashbury neighborhood where she lived. A teenage girl in Haight-Ashbury in the 1970s—it's no wonder Rypins was on course for a difficult life on the street. When she was exposed to river running, she saw new opportunity in the world, and latched onto it with extraordinary tenacity.

When Beth was fifteen, she lied about her culinary skills (stating that she in fact had some) in order to land a job as cook at Sierra Kayak School. The cooking gig offered her the chance to learn kayaking, which in turn taught her how to focus—an important life skill that had eluded her previously. She recalls the revelation, "I realized, 'Hey, I better pay attention here or I'm gonna flip and swim.'"

At sixteen she got a Perception Mirage for a high school graduation present, and soon started guiding raft trips for Whitewater Voyages—a cutting edge California raft company that was a hotbed for river running talent in the 1980s.

By the time Beth was twenty-one years old, she was on her way to the infamous Stikine for the made-for-TV first raft descent. It proved a pivotal event for Beth as she learned the intricacies of expedition team dynamics, and she met Lars Holbek.

"Lars was a huge influence on my paddling," Rypins recounts. The couple spent the next several years in pursuit of kayak dreams both at home in

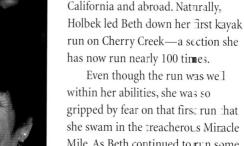

California and abroad. Naturally, Holbek led Beth down her first kayak run on Cherry Creek—a section she has now run nearly 100 times.

Even though the run was well within her abilities, she was so gripped by fear on that first run that she swam in the treacherous Miracle Mile. As Beth continued to run some of the Sierra's toughest whitewater, she developed techniques to deal with the inherent fear. Whitewater, it seems, had taught her another important lesson. Today she gives motivational talks to business executives on how to manage their fears.

One thing Beth has never been afraid of is foreign travel. She has run rivers worldwide, both in her kayak, and in a raft for Earth River Expeditions. She did some of the earliest kayak exploration in Chile, paddled in Peru, guided on the Zambezi, and spent significant time in Russia, where she speaks the native language.

Throughout her career in whitewater, Beth has gained a clear perspective on how the sport has developed, and she expresses this in *Tight Squeeze*, a film she co-produced with Jamie Cooper that focuses on the whitewater divas of today. Beth's passion for paddling is palpable in the video, no surprise for someone whose life was changed from the day she began to follow the path of the paddle.

Cherry Creek

The Cherry Creek section of the Tuolumne River is the benchmark class V run in California. Although commonly referred to simply as Cherry Creek, almost all of this 7-mile run is actually on the Tuolumne—a river that is symbolic of all Sierra Nevada Rivers.

Even at its origins, the Tuolumne is a whitewater stream. Its headwaters are a series of small creeks that splash and tumble off the granite slabs of the Yosemite high country. After slowing briefly in beautiful Tuolumne Meadows, the clear mountain river plunges into the dramatic Grand Canyon of the Tuolumne. In this narrow granite gorge, the river twists and plunges in an array of class V-VI whitewater. This upper 30 miles of the Tuolumne are about as spectacular as a river can be. Then it is swallowed by Hetch Hetchy Reservoir.

This reservoir project was valiantly opposed by the great John Muir and his Sierra Club, but the dam was nevertheless completed in 1923, flooding the Hetch Hetchy Valley. Now, most of the Tuolumne's water is funneled from the reservoir into the Hetch Hetchy aqueduct, where it is eventually sent to San Francisco. Significant water isn't returned to the Tuolumne until Cherry Creek enters roughly 20 miles downstream from the dam.

This tributary has much the same story as the Tuolumne. It starts high in the mountains, flows over many dramatic slides and waterfalls (this is the Upper Cherry Creek run, a three-day epic requiring a hike-in), and then dumps into a reservoir. Unlike the Tuolumne, however, much of Cherry Creek's water is returned to the river rather than being sent directly to the thirsty valley below. Not far below the power house where this water is returned to its bed, the standard Cherry Creek run begins. A half-mile downstream from the put-in, the creek joins the nearly dewatered Tuolumne.

This section didn't receive much attention from the California paddling crowd until a dam threat prompted Dick Sunderland and Gerald Meral to run it in 1968. This duo portaged 9 times on the exploratory. When Richard Montgomery and Chuck Stanley asked Sunderland about the river a decade later, he told the skilled paddlers in plastic boats that they would portage only 4 rapids. He was right.

A week after their first trip on Cherry Creek, Montgomery and Stanley returned with a group of raft guide friends who took paddle rafts on the run. The ace kayakers figured the rafters would portage at least the 4 big rapids, and maybe more. To the kayaker's surprise, the rafts started bombing over the "portages," and Montgomery and Stanley found themselves watching in amazement. After each successful raft run, the two kayakers would look at each other, shrug their shoulders as if to say, "It must be runnable," and then proceed to test the lines in their kayaks. At the end of the day, everything except Lumsden Falls near the take-out had been run.

Rafts had played a major role in Cherry Creek's river running history even before this aggressive display of paddle rafting. Throughout the '70s, Marty McDonnell made a number of descents on Cherry Creek in first-generation catarafts. He and Walt Harvest made the first ever raft descent in April of 1973. They went in armed with climbing gear for potential lining and portaging, and each carried a passenger to help with high-siding when necessary. The group got an early start, expecting two days on the river. By midday on day one, they were pleasantly surprised to find that not only were they going to finish the run that day, they were very likely going to run most of the rapids. McDonnell writes, "It was like a dream come true...We could hardly believe we were doing it." McDonnell's

Sierra Mac River Trips started doing the Cherry Creek run commercially in 1981, and it remains one of the most difficult commercial raft runs in North America today.

Rafts can often bridge holes that present problems for smaller boats, and this is one of the primary reasons Cherry Creek is within reach of skilled rafters. For kayaks, C-1s, and open canoes, the holes of Cherry Creek present good action throughout.

On a high water Cherry Creek day, freestyler Tanya Shuman recalls seeing one of her group make a "world champion freestyle ride for over a minute." The lengthy hole ride naturally ended with a swim. While retrieving the un-manned boat, a rattlesnake was encountered. Despite the large numbers of paddlers who run Cherry

Creek, this is still a wild class V place.

The riverbed is littered with big granite boulders that form rapids at fairly regular intervals along the entire stretch. Mushroom is the biggest rapid on the first half of the run. Two of the hardest rapids, Lewis' Leap and Flat Rock Falls, come in the last mile. If you're really feeling good, the normally-portaged Lumsden Falls awaits at the take-out.

Not far below here, the main Tuolumne run begins. This is a long one-day or short two-day trip through a beautiful canyon. The run ends in the New Don Pedro Reservoir. Here the Tuolumne is again put to use as an irrigator. Its fate is that of a true Sierra Nevada river.

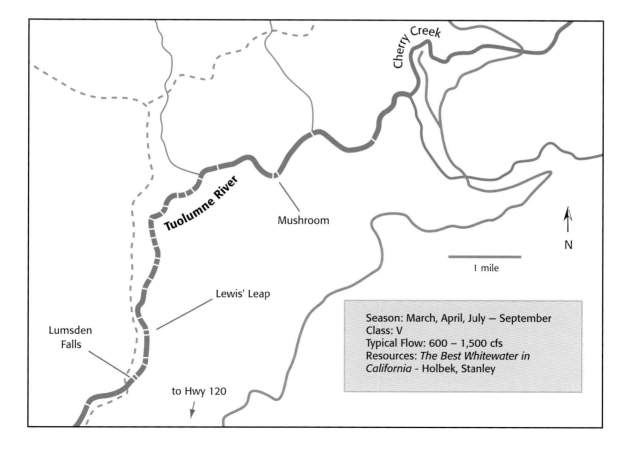

Season: March, April, July — September
Class: V
Typical Flow: 600 – 1,500 cfs
Resources: *The Best Whitewater in California* - Holbek, Stanley

A typical Middle Feather scene

Phil & Mary DeRiemer

Paddling together provides some of the best times a couple will ever have. It is only natural, then, that the sport of whitewater paddling has sparked a number of renowned relationships over the years. Leading the way as the model for paddling couples are Phil and Mary DeRiemer.

Although instruction is also a major aspect of Phil's contribution to the sport, his history in paddling has a bit more ragged edge. His storied career began with a shaky start on California's Trinity River, when Phil recalls "plowing through a gravel bar with my elbow." Eventually, however, kayaking struck a chord, and he was soon working at Sundance Kayak School.

Their paths did not join until after each had already achieved impressive paddling resumes individually. Since their union, the two have continued to make paddling the driving force in their lives. Winters find them teaching and guiding paddling trips in Ecuador, while summer brings the DeRiemers and their company—DeRiemer Adventure Kayaking—to the rivers of North America.

Paddling was not on the radar screen for either Phil or Mary early in life. Both got their introduction to kayaking after college. Mary, an RN, took a kayaking class on the suggestion of the doctors she worked with. She had such a natural talent for instruction, she was offered a job at Nantahala Outdoor Center within two years of taking her first strokes. Her tenure at NOC lasted ten years, during which time she raced wildwater in both C-2 and kayak, winning three national championships. Racing, however, was just "a social thing at that time," she says. Her greatest impact on the sport remains her tireless instruction. Mary has had legions of protégés over the years, among them celebrated paddlers Buffy Burge and the late Brennan Guth.

Unbeknownst to them, Phil and Mary's lives had taken parallel paths. While Mary raced in her spare time, Phil adventured. He traveled to South America, where he joined the fabled Paucartambo expedition, then went south to Chile and joined Lars Holbek on the first descent of the Futaleufu. In the north, DeRiemer ran the Stikine, and made the only river circumnavigation of Baffin Island ever attempted. Back home in California, he has run most of the Sierra Nevada classics, including a four-day grunt down the Middle Fork of the San Joaquin before the era of short boats.

The Middle Fork of the Feather, however, is the one that Phil calls "a run where you will drop anything to get on it with your buds." He has run both the Devils and Bald Rock Canyon sections, and first showed the upper run to Mary in 1994, when just the two of them went on a two-day trip. The river has since become one of Mary's favorites, too. She calls it "a doable yet challenging overnight surrounded by spectacular California granite." Sounds like a good place to go with your sweetheart, eh?

Middle Fork Feather

"This is it. The Middle Fork of the Feather River is the best self-supported wilderness trip in California," claims California paddling legend Chuck Stanley, co-author of *The Best Whitewater in California*. Some may disagree with Stanley's bold claim, but there is no question that the Middle Feather has all the ingredients of a classic.

To start with, the scenery is varied and pleasant throughout. The river is ensconced in smooth, slabby Sierra Nevada granite in Devils and Bald Rock Canyons, whereas the upper reaches are quite different. For the first days of a Middle Feather trip, the river canyon is reminiscent of Idaho's Salmon. Arid, steep slopes of broken gray granite intermingle with a forest of ponderosa pine and Douglas fir, and cold clear springs trickle into the river beneath flat bench lands littered with historic mining relics.

The whitewater, however, bears little resemblance to the mellow Salmon. Beautiful class IV rapids lace the entire river, with class V drops sprouting up intermittently until building to a climax of V-VI in Bald Rock Canyon.

Bald Rock was first run in 1980 by the usual suspects—Lars Holbek, Richard Montgomery, and Chuck Stanley. The trio arrived at the Milsap Bar put-in under ominous gray skies to find the river at a burgeoning 1,500 cfs, much too high for an exploratory run in a steep granite gorge. Another complication for the group was the shuttle. They didn't really have one. A combination of hitchhiking and bike riding was their planned return to their vehicle. All they had to do first was paddle seven miles of unexplored river and thirteen miles across a reservoir—no problem!

They all got pushed around in the first class IV rapid, and doubts about their plan grew. Two miles down, they arrived at the intimidating head of the gorge. Stanley writes, "Downstream loomed massive, sheer granite cliffs on both sides, below us lay a class V drop, and overhead dark clouds threatened." Considering the high water and poor weather, Montgomery and Stanley voted for a return to the vehicle, but Holbek was on a mission. He was willing to push through the gorge solo. "Once again, democracy failed, and we entered the canyon with a tremendous foreboding," writes Stanley.

The team quickly and smoothly made their way downstream, launching off the boat-scoutable horizon lines, and decisively portaging any questionable drops. Above the unrunnable Atom Bomb Falls, their portage route cliffed out, and they were forced to make the now-infamous ferry move just ten feet from the brink of certain death. They all completed the delicate move, and one at a time got out on a narrow ledge of granite to continue the portage. Had the river been 100 cfs higher, the ledge would've been lost underwater, and they would've been trapped in the canyon.

They made it to the reservoir without any more close calls, only to find a giant logjam that slowed their progress a half hour before dark. At midnight, they reached the take-out bridge, built a fire out of road signs, and started fighting off the cold. Only Stanley had decided to bring the extra weight of a sleeping bag. After a mostly sleepless night, Holbek completed their dubious shuttle plan, and the first descent of Bald Rock Canyon could be called a success.

The same type of scoured bedrock canyon that nearly trapped the Holbek party at Atom Bomb Falls also caused problems for the first descent party of the river's upstream canyons. In July 1975, explorers Bert Welti, Charlie Pike, and Dan Gaut launched on the Middle Feather at what they thought was an ideally moderate-low water level. Ironically, it was the low water that caused the group their scariest moment.

By day three of their run, Welti and his companions had negotiated a few of the Middle Feather's rock boxes, paddling and portaging without major difficulty. So it is understandable that they allowed themselves to drift too far downstream in one particular tight spot in Devils Canyon. The rapid below them was not fully visible, yet there was no returning upstream to a point from which to get out and scout. Higher water would've allowed access to a ledge, but it was too far out of the water to reach. The three paddled back and forth across the pool for several minutes feigning contemplation, but everyone knew what had to be done. Someone had to probe the blind horizon. Finally, Gaut charged off the lip, and luckily found it to be clean.

The Welti team thought that they were surely the first to run the river, and they indeed were the first to paddle all the way through Devils Canyon, but their first descent glory was dampened when a fisherman told them of a kayaker he had seen just a week previous. With some detective work, they discovered the culprit to be Joe Kholer, a Czechoslovakian immigrant who worked odd hours and wasn't well known in the paddling community. Apparently Kholer had soloed the first 22 miles of the 32-mile run, carrying his boat out of the river canyon on the Pacific Crest Trail at Hartman's Bar. Here's to the unknown adventurers out there!

From the early runs to today, the Middle Feather has retained its mystique. Bears still roam the thick forests of the upper canyons, and roads are still unable to penetrate the granite gorges downstream. Combining scenery with whitewater, the Middle Fork of the Feather is undeniably what most would consider classic.

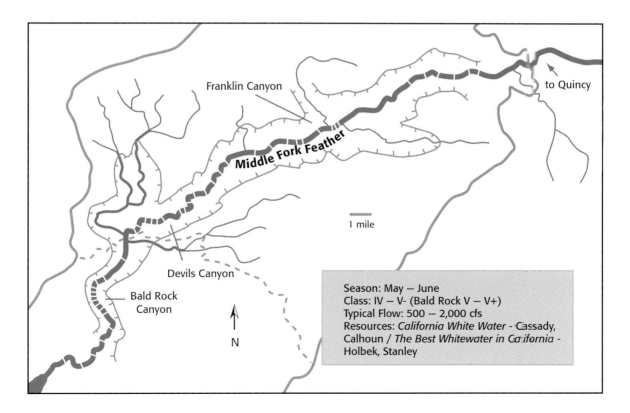

Franklin Canyon

Middle Fork Feather

to Quincy

1 mile

Devils Canyon

Bald Rock
Canyon

N

Season: May — June
Class: IV — V- (Bald Rock V — V+)
Typical Flow: 500 — 2,000 cfs
Resources: *California White Water - Cassady,
Calhoun / The Best Whitewater in California -*
Holbek, Stanley

Jed Weingarten

It's not a fantasy, it's the North Fork of the Mokelumne

Brandon & Dustin Knapp

Brandon and Dustin Knapp must view life's accepted norms as nothing more than unnecessary limitations. From their home-schooled education deep in the mountains of northern California, to their unconventional development as kayakers, the Knapps have always done things their own way.

Dirt-biking near their home was the brother's favorite pastime as youngsters. It wasn't until traveling to the jungles of southern Mexico as teenagers that their energies were directed toward whitewater.

Near the end of an adventuresome family tour to Mayan ruins, the Knapp's motor boat driver wisely refused to take them through the Usumacinta River's turbulent San Jose Canyon. The inaccessibility of the canyon captivated Brandon and Dustin's mother Julie, and she immediately resolved to return and explore the canyon by whatever means necessary. Kayaks were the most logical boats for the endeavor, so the family promptly picked up the new sport.

The next winter, the Knapp clan returned to the Usumacinta and ran the swirling canyon. Afterward, they ran other Mexican classics like the Agua Azul and Santa Maria.

Brandon and Dustin were hooked. Upon returning home, they found that their northern California homeland was laced with whitewater rivers, and they began exploring them. In the next year, the Knapp boys paddled a total of 320 days. Whether at a play spot, or on an expedition, the Knapps were almost always together, though each had slightly different strengths.

Brandon excelled at freestyle, making the U.S. team for four years in a row. He is also an accomplished whitewater photographer. Dustin's forte' has become foreign expedition paddling. He has kayaked in Japan, Chile, Africa, Myanmar, Europe, and traveled to Tibet as part of the Tsangpo's first descent team. Both brothers, however, are equally at home on the rivers of California's Sierra Nevada Mountains.

They first started exploring this granite wonderland in the mid-'90s with the help of the Holbek/Stanley guidebook. After blitzing some of the standard runs, they decided to give a few of the more steep and obscure rivers a try. One of the first was the North Fork of the Stanislaus. Holbek's guidebook read: "Chuck and I ran this in '81 and made 20 or 30 portages and came away thrilled, bone-tired, and proclaiming it a first and last descent." The Knapps ran it with a mere 4 portages, and loved every minute. Says Brandon, "We started realizing that those runs listed as portage fests were actually good to go."

The Fantasy Falls run on the North Fork of the Mokelumne is another one of those runs that was first done in the early '80s, with 13-foot-long boats. Back then, it was marginally runnable. Today, the Knapps consider it a classic.

Fantasy Falls

The North Fork of the Mokelumne's Fantasy Falls run is the classic whitewater adventure of the high Sierras. Stunning scenery, big clean drops, remoteness, Fantasy Falls has it all. Even driving toward the put-in is a memorable undertaking.

Highway 4 steadily climbs a forested ridge that divides the Mokelumne River drainage from the equally dramatic Stanislaus drainage to the south. Roadside elevation signs confirm the ascent: 5,000 feet, 6,000 feet, 7,000 feet...The highway finally crests a pass near Bear Valley ski area, and then suddenly narrows into a slender one lane road twisting through the forest. From here it takes on the appearance of a residential street as it winds past summer cabins before it boldly leaps from the forest into the granite splendor of the Sierras. The surreal road passes a picture-perfect mountain lake, then curves downhill until it crosses a narrow rock-bound creek that obviously leads into an emerging canyon to the west. The scene beckons adventure. The small swift creek which the road crosses is the North Fork of the Mokelumne, and just downstream lies the Fantasy Falls run.

This inviting put-in first gained the attention of paddlers in the late '70s. Lars Holbek gazed across the wild river canyon while skiing in the area, and began studying maps of the Mokelumne. He considered the 250 feet-per-mile gradient of the river to be too steep for a reasonable descent, however, and plans for a Mokelumne run were shelved. As Holbek explored progressively steeper rivers in the next few years, the Mokelumne crept back into the realm of possibilities. By 1981, Don Banducci, Rick Fernald, and Chuck Stanley joined Holbek for an attempt on the unknown run.

The group spent four days in the river canyon as they struggled through several long portages. Their payoff was the thrill of discovering a series of cascades so perfect that they seemed to be out of a dream. The cataracts were poignantly dubbed "Fantasy Falls," and the North Fork of the Mokelumne was forever renamed among the paddling crowd.

The run didn't see many descents for the next decade. Then bold young paddlers using the shorter boats of the next generation began trying the forgotten run, and found that it was more than just a wilderness portage fest. Most paddlers still make a dozen or more portages, but as of this writing, all but one rapid on Fantasy Falls has been run. Different lines come out at different water levels, so the fewest number of portages on any single descent is five.

The portages come throughout the 20-miles of whitewater, until the river is swallowed by Salt Springs Reservoir. Once hitting the flat water of the lake, 5 miles remain to the take-out. Theoretically, Brandon Knapp thinks the run could be made in a day, but as he says, "I don't know if your body could take the pounding for ten hours straight." Knapp has pushed through in two days, but that was only because "somebody had to get to work," as he recalls. Three days is the standard approach, allowing for unforeseen problems, which Fantasy Falls tends to dole out.

The first couple of miles below the put-in are pure punishment, plain and simple. If there is enough water to cushion this first part of the run, then the water level is going to be too high for the big drops downstream. Perseverance through the bony first few miles is part of the challenge on Fantasy Falls.

When paddler Jed Weingarten made his second run on Fantasy Falls, he was frustrated by the low water portages his group had to make, and was anxious to run the slides of the first gorge five miles in. He entered a 20-foot ramp with the same left to right angle he had used with success on his previous run, but the water was too shallow to allow a stroke this time. He skidded out of control with ever increasing speed toward a wall below the falls. Unable to correct his position in the drop, his boat pitoned in a violent head-on collision with the bedrock wall. He rolled upside down, washed into a hole below, and with his ankle burning from the wall impact, quickly swam.

With several critical portages still ahead, Weingarten was unable to continue. With a useless ankle, he couldn't hike out either. After camping for the night, the other six paddlers in his group paddled out to arrange a helicopter rescue, and left Jed there on the riverside rocks to wait for help. Although he had firewood, food, and water, Weingarten admits that with his ankle throbbing and cougar sign everywhere, his two days spent solo were "super not comfortable."

If paddlers make it beyond the troublesome first gorge, they can expect stunning scenery and great rapids all the way to Salt Springs Reservoir at the end of the run. When the river isn't plunging over huge slides, it winds through groves of sequoias. All the big drops have relatively simple portage routes, but a slip on one of the smooth granite slabs will likely send your boat tumbling into the class VI below. Between the portages, there are numerous must-make moves above huge falls. Fantasy Falls is pure Sierra Nevada paddling that demands three days of full attention, and provides three full days of unforgettable rewards.

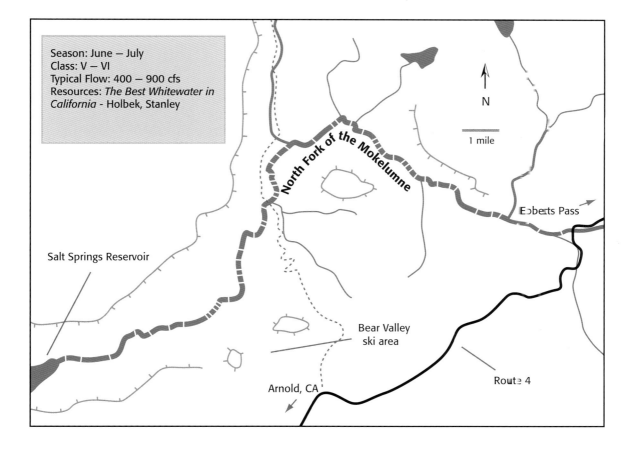

Season: June – July
Class: V – VI
Typical Flow: 400 – 900 cfs
Resources: *The Best Whitewater in California* - Holbek, Stanley

N

1 mile

North Fork of the Mokelumne

Ebbetts Pass

Salt Springs Reservoir

Bear Valley ski area

Route 4

Arnold, CA

Tom Okeefe

Winter paddling in the Green River Gorge

Scott Shipley

In the history of American kayak slalom racing, there have been two paddlers who have dominated the sport during their respective eras. In the 1970s, Eric Evans won the national title nine times, including eight in a row. Twenty years later, an even more decisive slalom domination was seen. The reign of this dynasty belonged to a young paddler from Poulsbo, Washington by the name of Scott Shipley.

It's no mystery why Shipley excelled at whitewater racing. His father Dick was a world class competitor in his own right. Dick raced at the 1965 world championships, and won the national C-2 slalom title that year. As Scott says, "every Shipley starts out in the front of a Grumman."

Scott, however, resisted the Grumman indoctrination at first, thinking that a ride in the canoe would be a lot like fishing, which he hated. At age six, he finally relented to the family canoe ride, and by third grade, he was in a kayak.

He got his first slalom boat at thirteen, and a year later he qualified for the junior worlds along with his brother Paul, who paddled C-1. At the junior national championships that year, the paddler starting after Shipley asked to start a minute late, thinking that Shipley would be so slow, he'd be flailing down the run and holding things up. Shipley, hearing of the cocky request, promptly blazed the course and won the race, along with every other junior competition he ever entered.

At sixteen, he became the youngest kayaker to ever make the U.S. team. Following high school, Shipley trained with teammates Eran Brown, and reigning national champ Rich Weiss. The three shared a tree house near British Columbia's Chilliwack River. Rent was a steep $50 a month—worth it, considering that the training course was only a half-mile away.

In 1992, Shipley won his first national championship in K-1 slalom, a title he wouldn't relinquish for the next eight years. In international competition, he won three world cup silver medals, competed in three Olympics, and was crowned world champion three times.

His life of traveling to competitions allowed Scott to paddle off of the race course as well. Among his favorites are Chile's Maipo, and the Peralta section of Costa Rica's Reventazon. Back in the States, his all-star list includes Georgia's Overflow Creek, and Washington's Green. This winter run near his hometown planted early seeds of adventure in a young Scott. He says, "The gorge is mystic...The whole stinks of adventure, and my dad, brother and I went back again and again. I'm sure I've run that river over 200 times."

Now retired from racing, Shipley designs riverbeds for a watercourse restoration company, re-creating features he has seen on rivers from the Green to his favorite race course. What better person is there for this task than a world champion?

Green River Gorge

No single aspect of the Green River Gorge is notably spectacular, but the run taken as a whole is one of the best in the West. The Green is within an hour of downtown Seattle, has good play spots, is challenging enough to keep expert paddlers entertained, yet easy enough for intermediates, and it runs through a scenic gorge. As author Jeff Bennett says in *A Guide to the Whitewater Rivers of Washington*, "The Upper Green River Gorge is a classic Washington whitewater trip."

The Green drains a relatively low portion of the central Cascades. Most of the watershed lies barely above the winter snow line between 2,000 and 4,000 feet, and the highest ridges of the drainage basin don't quite reach timberline. This low valley serves as a natural corridor through the mountains, and has historically been used as a route of travel. The Burlington Northern Railroad used the valley of the Green as a route across the Cascades. Rather than climb over the imposing range, however, they tunneled beneath Stampede Pass at the river's headwaters.

The railroad was one of many utilitarian uses the Green has endured. Once it was in, the valley was quickly stripped of its stately forests, providing the initial fuel for a construction boom in the nearby cities of Kent and Auburn. As development expanded onto the Green's floodplains near these towns, flooding became an increasing problem. Attempts to confine the river into a narrow channel only led to increased flooding, and a dam was proposed.

In 1962, the Howard Hanson Dam and Reservoir were completed by the Army Corps of Engineers. The dam flooded a narrow canyon of the Green known as Eagle Gorge, and trapped the logs and debris that once provided habitat for Pacific salmon.

Now as a new century begins, the descendants of that generation who built the railroad, to cut the forests, to fuel the construction boom, which led to flooding, that necessitated the dam, which killed the salmon, have decided that salmon are a good thing to have around. So, the same Army Corps of Engineers who constructed the gravel-trapping dam now adds 8,000 cubic yards of gravel to the river each year to aid in salmon recovery. Additionally, engineered logjams are being constructed on the Green to create fish habitat.

Paddlers have been working with the Army Corps on the logjams to ensure that the strainers aren't unnecessarily hazardous to boaters. The section of river where most of this restoration is taking place is called "The Headworks."

This is a bouncy little stretch located just below the dam. There is one 4-foot ledge on The Headworks that serves as the greatest challenge on the mostly class II run. Shortly below the ledge, a sign on river left cautions paddlers of dangerous rapids ahead. The whitewater prompting this warning is that of the Green River Gorge.

The Gorge is split into two runs; the class IV upper and the class III lower. The Gorge itself is a hidden cleft that meanders beneath the patchwork of forest and farm country above. Dark moody cedar trees loom over the water, and vertical cliffs covered in a miasma of green rise from water's edge. The experience of traveling through the depths of the gorge are reward enough for paddling here, but there is good whitewater too.

Below the upper put-in at Kanaskat-Palmer State Park, two ledge drops set the tone for the run before the river is deep within the gorge. As the canyon begins to form, class III rapids with decent play potential keep things busy. When powerlines pass over the canyon about 3 miles into the run, it's time to pay attention. The crux of the gorge is just downstream.

Mercury and The Nozzle are the two named rapids here, but the entire section surrounding these drops is a continuous set of class IV whitewater. Huge boulders send the river into a maze of swirling channels, the sound of the rapids reverberates between the canyon walls, and a damp mist often fills the canyon. It is an ominous, mystical place.

The whitewater eases in the next couple miles, but the canyon remains deep and dark. One of the most scenic sections of the Gorge comes when Franklin Bridge crosses the canyon. This location once served as the take-out for the upper run, but the rickety stairway that leads out of the canyon is no longer maintained, and private landowners have denied access. Paddlers must now continue downstream to a lengthy trail that leads out on river right. The added paddling is just as well, though. Paradise Ledge—the Gorge's best play spot—is located below Franklin Bridge.

Many paddlers continue through the lower Gorge

to Flaming Geyser State Park. This is a great class III stretch that changes into a scenic float after the river emerges from the canyon in the last couple of miles.

Scott Shipley learned on the lower Gorge as a youth, and still has acute memories of the cold winter trips there with his brother and father. He remembers: "We'd always take out at Flaming Geyser State Park where they had changing rooms with those hand blow-dryers installed next to the sinks. I can remember my brother and I standing with our shirt backs hooked over the nozzle of that thing for forty minutes while dad would run the shuttle. We'd just keep pushing the button and letting the hot air blow down our backs—politely stepping aside to let the visitors dry their hands."

Whether it serves as training ground for a world champion like Shipley, or offers an escape from the nearby city, the Green is clearly more than just a river of utility.

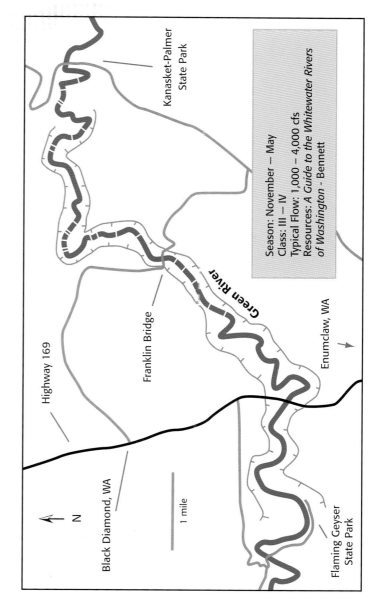

Highway 169

Black Diamond, WA

N

1 mile

Franklin Bridge

Green River

Enumclaw, WA

Flaming Geyser State Park

Kanasket-Palmer State Park

Season: November – May
Class: III – IV
Typical Flow: 1,000 – 4,000 cfs
Resources: *A Guide to the Whitewater Rivers of Washington* - Bennett

Brian Zderic

Heading into the depths of Robe

Tao Berman

Jock Bradley

The late 1990s youthful Generation X spawned a new breed of athlete. Bold, innovative, and fearless, Gen-Xers embraced non-traditional sports such as whitewater boating, and in turn popularized them by performing in non-traditional ways. Whether it was a snowboarder throwing a 720 in a half-pipe, or a kayaker hucking a 70-foot waterfall, extreme athletes turned hobby into career, gained media coverage, and inspired an even younger generation to get involved in sports outside of the mainstream. Like it or not, the growth of sports like kayaking owe much to these young "leaders of the extreme."

Tao Berman is one of those leaders. And although he may be leading a generation which shows disdain for old-fashioned ways, Tao's success has been achieved through something very old-fashioned indeed—hard work and determination. His boundless energy and intense drive have propelled him to a spot among kayaking's elite and gained unprecedented media coverage for the sport.

Tao's willfulness was apparent his first day on the water. Launching an inflatable kayak with his mother on the Skykomish River, Tao's first run was almost over before it began when mom demanded that they have helmets before starting. Not to be denied, Tao convinced mom to drive to the local rafting company where they might be able to borrow helmets for the run. His plan worked. Not only did Wave Trek's Kris Jonasson offer helmets to the energetic youth, she offered him an apprenticeship with the raft company. Tao was 14-years-old. Within three seasons, he was running his first "first"—Alpine Falls on the nearby Tye River.

With his run of the technically demanding 50-foot Alpine Falls, Tao feels he has established himself in the eyes of the local paddling community. "Before that, people thought I was just this out of control kid," he says. Anyone who paddles with Berman insists that he is very much in control, or he wouldn't still be here. His approach to running previously unrun drops is painstakingly thorough, taking extra time to set up safety beforehand. When it is showtime, his quickness and cat-like agility keep him out of trouble. Tao's most notable descent was a record run of Canada's 98-foot Johnston Falls. That one was a pretty straight shot compared to other class VI drops he has run like Log Choke Falls. The name says it all here. Other firsts are now adorned with Berman's less descriptive, but more colorful naming style. Rapids like Washington's "Friend of the Devil" and Mexico's "Welcome to Insanity" both sport the Tao label.

Although he never got the chance to name anything on the South Fork of the Stillaguamish's Robe Canyon, he has pushed the boundaries of what is possible there. Finding the river at a raging 10-feet after a winter storm (6 feet is high), Berman's partners quickly decided against running it, but Tao was drawn to the power. He admits, "I find it hard to walk away from something." He put in while his friends drove his shuttle, and cleaned the four-hour run in less than an hour. Tao especially likes this Seattle area classic because, he says, "The rock is loose in Robe, so it's always changing." With boaters like Tao Berman on the loose, the sport of kayaking is likely to keep changing too.

Robe Canyon

In a land where winter is the prime season for paddling, Robe Canyon is the classic winter run. Throughout most of the summer dry season, Robe's South Fork of the Stillaguamish River is nothing more than one of many small streams that dissect the rural landscape of the Cascade Mountain foothills. Robe doesn't usually come to life as a whitewater run until the famous gray of western Washington's rainy season sets in around mid-October.

From then until late spring, whitewater paddlers in the area keep a keen eye on a meteorological term known as the freezing level. This, of course, is the elevation at which temperatures are cold enough to freeze the surrounding snowpack. The higher the freezing level, the greater the likelihood that rivers will rise. Combine a little rainfall with a high freezing level, and nature's faucets are on. These rain-on-snow conditions normally occur a few times every winter on the relatively low elevation Stillaguamish drainage, producing prodigious floods that regularly re-shape the jumbled riverbed of Robe Canyon. The dynamic forces of nature can be seen here more than on most rivers, and upon seeing the narrow granite canyon of Robe, it's easy to understand why.

Robe Canyon starts dramatically. The relatively wide river turns abruptly left, entering a cleft of slick gray walls that suddenly emerge from the dank carpet of green covering the upper slopes of the canyon. An abandoned railroad bed amazingly clings to the steepness on the right before getting forced into a blasted hole in the canyon wall, immediately providing Robe with a name for its first rapid—Tunnel.

Tunnel's stout holes lead paddlers into a demanding first quarter mile of whitewater that races around the corner into the next named drop, Last Sunshine. If you're lucky enough to catch Robe on a sunny day, don't

expect to see many rays below here. This is a dark, foreboding place, eerie, but also mystical. Fortunately, the river becomes more pool-drop in character after the initial flurry, with rapids coming at fairly regular intervals. One of the most changeable rapids on the river is Landslide, a chunky boulder mess that is often portaged, depending on its current configuration. Just below this is Garbage, the one rapid that might just change more than Landslide. One of the final major drops on Robe is called Conversation, named on a high water descent by Paul Morganthal and noted Seattle-area boater Rick Williams.

The uncommonly high water level that day made many of the standard routes on the well-known run obsolete, and nerves were high as the two neared the end of a day filled with last second surprises. As they approached a recognizable horizon line toward the end of the canyon, Williams led over a river left chute, and was spontaneously cartwheeled a time or two in the punchier-than-normal hydraulic at the base. Thinking anything must be better than this dynamic line, Williams directed Morganthal to try a different route on river right. The new line was hardly any better than Williams' chute. In fact, it was worse. Morganthal only escaped his hole ride after the powerful river had its way with him, and when he finally emerged, he was none too happy with Williams and his errant instructions. His displeasure was expressed with some, shall we say, strong language. When the two were able to let the intensity of the run ebb away at the take-out, they realized the rapid that had precipitated Morganthal's virulent words had a logical new name—Conversation.

Although Rick Williams has paddled Robe about as much as anyone, he was not the first. That distinction goes to Don Sessions and Jerry Buford, two Eastern boaters that moved to Washington in the '70s.

Sessions came from Alabama, and immediately started searching for interesting new rivers that were on par with the Little River Canyon, a favorite of his from back home. Upon asking around about the class V streams he suspected existed in the area, he found that most of the local paddlers "weren't too fired up" about difficult unrun creeks in their backyards. When he explained to a Seattle area club paddler that "our favorite thing to do in Alabama is to find new runs," he was told matter of factly, "All the runs have been found out here." The challenge was on.

Sessions got out his topographical maps, and began investigating unknown rivers, first on foot, then by boat. He explored runs that are now standards like the Miller, Foss, Sultan, and Deer Creek. Sessions was also the impetus behind the exploration of the Cispus and Carbon. Before the rainy season hit in 1980, Sessions hiked through Robe, confirming the canyon's

escapability. When the rains came in October, he and Buford, a C-1er with creek boating experience from the Southeast, launched on 500 cfs.

At the intimidating first set of rapids, Sessions considered a lengthy portage, but Buford was unfazed. Sessions says of his partner, "Jerry had come to paddle." The two survived the initial Tunnel/Last Sunshine series, and then continued through the entire run with only one portage, that one coming at the class VI Landslide. Sessions admits Robe was "the wildest thing I'd done at that point." He returned later in the winter to run it at a slightly higher level, then Williams and others began making it a regular stop and pushing ever higher water levels. The single most audacious high water descent thus far is probably Tao Berman's solo run at 10 feet. It doesn't take high water to make Robe memorable, however. Every run on Robe reveals something special, and often something new.

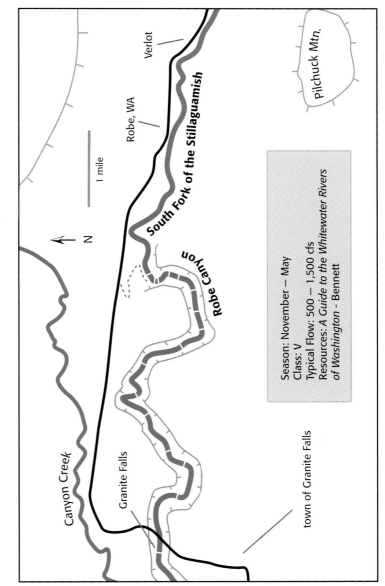

Season: November – May
Class: V
Typical Flow: 500 – 1,500 cfs
Resources: *A Guide to the Whitewater Rivers of Washington* - Bennett

Low water on the scenic Sky

Jennie Goldberg

If you paddle in western Washington for long, chances are that you'll cross paths with Jennie Goldberg. Maybe you'll see her out with the young bucks on the hottest new class V run, or perhaps you'll see her paddling a canoe across Puget Sound. You'll almost certainly see her if you attend a meeting for the League of Northwest Whitewater Racers, or any American Whitewater event. She is on the board of directors for both organizations. Her leadership is testament to her determination, especially when considering that paddling wasn't even her original athletic passion.

Climbing is what drew Jennie from southern California to Colorado State University in the early '70s. While earning a degree in wildlife biology, she made several first ascents in the Colorado Rockies, and traveled to Europe to sample some of the Alp's classic routes. Then one sunny June day, her life changed with the swiftness of a falling 300-pound slab of granite. The boulder crushed Jennie's lower left leg, and instantly snapped her femur. As she hung from her airy belay position bleeding to death, her climbing partner made a valiant dash off the cliff to get help. She was rescued with little time to spare.

Three surgeries, and one year later, Goldberg got out of her full leg cast, and began a new life with a fused ankle and an atrophied leg three inches shorter than before. Her first-ascent days may have been over, but her drive to find fun and excitement in the outdoors was definitely not. Almost two years to the day after the climbing accident, Jennie was taking her first strokes in a kayak.

Her third paddling trip was a cold, blustery day on Brown's Canyon of the Arkansas River—no place for beginners even on a warm day. Underprepared and in over her head, Jennie swam four times that day, and loved every minute of it. She had her adrenaline rush back.

Shortly thereafter, Goldberg moved to Seattle to pursue a masters degree, and was quickly adopted into the local paddling scene. Still new to kayaking, she had to learn how to overcome the challenges of paddling with her damaged leg. One obstacle was her bulky leg brace. It didn't come out of the boat easily, and once out it floated to the surface, making swimming difficult. This provided Goldberg incentive to hit her rolls. "I was famous for the 11-attempt roll," she says with a chuckle.

Before long she was taking on class V adventures with the West Coast's elite, paving the way for other female paddlers to follow. Though she always enjoys a good adventure, much of Jennie's paddling of late has been dedicated to racing. She has competed in several Olympic festivals in K-1 slalom, but her strongest event is the downriver race. She was the Northwest Whitewater Cup wildwater champion from 1998 to 2002, and national K-1 wildwater champ in 2000.

Many of her races have taken place on her classic pick—the Skykomish. Goldberg says of this reliable gem, "When nothing else is running, the Sky is. Locals cut their teeth on it. I know it was a landmark run for me." Show up on a July weekend, and you might just cross paths with a local who cut her teeth there long ago.

Skykomish River

The Cascade Mountains of western Washington are a labyrinth of rocky snow-draped ridgelines, and verdant river canyons. Whether one proposes to climb the snowy peaks, or descend the shrouded gorges, the place is made for adventure.

A multitude of streams carve the western slopes of the northern Cascades into a many-fingered maze of blue-green waterways. The Skagit, Nooksack, Snoqualamie, and Pilchuck river basins are all inviting whitewater playgrounds, but the drainage that stands at the top of the list for all-around paddling possibilities is the Skykomish.

Just a quick scan of the Skykomish (called simply the "Sky" by locals) watershed reveals several outstanding runs. The North Fork of the Skykomish, Foss, and Miller Rivers are all favorites of dedicated Seattle boaters, while class V junkies head for the tributary streams of Money Creek, and the Tye River.

Daredevils seeking the limits of navigation have been attracted to the Skykomish and its tributaries for many years. Today Tao Berman and his posse push themselves by making calculated descents of the unrun waterfalls in the area, but they are not the first to go *big* here. In 1926, a lumberjack named Al Faussett made history by being the first to run the South Fork of the Skykomish's class VI Sunset Falls.

It all started when Hollywood rolled into town looking for a stunt boater to play the part of an Indian paddling a dugout canoe over the horrendous drop. Faussett jumped at the movie executive's $1,500 payday for the stunt, and quickly set to making a boat that was equal to the task. When lumberjack Faussett returned with his dugout-whitewater-kayak design, the movie folks backed out, saying his craft wouldn't look good in the shot. The push to run Sunset Falls had gained momentum by this time however, and Faussett would

not be denied. He charged a $1 admission to watch his run, and well over a thousand people came and lined the banks of the South Skykomish for the event.

He had a spectacular run, catching air in mid-drop, and submerging briefly at the bottom before floating clear of the hole at the base. The crowd gave a cheer, and extreme boating in the Northwest was born.

By the '60s, the main Sky was a popular weekend run, and it continues to be so today. Its moderate whitewater attracts everything from beginners to full-on experts. Most of the rapids are class II and III, but the class IV Boulder Drop maintains its fierce reputation by thrashing paddlers and flipping rafts on a regular basis.

At Boulder Drop, the river is blocked by a fence of large polished blocks that force the paddler to make a decision and handle their boat in turbulent water, the type of rapid with enough character that even the different lines have their own names; The Needle, Mercy Chute, The Airplane Turn. Class III boaters will want to practice their portage skills here, while experts will enjoy the challenge of darting between the eddies.

Below Boulder Drop, the river begins to mellow before ratcheting up the action again with a series of class III boulder gardens. When the railroad bridge crosses overhead, the class III comes to an end. Below this point the river snakes beneath big cottonwoods, and tumbles over a few class I-II gravel bars—a great beginners stretch.

Although the main Sky is much tamer than the waters Faussett rode upstream, that doesn't mean local experts haven't had their share of excitement on it. High water trips have produced notable humility even in Sky veterans. One memorable swim at 50,000 cfs sent the un-manned kayak all the way down the Skykomish, into the larger Snohomish River, and out to the Puget Sound, where it was found days later. Racer Andy Bridge once re-traced the mountains-to-sea route (in his boat, no less) by paddling from his home on the Sultan River, out into the Sky, downstream to the Snohomish, and across the Puget Sound to the wooden boat show in Port Townsend.

The Skykomish might lend itself to extraordinary feats, but its real charm is in its regular, everyday presence. This is the river western Washingtonians count on for its reliable flows, its rapids, or simply its clear green pools that reflect the somber hemlocks along its banks. Generations have grown up with the Sky, whether paddling, fishing, swimming, or driving alongside, this river has touched nearly anyone who has come near it.

The North Cascades loom over the Skykomish

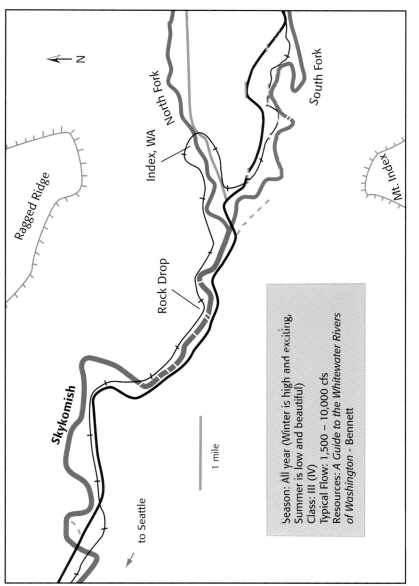

Season: All year (Winter is high and exciting, Summer is low and beautiful)
Class: III (IV)
Typical Flow: 1,500 – 10,000 cfs
Resources: *A Guide to the Whitewater Rivers of Washington* - Bennett

Surfing onto the wave at Skook

Tanya Shuman

Tanya Shuman has been described as "the glamour girl of freestyle kayaking." This may be true, though only in a relative sense. Even a "glamour girl" in whitewater would be considered down to earth by mainstream society. She may be blond and beautiful, but she's still a boater, a boater whose consistently high finishes in freestyle and high-energy marketability have helped mold the sport.

Her whitewater life didn't start until the relatively late age of 23, when her parents gave her kayak lessons as a birthday gift. Before that, soccer had been her passion, culminating with a four year career as center midfielder at nationally ranked Villanova University. A torn knee ligament cut short her senior season, but bitterness at her misfortune was never part of the equation. Says Shuman, "I was definitely ready for a change." She started kayaking soon after the knee had healed.

Her first lessons took place on the C&O Canal adjacent to the Potomac River near her home. After mastering flatwater techniques, she moved on to the Potomac itself. It was a series of river trips on multi-day wilderness rivers of the West, however, that really hooked Tanya on paddling. Hanging out with Eric Southwick helped, too. Wick and Tanya went on the freestyle circuit together in 1997.

They traveled the country, playing and competing with friends Shannon Carroll, BJ Johnson, Katie Nietert, Erica Mitchell, Jamie Simon, and others. During the late '90s, this core group of dedicated paddlers changed the face of whitewater boating. It was freestyle kayaking's golden age, and Tanya developed into top pro form during the period.

In 1998, Tanya and freestylers Erica Mitchell and Jamie Simon talked with Wave Sport's Chan Zwanzig about making a boat for women. The revolutionary XXX was the result. The new boat, besides making the flat spin an attainable move for the bulk of recreational paddlers, helped Shuman make her first U.S. team in 1999.

She continued her steady ascension in the ranks of freestyle the next year, finishing in the top five of every event she entered except one. Tanya took third at the prestigious Ottawa competition, and notched a first place in the Japan Open. By 2001, she was national champion. Shuman is now considered the wise veteran of the freestyle team, the one who knows just what it takes to win. She has seen the growth of pro freestyle, and been a key player in that development all along.

To take a break from the bustle of the circuit, Shuman often makes a pilgrimage to her classic pick, Skookumchuck. This surreal set of tidal rapids is more than just a good wave to Tanya. When speaking of it, her eyes take on a genuine shine as she asks rhetorically, "Isn't it a magical place?"

Tanya has been to many special places in her years as a professional kayaker, maybe that is why she is such a firm adherent to the whitewater lifestyle. She speaks fondly of the good friends and good times the sport has brought her. Of playboating, she says, "I love how dynamic and spontaneous and random it is." Those are pretty free-spirited words for a glamour girl.

Skookumchuck

From the air, the west coast of British Columbia looks like a scattered jig-saw puzzle of dark green mountains sitting atop a quiet sea. It is a mostly uninhabited labyrinth of islands, peninsulas, bays, and channels. At a few special locations along this coast, large bays several miles across are connected to the open sea by narrow channels only a few hundred yards wide. When the strong northern tides flow in and out through these gaps in the coastal maze, amazingly powerful currents result. One of the most impressive of these tidal rapids is the Skookumchuck Narrows.

"Skookumchuck" means "strong water" in native Chinook. That it is. The tide rushes through Skookumchuck (also known as Sechelt Rapids) at up to 14 knots, making it one of the fastest salt water rapids in the world. At maximum flood tide, the entire half-mile-wide channel rips with powerful current on a scale that dwarfs most rivers. For a paddler to ferry from one shore to the other takes several exhausting minutes. The tidal flow at Skookumchuck is the biggest water most paddlers will ever see.

This awe-inspiring display takes on a surreal quality when juxtaposed with the calm that exists between tide changes. Just after the ebb tide has drained the Sechelt Inlet, and before the flood tide begins its march inland, the Skookumchuck Narrows is a peaceful harbor of sea water, just like any number of protected waterways in the region. Dark purple starfish and slippery intricate sea anemones cling to the rocks. Low gray clouds swallow the tops of the forested mountains rising from the rocky shoreline. Even without whitewater, the place is very cool.

Then the tide begins to come in. Almost imperceptibly, eddylines appear along the margins of land, a gentle current glides where only minutes ago there was a flat sea. Next to a rocky point on the west side of the channel, a wave begins to form.

The wave starts out as a small surf-able ripple about 10-feet across, with sea kelp visible waving beneath the smooth accelerating tongue of water. The wave slowly but steadily grows into one of the nicest glassy waves you've ever surfed, then it gets *big*. A foam pile starts breaking on the wave crest, which grows into a giant fluffy pillow of white.

The sheer size of the Skookumchuck wave can be intimidating, but the perfect shape and flushiness make it a relatively safe feature. The only real scary part of surfing at Skookumchuck is what comes downstream of the wave. The eddyline below is strong and full of whirlpools, and it can send little play boats on a wild ride. A missed roll, or an unexpected surge is all it takes to send paddlers spinning downstream beyond the bottom of the eddy. Once this happens, a massive boil prevents any progress toward shore, and the powerful current ushers you several hundred yards farther into the bay. It's going to be awhile before you're back at the wave, so you might as well relax and go with the flow. You're going on "The Tour."

The worst tour experiences usually come when paddlers fight to get to shore right away. This often results in a battle with the giant swirls. Plenty of top paddlers have had swims here, usually following intimate deep-sea encounters while still in their boats.

The late Olympian Rich Weiss once went deep into the underworld at Skook. Not wanting to part with his expensive race boat, he hung on tight after ejecting, but the boat kept taking him deeper and deeper. Finally he had to abandon the kayak, and swim for the surface with his last breath. Both he and the boat survived, but it was a memorable flushing.

Drifting too far into the middle of the sea channel has its hazards too. This is the realm of "The Crusher."

This 100-foot-wide flopping wave crashes on a cycle. If you're there when it breaks, you're, well, crushed. Surfers recognize the Crusher's characteristics as those of an ocean wave that closes out. Its exploding force can easily blow off sprayskirts.

All of this might sound like big water survival boating, and it can be, but the essence of Skook is pure playboating fun. If you catch the eddy promptly after washing off the wave, you will be auto loaded right back to the top, where the fun starts again. Just about every freestyle move in the book is attainable here. At full flood tide, the top wave washes-out into a smooth green giant only surf-able with long fast boats. When this happens, the other waves of the rapid often form nice piles, although they tend to be more erratic than

the top wave. As the tide slows on the backside of its peak, the Skook wave starts to break again, providing the retentiveness needed for the ultimate play spot.

Whether you plan to come for an exhaustive surf session, or just paddle around the inlet looking at the amazing tidal life, Skookumchuck is magical. It is as powerful as one might expect from a place controlled by the astronomical forces of moon and sea.

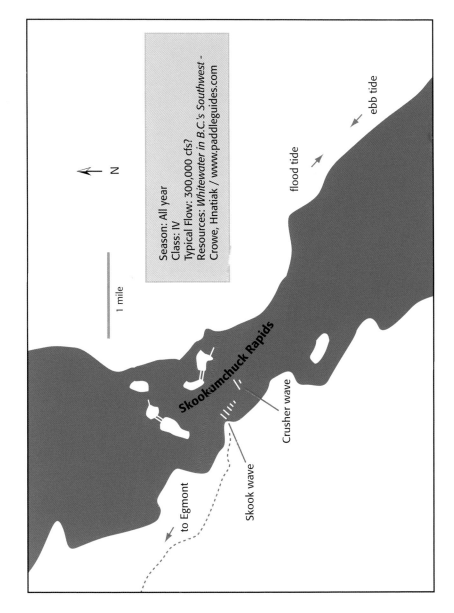

N

1 mile

Season: All year
Class: IV
Typical Flow: 300,000 cfs?
Resources: *Whitewater in B.C.'s Southwest* -
Crowe, Hnatiak / www.paddleguides.com

Skookumchuck Rapids

Crusher wave

Skook wave

to Egmont

flood tide

ebb tide

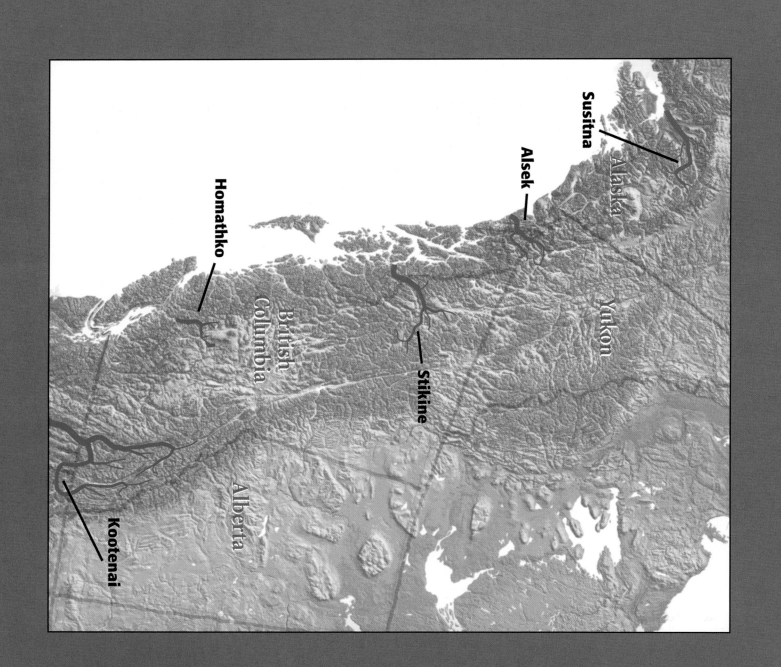

North

"But under it all they were men, penetrating the land of desolation and mockery and silence, puny adventurers bent on colossal adventure, pitting themselves against the might of a world as remote and alien and pulseless as the abysses of space."

Jack London

The North—big wilderness, big water, big adventure. From the broad expanses of tundra above the Arctic Circle to the endless spruce forests of the interior, the majestic Rockies in the south to the verdant glaciated mountains on the coast, this region is a living seething land of water. From a purely geographical standpoint, the North is the most under-represented region in this book. Either Alaska or British Columbia alone possess more whitewater than any other state or province in North America.

The limiting factors to this virtually endless array of rivers are access and season. The access is difficult, and the season is short.

In much of this region, the rivers are frozen ice highways between mid-October and early May, leaving only four to five months of good paddling. But what a season it is! Round-the-clock daylight means the only parameters to your paddling session are your energy level and your cash flow. Many rivers in the North require expensive backcountry flights just to reach the put-in. Once there however, it's just you and the bears,

moose, salmon, mosquitoes, hostile weather, frigid water, and awesome scenery.

Complicating matters further, high water can often shut down expeditions on the difficult rivers. Unlike the more temperate regions in the south, warm sunny weather means high water in most of the North, as perennial snowfields and glaciers gush into meltwater during the brief summer.

Despite the logistical hurdles, the North offers wilderness whitewater like nowhere else on the continent. It's not all epic multi-day exploring either. There are plenty of backyard haunts too. Rivers like the Allen, Clearwater, Kicking Horse, Sixmile, and Thompson are all commonly-run after-work classics.

The North will always be defined by its intimidating, untamed landscape, however, and the rivers featured here all fit that theme. For the paddler who is driven to explore wild places, the North is the place to be.

Doug Marshall

Running the far left line at Kootenai Falls

Brad Ludden

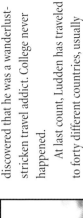

Orson Welles wrote the classic movie *Citizen Kane* at age twenty-two. For many of us, Welle's youthful genius is a nagging reminder of how little *we* have accomplished in our time. It is doubtful that Brad Ludden can share in our regret. Few outdoor athletes have embraced the title of professional so early, or earnestly.

From the time Brad learned to kayak with his family on the Lochsa River at age nine, he explored nearly every facet of the sport. First it was slalom, then rodeo, then expeditions. By the time Ludden was the same age as that plucky author of *Citizen Kane*, he had graduated to the altruistic phase of his career that too few ever reach.

After Brad's early introduction to whitewater on the Lochsa, he quickly shifted into a mode of commitment to the sport, living and training on Idaho's Payette River at the Cascade Kayak School. This led Brad into slalom racing, where he competed at the junior nationals by age fourteen.

Brad was hooked on kayaking, but slalom wasn't his medium. He says, "The structure of the slalom world didn't stick, but it embedded a competitive edge in me." He moved on to freestyle the next year while attending Adventure Quest alternative high school. His freestyle results continued to improve, landing him a victory at the Japan Open when he was just seventeen years old. The next year, he became the United States junior freestyle champion.

As expected, Ludden graduated from high school a year early with big plans for a successful college career. That is when Mr. Responsible impulsively bought an around-the-world ticket with his tuition money, and

discovered that he was a wanderlust-stricken travel addict. College never happened.

At last count, Ludden has traveled to forty different countries, usually with his kayak in tow. Along the way he logged first descents in Southeast Asia, Indonesia, and Africa, where he has journeyed seven different times. He talks about future expeditions there with bounding enthusiasm.

His legacy to the sport, however, will likely be his founding of First Descents, a motivational kayak camp for young adults with cancer. Based in Vail, Colorado, First Descents uses the sport Ludden knows so well in order to accomplish goals much bigger than kayaking. This fits perfectly with Ludden's overall philosophy of paddling. "Kayaking is a vehicle to do the things I enjoy," he says.

One of the things he enjoys most is paddling the powerful water on the Kootenai River. "Every time I run that river I'm impressed," says Ludden.

Kootenai Falls

Montana's Kootenai River might have been included with the rivers of the Rocky Mountain region in this book, but its characteristics are more those of a northern river. The Kootenai is big, beautiful, and uncrowded, just what you'd expect from a river originating in the Canadian Rockies.

Most of the Kootenai River is broad, flat, or dammed, but a few miles west of Libby, Montana, this sluggish river tumbles off a river-wide ledge known as Kootenai Falls, and instantly turns into a dynamic scene of awe-inspiring power. The falls themselves are impressive enough, but it is the two miles of swirling, surging whitewater below that makes the Kootenai a worthy destination for whitewater paddlers.

This has been called Montana's Zambezi, and though it might not be quite on par with that world famous river, the Kootenai does share big water features with its African cousin.

For those in search of class V waterfalls, the Kootenai's 300 yard-wide ledge offers numerous options. River right is the main channel, providing a class VI experience at most levels. As the water level gets higher, ledges in the middle and left sections of the riverbed get covered, opening a multitude of burly possibilities. Far left is the easiest and most commonly run line.

Below the initial falls, the river splits briefly into three channels, each with its own character. The left channel, which is dry at lower levels, finishes with a 12-foot waterfall. The middle channel is a standard big water wave train with epic surfing possibilities. The right channel holds a difficult-to-reach 25-foot drop known as Tahiti Falls. The moniker refers not to the tropical isle in the South Pacific, but rather to the type of inflatable kayak that was sent over the drop as a probe during the filming of Universal Studio's *The River Wild*.

In the Fall of 1993, Kootenai Falls and its environs were a full-time movie set for the multimillion dollar production. The film starred Meryl Streep as a retired river guide who meets up with the ubiquitous bad guys (actors Kevin Bacon and John C. Reilly) while on a wilderness rafting trip. The climax of the movie is a whitewater frenzy, as Meryl rows to salvation through the dreaded "Gauntlet." Hollywood's "Gauntlet," of course, was a selectively edited series of clips from the Kootenai, and the person running the big stuff was actually Cherry Creek guide Kelly Kalafatich.

Despite several weeks of intensive whitewater filming, including mechanical raft platforms, creative camera angles, and some genuinely expert class V runs, the filmmakers were still looking for that ultimate shot. This, you might have guessed, is where the Tahiti inflatable comes in.

The poor dispensable craft was sent over the far-right falls with only distant hopes that it might actually have a good run with filming potential. When the little boat was cast over the lip, it had a graceful plunge to the bottom of the class VI cataract, where it promptly vanished. After a couple minutes of staring into the frothing abyss, all onlookers gave the Tahiti up as forever lost, and went back to their various movie-making tasks. Approximately one month later, as the film crew arrived for work early one morning, a disquieting call came over the radio saying, "There's a loose boat in the far channel." The Tahiti, it seems, following four weeks under the waterfall, had come free. One tube was completely deflated, but it still floated. Its return from the waterfall nether-world demanded an honorable name for the unrun cataract, and it was dubbed Tahiti Falls.

To view Tahiti Falls, one must ferry across to a large island which separates the middle and right channels. The island carries a special significance to native tribes in the area. Legend states that aspiring chiefs were required to swim out to the island, find a particular sacred rock that didn't match the surrounding geology, and then swim back and describe the rock to the existing chief.

The native's swim must have taken them directly through a huge breaking wave that made the challenge exceptionally treacherous. Today, the wave is one of the best play spots on the river, known as Super Wave. Brad Ludden calls this "one of the world's best kayaking features." Located on river left a couple hundred yards below the falls, Super Wave is big, fast, and retentive. It will keep good playboaters mesmerized for hours. If Super Wave isn't at an optimal level, (16,000–18,000 cfs) there are likely more play spots downstream that are.

Less than a mile below Super Wave lies Swinging Bridge, a giant wave train reminiscent of Grand Canyon's Hermit Rapid. Hermit, however, terminates in a big pool, whereas Swinging Bridge leads directly into a very tricky rapid where the river makes a hard left turn. During the filming of the movie, this rapid was called The Door. Not to be trifled with, its huge seams earned the respect of several big name kayakers who were working on the film.

The last big rapid on the Kootenai is a river-wide ledge sometimes called Number Six. Below this, the river runs through a scenic swirling gorge out of sight of the nearby highway. Eagles, osprey, and bighorn sheep are commonly seen along the cliffs, and it's apparent that you are floating a big river of the North.

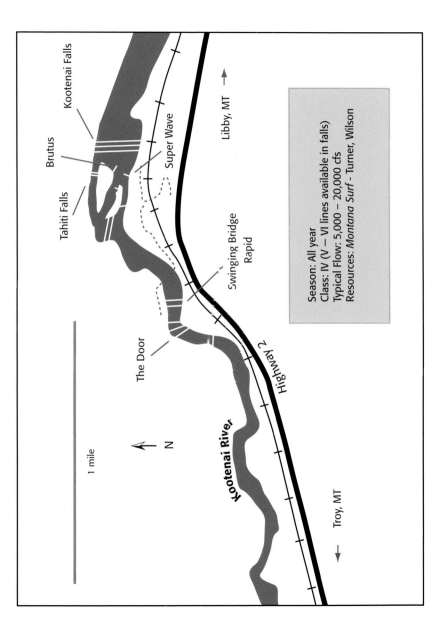

Season: All year
Class: IV (V – VI lines available in falls)
Typical Flow: 5,000 – 20,000 cfs
Resources: *Montana Surf* - Turner, Wilson

Johnnie Kern

In the zone on the humbling Homathko

Kern Brothers

Brothers have always shared a special relationship that embodies both the bonds of friendship, and the ties of ancestry. As with many human endeavors, white-water paddling has certainly been shaped by different groups of brothers. Brothers often teach one another the sport, and continue to fuel each other's success. These bonds that whitewater helps form and strengthen are exemplified by a trio of siblings who grew up together in New England—Chuck, Willie, and Johnnie Kern.

Big brother Chuck was the first to get a taste of whitewater paddling when he attended a summer camp at age fifteen. Chuck's whitewater experience whetted the little brothers' appetites. Within the next two years, they too attended a summer camp that taught the basics of whitewater kayaking.

With the money they earned from working in the corn fields of rural New Hampshire, they bought their first boats, and quickly embarked on a cross-country summer paddling trip with older brother Chuck, the only legal driver of the bunch. Their worried mother sent the boys off with a Mobil gas card, unaware of the fact that Mobil stations were non-existent west of the Mississippi River. Cash ran low, but spirits were high as they paddled dozens of new and ever more challenging rivers. In Sun Valley, Idaho, the brothers halted their paddling long enough to do some ditch digging work, and make some more gas money. Near the Lochsa River, the car finally broke down, and they decided it was time to head for home.

destinations. "We did a lot of park and sink," says Willie. River running has always been the Kern's niche, however, and the ensuing years saw plenty of good times shared in wild places. There was Quebec's Tareau, high water lessons on the Chattooga, and safety boating gigs on New York's Black. In 1995, they got their first real taste of California's Sierras, where they re-defined many of the classic high Sierra runs by successfully paddling what were once considered portage fests.

In 1997, the brothers were running the majestic Black Canyon of the Gunnison when Chuck, leading through a rather ordinary looking rapid, pinned severely, and drowned. His death rocked the paddling community. Johnnie and Willie stopped paddling for the better part of a year. It took a trip to far away Europe to re-kindle their relationship with the sport that had taken their brother, but had also brought them so much.

Other overseas jaunts have included Tibet's Tsangpo, where they were part of Scott Lindgren's "dream team" on that monumental expedition. Like the Tsangpo, their classic pick—the Homathko—is a big river in a deep wilderness canyon. While Johnnie and Willie ran the Homathko on separate trips, they both feel it is emblematic of their connection to the sport—a wild, beautiful, and challenging river that requires teamwork for success, and offers spiritual renewal as a reward.

Over the next few years, they explored various aspects of the sport, including squirt boating. This paddling phase led them to seek out the best mystery move

Homathko River

British Columbia's Coast Range is archetypal wilderness, a land of big glacier-draped peaks, dense mist-shrouded valleys, high alpine lakes, and fresh cascading mountain streams. There are several big rivers that bisect this range, and the finest example of these is the Homathko.

Part of the Homathko's appeal lies in its uniquely interlinked geography. A Homathko trip starts on Tatlayoko Lake in the relatively dry interior, and finishes on the sodden West Coast at Bute Inlet. En route, the river runs through the heart of the Coast Range, cutting a series of canyons at the foot of 13,177-foot Mt. Waddington. The first of these Homathko gorges, called Great Canyon, comes roughly 20 miles below Tatlayoko Lake. At this point, the river has already grown from a little creek to a medium-sized river, as melt water from the surrounding glaciers swells the river volume exponentially; Great Canyon has the steepest continuous gradient on the entire trip, a fact not lost on the river's first descent pioneer Ifor Thomas. He suspected that his group might have to portage the entire canyon.

Thomas was planning the trip along with fellow Canadian Stewart Smith, who now has more Homathko descents than anyone, and German Wolfgang Haibach. Thomas and Haibach were destined to paddle big whitewater together ever since their first chance encounter several years previous.

It was 1980, and the national slalom championships were being held on the Maligne River in Thomas' home of Jasper, Alberta. With all the hot paddlers in town, talk was beginning to circulate that the forbidden Staircase Rapid upstream from the race course might actually be attempted. While Thomas was showing the off-limits Staircase to friends, Haibach and his European crew came barreling around the corner in their kayaks, and swiftly ran the "unrunnable" cataract without so much as a scout. Thomas and Haibach became instant friends, spurring Wolfgang and his European contingent to return to Western Canada for multiple more first descents over the next decade.

By 1988, Haibach had a few major Himalayan descents under his belt, and was looking for a similar adventure in British Columbia. The Homathko was the natural choice.

Haibach traveled to Canada along with his friend Markus Schmidt and six other Europeans in the summer of '88 for a month of paddling that would culminate with a Homathko descent. Not everyone in the group was sure that they wanted to take on the mighty Homathko, however. Prior to launching, a helicopter fly over was done by a few of the team members in order to shoot video of the canyons, and to drop a food cache. Everyone was planning to view the video footage back at the base camp, so that those who didn't like what they saw could opt out of the trip. When connecting the video camera to the television, however, it was discovered that the European camera was not compatible with the American TV. Their video scout was useless. Concluding that fear of the unknown was better than fear of the known, everyone decided to go.

At Great Canyon, they were relieved to find the rapids either runnable, or easily portaged at river level, and they moved through in good time. The next gorge a few miles downstream proved more problematic.

Scouting the canyon from the rim before committing to its smooth sheer granite walls, they found a large side creek pumping tons of unwanted water into the river as a result of the warm sunny weather. Additionally, the Homathko plunged over a huge waterfall halfway down the canyon, thoroughly squelching any thoughts of running the gorge. A three-hour portage ensued. They rappelled back into the canyon below the waterfall, and were able to successfully run the final rapids of what they later named Fall Canyon.

Not far below here, Mosley Creek joins the Homathko, instantly doubling the already burgeoning flow. Even at low water, it is a big river from this point onward, and the first descent party did not have low water.

Following a layover day spent locating their food cache, the group launched in another cursed day of bright sunshine and rising water. The last major hurdle of the trip—Waddington Canyon—was several miles downstream. If the maps were correct, it promised an unrunnable series of falls near its mouth, and another lengthy portage loomed. They were ready for what they thought was ahead. They were not ready for what the Homathko had in store.

Haibach and company were hardly out of camp the next morning when the Homathko plunged into an unexpected granite gorge. The overhung 50-foot walls of this canyon didn't even register on the topographical map, and the group was caught off guard. All ten paddlers portaged the gorge.

At the next cleft just downstream, most of the group continued their boat dragging, but Stewart Smith had had enough. He scrambled down to the bank, and solo paddled what is now known as Tragedy Canyon-Act Two. The ominous title refers not to ill-fated kayakers, but to the slayed Alfred Waddington, who was attempting to put a road up the Homathko in 1893 as a route to the interior. The Chilcotin Indians took exception to his plan, and all but one of Waddington's party were killed.

After some more runnable but hair-raising white-water, the paddling crew finally reached dreaded Waddington Canyon. To their surprise, the gorge was clean, and they were able to paddle right out its mouth. Curiously, the maps had lied again. The mystery was solved upon reaching the mouth of Klattisine Creek, where a massive debris pile had recently dammed the river, and backed water up into the lower end of the canyon, smothering the falls. The cataclysmic debris flow was likely the result of a glacial outburst flood a few years earlier. Smith and crew were able to run the newly formed rapid, which leads to the open valleys of the coast. Its name—Exodus.

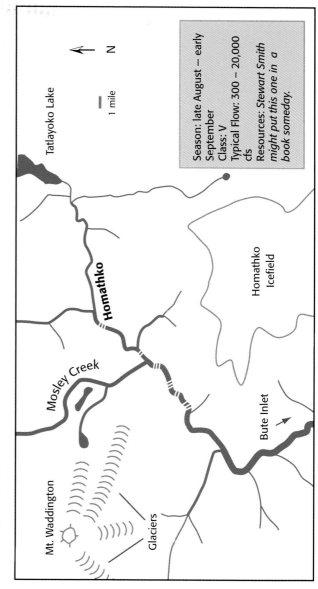

Season: late August – early September
Class: V
Typical Flow: 300 – 20,000 cfs
Resources: *Stewart Smith might put this one in a book someday.*

Charlie Munsey

Can you say commitment? The Grand Canyon of the Stikine is the ultimate big water challenge in North America

Rob Lesser

The term "living legend" is often overused, but in this case, it applies. Few river runners were as prominent during kayaking's coming of age as Rob Lesser. He is best known for his exploratory runs on some of the continent's greatest big water challenges, but Lesser was also a driving force in the early days of whitewater rodeo. He organized two of North America's first freestyle competitions—the Payette Roundup, and the Stanley, Idaho Rodeo. Expeditions have always been his true calling, however, and he is paddling's leading expedition historian, primarily because he appears in most of that history.

Just minutes after crawling into a friend's kayak in 1969 on Montana's Blackfoot River, he was hooked. Says Lesser, "A light went on in my head. It instantly invaded my psyche." The next day he ordered his own boat.

After teaching himself to roll in a frigid 38-degree stock pond outside of Missoula, Montana, Lesser began honing his self-taught skills on the rivers of the area. Soon he was not only camping out of his boat, but also beginning to figure out what he calls the "delicious puzzle" of whitewater. Two years after Lesser took his first paddle strokes, he was running the glacial meltwater of Alaska's Nenana Canyon and exploring every wild river he could find while working seasonally at Denali National Park.

In 1977, Lesser took on Devil's Canyon of the Susitna—an infamous stretch of river that he still describes as "the most intimidating water anywhere." On the trip was Walt Blackadar, who was making his third attempt at the canyon, having swam twice during

a high profile made-for-TV descent the year before. Also along were Idahoans Ron Frye and Al Lowande. The legendary Blackadar, at age 54, was overmatched by the powerful Susitna. He again swam, this time narrowly escaping with his life. Frye and Lowande were also forced to abandon the canyon. Lesser finished the run solo.

Lesser's comfort with huge whitewater was apparent again three years later when he ran Turnback Canyon of the Alsek. After completing the glacier-pinched gorge with his team members, he walked back upstream across the massive and stark Tweedsmuir Glacier, hopped into the boat of a team member who had walked around the canyon, and ran Turnback again, this time alone.

It was no surprise, then, when Lesser spearheaded efforts to run the greatest big water challenge of them all—British Columbia's Grand Canyon of the Stikine. Although helicopter filming logistics forced Lesser and his team to portage some of the canyon, the essence of the run had been completed. Lesser says of that first attempt, "It's historic, period." Lesser returned in 1985 to make a complete descent of the canyon, and in 1990 he made the first self-supported trip. Currently, Lesser has run the Stikine a total of four times, more than anyone else.

Stikine River

Expedition paddler Phil DeRiemer calls British Columbia's Grand Canyon of the Stikine "the ultimate test piece." There couldn't be a more perfect description. The Stikine has big water, runnable yet supremely challenging rapids, a narrow committing canyon, capricious water levels, and unforgiving wilderness surroundings. No other river elicits such widespread respect among the world's best paddlers. For one to say he is a veteran of the Stikine instantly places him in a select club of the sport's elite.

The Stikine drains a large swath of northern British Columbia, and runs generally westward to the fjords of southeastern Alaska, where it empties into the Pacific Ocean. There are excellent river running opportunities both on the upper river, where it flows across wild interior plateaus, and the lower reaches, where the Stikine glides through the scenic Coast Range. In between these two stretches, the river passes beneath the Cassiar Highway. Just below here, it enters the narrow and dramatic Grand Canyon of the Stikine.

Rob Lesser had passed over this Cassiar Highway bridge several times on his seasonal migrations to Alaska in the 1970s, but never had an inkling that anything remarkable lay downstream until fellow paddler Bob Walker mentioned "a big canyon" that he thought the river ran through. In 1977 on his way north, Lesser decided to stop and have a look. He chartered a plane to fly over the canyon so he could see if it was runnable or not. Upon seeing the unrelenting whitewater and vertical canyon walls he thought, "No way." Still, he was captivated by the place enough to research water levels and river gradient. During his research, he discovered that his overflight had been during high water, and the river gradient was a modest 43-feet-per-mile. With a little wishful thinking, Lesser decided that under the right circumstances, and with a little luck, the Stikine might just be runnable.

In August of 1981, Lesser got his chance. Joining Rob was Don Banducci, Rick Fernald, Lars Holbek, John Wasson, and an ABC television film crew. The quintet of paddlers had a medium to high water level (12,000 to 15,000 cfs) for the run, which helped create the most amazing whitewater film footage ever shot to that point.

Ironically, it was the successful filming that cut the descent short when the producers told the paddlers that they had all the shots they needed, the budget was used up, and they would be flying the kayakers to the Tanzilla Narrows at the mouth of the gorge for a closing scene. There was naturally disappointment at this news in the paddling camp, but also some relief. Wasson had already taken the swim of his life on day two when he was uncontrollably drawn into the backwash of a colossal pourover and ripped from his boat. The place where this occurred remains one of the canyon's most feared rapids, memorably titled Wasson's Hole.

Lesser and Holbek returned to the Stikine with Bob McDougall four years later to make the first complete descent of the canyon. Like the first attempt, it was again a filmed production, this time featuring the first raft descent of the river. A second rafting attempt that ended with an unplanned hike out to avoid rising water was made several years later. It wasn't the only time paddlers have had to abandon the Stikine and take their chances with the surrounding grizzly-inhabited wilderness.

Some might remember a story by Bob McDougall printed as field notes in a Patagonia catalog, in which McDougall related his life-changing swim at Entry Falls. It occurred on a 1989 trip with Lesser and Doug Ammons. The threesome scouted Entry, the first significant rapid of the trip, and decided on a line through a slot down the right, rather than the sloppy big water route in the middle of the river. As Lesser remembers, "We thought we were doing a total sneak route." McDougall ran first, and was thrown into a hole where he gave a valiant but energy sapping 45-second effort at riding it out. He finally swam and was sent deep only to lodge on an underwater rock just downstream. When he finally surfaced and made it to a riverside boulder, he clung desperately. He had come about as close to drowning as one can without actually crossing into that unknown void. Lesser and Ammons hurriedly ran the middle of the rapid in an effort to give aid, but Bob was unreachable. Below him was a continuation of class V Entry Falls, and shoreline was nothing more than sheer cliffs. After a long vomit session, McDougall regained some of his strength, and embarked on the

only option he had left. In one of the most desperate forced rock climbs of all-time, he scaled the black walls of the Grand Canyon of the Stikine. With Bob's boat gone, the McDougall trio used a trail to help them retreat from the Canyon.

World champion freestyler Jay Kincaid and Taylor Robertson weren't so lucky. These two caught the river in the year 2000 at a ridiculously high 35,000 cfs, and planned to paddle to Entry Falls for a look. An hour later, they were stashing their boats and hiking out after going for wild rides in Entry and catching the first eddy they could, which was thirteen miles below the put-in. A two-day bushwhack back to the car ensued. Two decades after the first descent, running the Stikine remains a challenge of the highest magnitude.

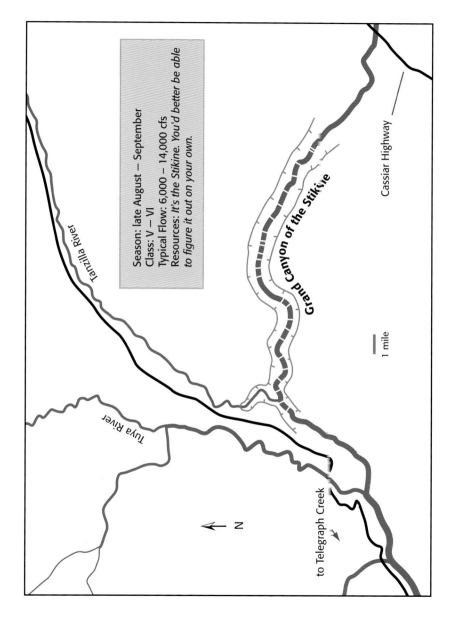

Season: late August – September
Class: V – VI
Typical Flow: 6,000 – 14,000 cfs
Resources: *It's the Stikine. You'd better be able to figure it out on your own.*

Grand Canyon of the Stikine

Tanzilla River

Tuya River

Cassiar Highway

to Telegraph Creek

N

1 mile

The Alsek River beneath the St. Elias Range and the Lowell Glacier

Walt Blackadar

Frank Wilcox

Throughout history, every arena of human endeavor has had a figure who is so charismatic and bold that his persona becomes larger than life, and his exploits can only be accurately described as legendary. For whitewater paddling, that figure is Walt Blackadar.

Blackadar did not even start kayaking until age forty-six, but he made up for the late start by embracing the sport with the same trademark zeal he exhibited in all facets of life. He was a respected doctor in the town of Salmon, Idaho, an avid hunter, and a brave wilderness activist within that conservative western community. He also happened to be America's most illustrious kayaker.

Blackadar was already an accomplished oarsman in 1967 when he launched his first kayak on the frigid snowmelt-swollen Salmon River. It was no place for a first day in a kayak, as Walt and his partner quickly learned. He writes, "We were both swimming and horribly unprotected...I learned fast...and swam for my life." Both boats were lost, and the two exhausted paddlers barely made it to shore, but Blackadar was undeterred. The next summer, he organized a trip on the Middle Fork of the Salmon, inviting an all-star cast of paddlers from across the continent whom he learned basic kayaking skills from. With the experience he gained on the Middle Fork, Blackadar ran ever more challenging whitewater, becoming a top paddler in just a few short years. He was never a technically proficient paddler, but his poise in the midst of overpowering chaos was remarkable, and he is certainly considered the greatest big-water paddler of his time.

His crowning moment came in 1971, when he made a solo run of the Alsek River's Turnback Canyon. His descent of the surreal gorge ranks as one of the most audacious and inspiring river runs ever made. The trip was a catalyst for all adventure boating that followed.

After Turnback, Blackadar starred in some of the first whitewater films. He thrilled audiences with his flamboyant runs through Lava Falls in Arizona's Grand Canyon, and Devils Creek Rapid on Alaska's Susitna. It was Devils Canyon of the Susitna that obsessed Blackadar as his kayaking career waned. He made three trips to the intimidating northern river, and although none of them were considered a complete success (they all involved an epic swim or difficult rescue), each were vintage Blackadar with the requisite big water, fun times, and high adventure.

By his third attempt at the Susitna, Blackadar had an ailing shoulder and faltering stamina that prompted thoughts of giving up kayaking. It was a hard thing to quit, however. The sport had rekindled his youth and made him somewhat of a celebrity, and he of course always had plans to explore one more new river. Ultimately, Walt was spared the decision when he pinned on a log and drowned on the South Fork of the Payette on Sunday, May 13th, 1978. He was fifty five years old. His inclusion in this book is meant to represent and honor all those who have lost their lives in the embrace of the river, while living life at full speed.

Alsek River

The Alsek River runs through some of the most stark and intimidating terrain in North America. The immense landscape is alive with groaning glaciers, unstable house-sized icebergs, and roaming Alaskan brown bears. To travel the river solo, as Walt Blackadar did, is an indescribably humbling experience.

The Alsek's upper tributaries start in the rolling forests of the interior north, where bogs of black spruce sluggishly drain into one another to form a winding stream known as the Dezadeash. The milky-green Dezadeash glides beneath cut-banks of alder as it swiftly flows past the town of Haines Junction, Yukon. This is the simplest place to launch for an Alsek journey, and the last outpost of civilization for the next couple hundred miles, before reaching a dismal smattering of structures near the river's mouth.

About 20 miles below Haines Junction, the river enters mountains; a swift glacial stream called the Kaskawulsh flows in on the right, and where the two rivers join, the Alsek is born. At this point, the river is 1,000 to 3,000 cfs. By the time it empties into the Pacific Ocean roughly 160 miles downstream, it will have grown to a massive 100,000 cfs.

Classic northern scenery consisting of open tundra, dark grottoes of spruce, and broad snow-flanked mountains borders the braided and steadily growing river for the next couple days of travel. The landscape is huge and powerful, and the glacial silt of the river swirls and hisses at your paddle as it moves through the water. Just as your senses become adjusted to the big scenery, the river makes a right turn and races into an iceberg-littered lake at the foot of awe-inspiring 15,015-foot Mt. Hubbard and the Lowell Glacier.

As the river exits the far side of Lowell Lake, the flow is noticeably bigger, typically 20,000 to 25,000 cfs in mid-summer. A couple of class III rapids and a class IV below the lake provide the biggest whitewater of the trip. Unless of course, you choose to run Turnback Canyon.

At Turnback, the sweeping rock and ice valley of the Tweedsmuir Glacier has pushed the mighty river against the steep flanks of the mountains on the far side of the valley, creating a tortured canyon of sinister gray walls, and a river of utter chaos. This is the section of river Walt Blackadar became the first to run in August of 1971.

We'll never know exactly what led Blackadar to the icy confines of Turnback. Certainly his brazen, even macho approach to kayaking helped, but more essential in his decision was probably the bitter mortality he saw all around him. His father had endured a slow death to Parkinson's Disease two years previous, and being a doctor, Walt was witness to the suffering of several cancer victims in his small town. On his forty-ninth birthday he wrote: "My birthday! Looked in the mirror and realized I wasn't getting any younger. After spending a sleepless night, I decided to paddle the Alsek and to do it this year solo if I can't get a competent boater to go with me." There is also one more factor that probably landed him in the biggest whitewater ever attempted to that point. He didn't know what he was getting into.

His journal indicates that when he reached Turnback, the gorge caught him somewhat off guard. By the time he realized that he was in the thick of it, it was too late to do anything but paddle.

At his first scout, he nearly swam while getting out of his boat in a precarious spot. Regaining his composure, he made it through the first couple rapids with two quick rolls. At the next rapid, subsequently named Dynaflow, he tried to portage but was backendered and flipped on the giant eddyline guarding his exit point. After a few failed attempts at crossing the swirling eddyline, he tried to attack it farther downstream, and was swept toward the rapid. He writes, "I knew I had a paddle ahead...Just then I saw an iceberg the size of my bedroom immediately alongside me and both of us charging for the 30-foot drop." He paddled upstream to avoid the iceberg, dropped into the rapid backwards, flipped, and rolled up at the bottom.

Below this he braced his way through a mile of survival boating that prompted his most famous journal entry: "Reminded me of trying to run down a coiled rattler's back. And believe me, the rattler was striking at me from all sides." If this weren't enough, just downstream he got hammered in two consecutive holes, broke the knee brace and cockpit rim of his fiberglass boat, rolled on his sixth attempt, and struggled to shore with a boat full of water. Here he camped for the night,

wrote in his journal, and drank his vodka.

The next day he repaired his boat and ran the remaining two rapids of the gorge. In all, he rolled seven times in Turnback, surviving one of the wildest sequences of water ever attempted. The canyon has been run many times since, but never again at Blackadar's high water level, and in constricted Turnback Canyon, water level makes all the difference. Estimates place the flow on Blackadar's descent between 20,000 and 30,000 cfs.

Regardless of water level, or whether you run Turnback or not, a trip down the Alsek is a view into the naked uncivilized world of the past. Few places on earth display the overwhelming power of nature like Alsek country.

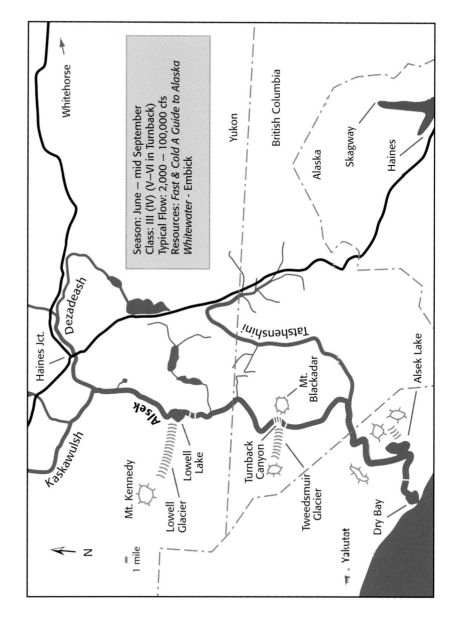

Season: June — mid September
Class: III (IV) (V—VI in Turnback)
Typical Flow: 2,000 — 100,000 cfs
Resources: *Fast & Cold A Guide to Alaska Whitewater* - Embick

Rob Lesser

Devils Canyon of the Susitna

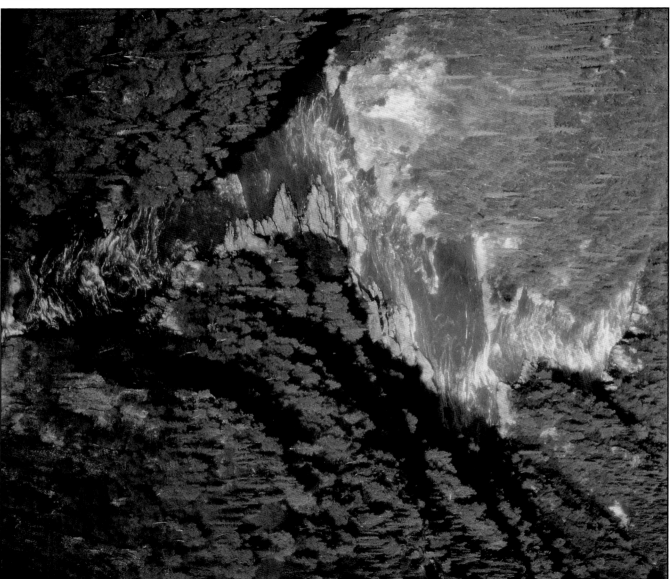

Bo Shelby

Few people are able to combine their passion with their job, and have the result be meaningful, purposeful work, but Bo Shelby does just that. Officially, Shelby is a social science professor of forest resources at Oregon State University. The significance of this to you and me is that he has weighty input on issues that affect whitewater paddlers, like minimum recreational streamflows, and wilderness carrying capacity. The vagaries of government might sometimes take Shelby's conclusions and process them into watered-down bureau speak, but at least he is a voice for river advocates, a voice that speaks from experience.

Shelby was first thrust into river running as a teenager when the outdoor school where he was teaching added it to their curriculum. Shelby was a trained climbing instructor. He knew virtually nothing about whitewater. Nonetheless, he was told, "You'll learn," and he did.

He started by rafting on Colorado's Yampa River, then finished the season with a Grand Canyon trip. Shortly thereafter, when he and his friend John Wasson were introduced to kayaking, Shelby recalls thinking, "Hey, these kayak things are really cool." Bo practiced with the new boat while studying for his masters degree in Wisconsin, and when he returned to the West in the mid '70s, he was good enough to join his friend Wasson in exploring the rarely traveled rivers of Colorado and Idaho.

By 1980, Shelby was ready to challenge himself on the biggest known whitewater on the continent. The Alsek River's Turnback Canyon had only been run once before, and that was by a possessed Walt Blackadar nine years earlier. Even though he had survived,

Blackadar called the canyon "unrunnable." The top expedition paddlers of the next generation were determined to find out just how "unrunnable" the canyon really was.

Shelby put on with Don Banducci, Rob Lesser, and John Wasson. Their descent was successful not only in paddling the canyon, but also by mapping and naming the rapids. One of the constrictions was coined after Bo. While fighting the massive boils of the river, he drifted past his scouting companions without seeing them, and was forced to run the narrow passage by himself and on the fly—a la Blackadar. When the group found Bo waiting in an eddy downstream, the name for the rapid they had just run was apparent—Looking for Shelby.

A few years later, Shelby returned to Alaska for a run down the Susitna, again with Lesser and Wasson, and Alaskan John Markel. Initially, the water level was too high for a reasonable attempt at their objective Devils Canyon, but a few days of patience paid off, and they were able to make the run as the river dropped to a high but feasible level.

Other Alaskan adventures of Shelby's include trips on the Talkeetna and Nellie Juan, where bad weather prevented a float plane pick up, forcing a two-day diet of "hot water soup," as Bo recalls. Finally, Shelby and his party rescued themselves by paddling out to sea and hitching a ride on a fishing boat. Descents on Alaskan rivers like Beaver Creek and the Fortymile River have been less eventful. These runs were done as Shelby conducted studies for the Bureau of Land Management on those rivers' Wild and Scenic status. Talk about another tough day at the office.

Susitna River

The Susitna River is vintage Alaska—big, wild, and filled with stories of adventure. The river starts in a stark landscape of rock and ice at the foot of the Alaska Range, then winds through the spruce-covered Alaskan interior for nearly 300 miles, growing into a moving gray sea of over 100,000 cfs before reaching the Cook Inlet near the city of Anchorage.

A run down the Susitna would be nothing more than a typical wilderness float trip were it not for one 11-mile section of the river ominously known as Devils Canyon. Here the cold silty Susitna explodes into a minefield of holes, giant exploding waves, and unruly whirlpools. The first and most storied rapid of the canyon is Devil Creek, a drop that nearly brought disaster on the first descent of the river.

It was the summer of 1970 when adventurers Jack Hession and Dave Christie put in near the river's source at the convenient Denali Highway bridge. The duo had anticipated some whitewater on the river, but planned to portage their canvas Klepper kayaks around anything significant. Running big rapids was not the focus of their trip, they simply wanted an adventure in Terra Incognita. They found it.

At class III—IV Watana Canyon 64 miles below the put-in, they found the first of the expected rapids, and portaged without mishap. Roughly 60 miles below this first short canyon, Christie swam out of a hole in a class III rapid. Hession was right there for the rescue, but progress toward shore was slow and laborious as he towed Christie and his water-logged boat. The huge swift Susitna swept them downstream. Boulders and the river's big swirling eddylines prevented them from making shore, and the rescue dragged on. As they rounded a bend, the jet-like roar of Devil Creek Rapid suddenly put a heightened urgency to the scene, and Hession yelled at Christie to let go of the boat they

were towing. Fatigue now wearing on both men, they paddled and kicked for shore at frantic speed with the last of their energies. At the brink of the rapid, Hession got his bow onto a submerged ledge as Christie lunged for shore and scrambled to his feet. Hession's boat began to slip off the rock, but Christie grabbed it and hauled it onto the bank where both men sat and let the realization of their near-miss sink in.

Four days later, they staggered out of the woods at the lonely railway stop of Gold Creek. Christie had been forced to make the wilderness march barefoot.

Two years later, Hession paddled with Walt Blackadar while the famous Idahoan was on a paddling trip in Alaska, and it wasn't long before Blackadar had his eye on the Susitna. Following a nerve-wracking treetop buzzing overflight of the canyon with legendary bush pilot Cliff Hudson, Blackadar drove to the put-in and launched on the mighty Susitna with Kay Swanson and Roger Hazelwood.

When they arrived at Devil Creek Rapid, it was late in the afternoon. Blackadar took one good look at the big water mess and proclaimed, "If you're running that, you're running it by yourselves." That was enough for Hazelwood and Swanson. Despite being behind schedule, with a search plane due to arrive in 36 hours if they didn't make the take-out on time, they decided to make the long portage up and around the rapid.

After a few hours' sleep, they began the portage at 3 A.M. in the northern twilight. Following an arduous six hours of boat hauling and a good dose of hairball boating, the threesome got out to scout yet another rapid as afternoon turned into evening. The river roared in a continuous series of massive waves that led out of sight into an ever-narrowing canyon. The sun shone a blinding glare, casting dark shadows on the walls of the huge resting gorge, and illuminating the spray from the huge restless pulsing waves. The scene was terribly intimidating. There was talk of camping right there in the canyon's last open spot, and waiting for the search pilot to find them the next day, but Blackadar quickly discarded the idea. He growled, "I'm not having anyone come in after me," and returned to his boat. Hazelwood followed, and Swanson paddled third.

As Hazelwood crested one of the 20-foot waves of the rapid, he saw Blackadar in front of him, caught side surfing in a huge hole. Hazelwood barely missed hitting Walt, flipped over, and rolled up below the hole. He had made it through, but he was now in the lead, and bombing down a freight train of unknown water. He stroked for the first eddy he could reach, and caught a small surging pocket against the right cliff just above an awful looking drop. A tense minute later, he heard the voice of Blackadar yelling from upstream, "Swim Kay swim!" It seems Kay had also gone for a ride in the big hole, and now he and Blackadar were in a desperate rescue attempt. They flushed by Hazelwood, and were out of sight around a corner.

Blackadar and Swanson flushed through the rapid below Hazelwood's eddy, made it to shore, and paddled the diminishing rapids to the take-out, but Hazelwood knew none of this. He felt one or both of his partners had surely drowned in the terminal looking rapid below him, and any attempt to give chase would only result in another victim. Hazelwood delicately climbed out of his kayak onto the near-vertical cliff, and spent a fitful night of sleep roped to a narrow ledge above the water. The next day, he scrambled out of the canyon, and was prepared to start his survival hike downstream when an Air Force helicopter swooped in and plucked him out of his predicament. In the front seat of the chopper was a grinning Blackadar, giving a thumbs up.

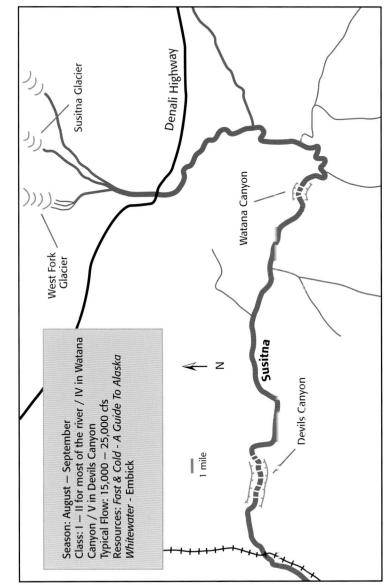

Season: August — September
Class: I — II for most of the river / IV in Watana
Canyon / V in Devils Canyon
Typical Flow: 15,000 — 25,000 cfs
Resources: *Fast & Cold - A Guide To Alaska*
Whitewater - Embick

Additional titles from Funhog Press

This is *the* book for finding just the right side hikes on your Grand Canyon river trip. The Canyon's standard routes like Thunder River and Nankoweap are covered, as well as numerous lesser-known hikes. Handy information specific to Grand Canyon is listed with each route in this easy to use guide. As with all Funhog Press books, maps and photos accompany every route description.

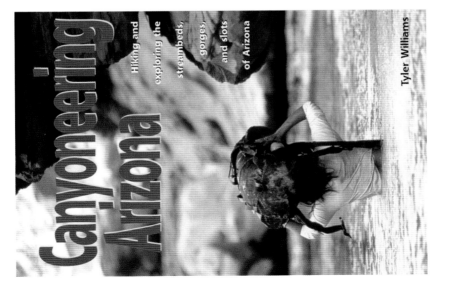

One of the most successful canyoneering guides ever, *Canyoneering Arizona* is the quintessential tool for exploring Arizona's streambeds, gorges, and slots. All the best canyon routes in the state are covered, from easy canyon trails to waterfall-choked chasms. This is the book that helped redefine backcountry play in the Southwest.

Available from: REI Stores, your local bookseller, and Funhogpress.com.

Glossary

boof: To launch a boat horizontally off a vertical drop so as to land flat, and not plunge deep underwater.

C-1: Decked canoe

C-2: Decked canoe for two people

continuous: River characteristic in which rapids are not separated by pools, but rather run together in an unbroken nature.

cfs: Acronym for Cubic Feet per Second. This is the standard measure of water volume in a river in the United States. The Metric version of this is Cubic Metres per Second, or Cumecs.

eddy: River current that is either virtually calm, or moving upstream and contrary to the main flow.

ferry: To move across any given current.

fpm: Acronym for Feet Per Mile. This is the standard measure of river gradient in the United States.

K-1: Kayak

pool-drop: River characteristic in which rapids are separated by relatively calm pools.

squirt: Sinking all or portions of a boat by using currents and strokes.

wildwater: Racing term for down river racing

American Whitewater

American Whitewater has been the voice for whitewater paddlers for 50 years. Whether a river is being threatened with development, or having its access restricted, AW is the one organization that will stand and fight for whitewater paddlers and the rivers we love. AW's vision is: "founded on the need to protect whitewater rivers from destruction or degradation, and to build a constituency that cares about these issues." If you are reading this, you are part of this constituency, and you should be a member of American Whitewater. AW works hard for whitewater paddlers, and they need and deserve our help. There is a membership form in the back of this book. Please use it. Besides supporting the good fight at AW, membership gets you a subscription to the AW Journal—a very cool bimonthly publication that is worth the price of membership on its own accord. If you are already a member of AW, good for you. You are doing your part, and the river Gods will treat you well.

If you are still unconvinced that supporting AW is the right thing to do, hopefully the appendix below will help you see the light. The following is a list of *Whitewater Classics* rivers on which American Whitewater has protected paddler's interests. As you can see, their efforts are worthwhile, and protect the resources we use.

RIVER	ST	ISSUE	AW INVOLVEMENT
Ottawa	ONT	Conservation	In 2001, the Canadian government proposed building 36 low power dams on 24 classic whitewater rivers near the Ottawa by 2005. AW's Access Director Jason Robertson led an American effort to support the Federation Quebecois de Canot et du Kayak in opposing these dams. Largely as a result of opposition, the government scaled back plans and, as of 2003, construction had not been initiated on any of these dams.
Moose	NY	Restoration	The first landmark relicense in the United States has restored and guaranteed releases on this Adirondack treasure.
Kennebec	ME	Access & Conservation	AW board member Tom Christopher signed a hard earned dam relicensing settlement in July, 2001, that provided daily boating releases and a constant fisheries flow, removed an access fee, protected over 1,300 acres of the Kennebec gorge, and secured more than $670,000 in fisheries enhancement projects. This effort took many years of hard work by AW staff and volunteers and is a shining example of what we are capable of accomplishing through dam relicensing.

RIVER	ST	ISSUE	AW INVOLVEMENT
Niagara	NY	Access	In 1987, AW Directors Bob Glanville and Pete Skinner succeeded in opening the door to legal boating for one fall season, and several runs took place. In more than 50 canoe and kayak descents of the Gorge, not one boater was killed or seriously injured. Nevertheless, on November 10, 1987, the New York State Department of Parks, Recreation and Historic Preservation amended its regulations to close the Gorge to all whitewater boating. Public comment on the proposed regulations uniformly opposed closure of the Gorge to boating, and the agency acknowledged that it lacked the expertise to evaluate these comments.
Big Sandy Creek	WV	Access & Conservation	In the 1990s AW leased public access to the Big Sandy. With the sale of the land in 2002, AW director Charlie Walbridge and Access Director Jason Robertson began working with new landowners on the Big Sandy to protect access and ensure a buffer from logging near the river.
Youghiogheny (Upper)	MD	Access & Conservation	AW manages the Sang Run put-in for Maryland under a cooperative agreement, and built a changing facility at the Mountain Surf take-out in Friendsville. AW also worked with outfitters to originally secure access to Sang Run, and has supported State efforts to designate and manage the river as a Wild and Scenic corridor.
Blackwater	WV	Access & Conservation	In 1997 AW purchased a legal public take-out at the confluence of the Blackwater and Dry Fork of the Cheat. Between 1998 and 2002, AW also worked successfully with the new landowners (a logging company) along the North Fork and Lower Blackwater to protect access to the Upper Blackwater take-out and Lower Blackwater launch trails, as well as parking at the put-in for both. AW efforts to protect the scenic values of the corridor culminated in 2002 with the acquisition by the State of West Virginia of land on the Upper and North Forks of the Blackwater.
New	WV	Access & Conservation	AW worked with the Park Service, Congress, and others to secure legal protection and designation of the New River as a National Recreation Area.

RIVER	ST	ISSUE	AW INVOLVEMENT
Gauley	WV	Protection & Access	Secured National Recreation Status in collaboration with commercial outfitters, to guarantee public access to the river. AW leases a field during fall release season for paddlers so they're able to take out at Mason's Branch, or Panther Mountain. AW provides the only free and open public access to the Gauley below the Dam, and is working with the National Park Service to improve public river access throughout the river corridor.
Potomac	MD	Access & Conservation	In 2001 AW's Access Director Robertson convinced the State of Maryland to change its regulations and allow unrestricted access to Great Falls on the Potomac; this was a pinnacle of success capping 20 years of work by dedicated volunteers. Earlier, in 1986, AW volunteers in our affiliate Canoe Cruisers Association of Greater Washington, D.C. (CCA), including Mac Thornton, met with Great Falls Park and reached a voluntary agreement designed to head off formal regulations on, or a prohibition against, falls running. This voluntary agreement was adequate for 15 years; however, changes in use and Park staff led to AW's advocacy for unrestricted access. Between 1999 and 2002, AW also worked with the CCA and Potomac Conservancy to protect the river corridor near Little Galls from development and deforestation.
Green Narrows	NC	Access	Protected an early effort to shunt water during daylight hours by local landowners, and has worked to maintain put-in, take-out and emergency access to the Upper and Narrows sections.
Chattooga	SC	Access	AW supported designation of the Chattooga as a Wild and Scenic River, and has worked to protect that status for three decades. AW also organized a stakeholder conference which served to uphold the self-managed private user system; and has led the work to reestablish access to the headwaters, limited to angling interests since the 1970s.
Rock Island	TN	Access	In 2002, AW supported efforts by volunteer Clay Wright and others to secure notice of releases and changes in flow from the dam operators; these efforts are ongoing.

RIVER	ST	ISSUE	AW INVOLVEMENT
Ocoee	TN	Access & Conservation	AW publicized the threat of a permanent end to water releases on the Upper Ocoee, site of the Ocoee Whitewater Center and host to the 1996 Olympics. Articulating the long term economic importance of this resource in southeastern Tennessee and the relatively negligible impact on lost power revenue by the Tennessee Valley Authority, local businesses and Congressman Zach Wamp took up the banner for viable outfitter fees and public releases for non-commercial users for the forseeable future.
Tallulah	GA	Restoration	With the endorsement of paddling clubs and regional environmental groups, AW secured recreational releases that have reintroduced the most spectacular river resource in northern Georgia, the backdrop for scenes from *Deliverance*.
Colorado (Grand Canyon)	AZ	Access & Conservation	In the 1950s and 1960s, AW worked with many other organizations to prevent any dams from being constructed in the Grand Canyon. Later, in the 1970s, AW worked with the Park Service to draft a River Management Plan; unfortunately this plan was damaged by Congressional meddling in the early 1980s. During the late '80s and early '90s, AW tried to work with the Park to fix the plan; however the Park caved over and over again to Congressional pressure. Finally in 1999, AW joined with the Grand Canyon Private Boater's Association and other AW affiliates to sue the Park service to recommence planning and fix the Private Boater Permit Wait List, which had grown to over 7000 names and a 25-year wait! The park settled the suit and commenced a new river plan. This revised plan will be released late 2004 and implemented in 2005.
Roaring Fork	CO	Access	Lawyer and AW Director Jay Kenney has been working successfully to protect the public right to float in Colorado. Working with AW and affiliate Colorado White Water Association, AW has protected access to Colorado's rivers and streams despite annual challenges from landowners and legislators. AW established the Paul Zirkelbach Memorial Access Fund to defend the right to float in Colorado.

A p p e n d i x

RIVER	ST	ISSUE	AW INVOLVEMENT
Arkansas	CO	Access	AW volunteers worked closely with the BLM and Arkansas Headwater Recreation Area to protect access, to draft a management plan, and to establish a model permit system if certain high use triggers are met.
Animas	CO	Conservation	AW supported efforts of local conservationists and volunteers to prevent passage of the Animas La Plata project, which was one of the most controversial and contentious water development schemes in U.S. history. The project included a dam, reservoir, pipeline, and pumping system at a site near Durango known as Ridges Basin. Congress approved the project in 2001; however, the project was significantly scaled down in response to environmental concerns raised by many groups including AW and our volunteers.
Colorado (Gore)	CO	Access	AW worked with the BLM between 1995 and 1998 to secure a large land exchange with a private ranch (Eagle Pass) in Grand and Summit Counties, Colorado. One of the parcels that the BLM picked up is the current access site that boaters use to access Gore Canyon (on the south side, at the confluence of the Blue and Colorado).
Clarks Fk Yellowstone	WY	Conservation	In 1996 AW opposed plans to establish a gold mine that would span the headwaters of three drainages: Montana's Stillwater, the Clarks Fork, and Soda Butte Creek.
Middle Fork Salmon	ID	Access	AW, along with others, has participated in the USDA Forest Service management planning process to make sure access for non-commercial users is maintained or improved.
Lochsa	ID	Conservation	AW supported designation of the Lochsa as a Wild and Scenic River.
Kings	CA	Access	In 1995 protected access to the Kings River. AW successfully prevented the closure of the Class I-II section from Winton Park to Hwy 180 after the sheriff proposed closing the river due to the fact that there are a couple of mandatory portages around weirs on the river. In 1996 AW worked to secure recreation and

RIVER	ST	ISSUE	AW INVOLVEMENT
N Fk Mokelumne (Fantasy Falls)	CA	Restoration	With the support of members of the California Hydropower Reform Coalition, advocated for and secured releases beginning in 2002 that will restore the "dewatered" section for decades.
			instream conservation flows through the Class IV-V North Fork Kings from Balch Afterbay to Dinkey Creek below PG&E's Blackrock Reservoir.
Green River	WA	Conservation	AW is working with Friends of the Green River and the Army Corps of Engineers to preserve and enhance recreational opportunities on the Green River, primarily by keeping water in the river which benefits both paddlers and endangered salmon.
Skykomish	WA	Access	In 1998 AW started the Skykomish River Fund to secure legal access up and down the Skykomish. AW volunteer Tom O'keefe has been successful in creating a dialogue with landowners and the state to protect existing access.
Kootenai	MT	Access	In 2003, AW's Conservation Director John Gangemi successfully convinced the State of Montana not to implement a boater fee and registration. AW also successfully protected state navigability and recreation laws from changes that would have significantly limited public access under the Constitution.
Alsek	AK	Conservation	AW supported designation of the Alsek as a Wild and Scenic River.
Susitna	AK	Conservation	In 2003, AW volunteers began organizing to oppose the construction of a hydroelectric dam on the Susitna River.

American Whitewater Membership Application

American Whitewater is dedicated to the conservation and restoration of America's whitewater resources and to enhance oportunities to enjoy them safely.

NAME _____

ADDRESS _____

CITY, STATE, ZIP _____

TELEPHONE _____

EMAIL _____

CLUB AFFILIATION _____

(circle)

NEW MEMBERSHIP / RENEWAL

MEMBERSHIP LEVELS

- $25 Junior / Senior (Under age 18 and over 65)
- $25 Indivudual for Affiliate Club Members (Save $10 if you are also a member of an AW affiliate club)
  Name of club _____

- $35 Individual
- $45 Family (Two or more immediate family members excluding children over age 18)
- $100 Ender Club★ (Receive AW's annual Ender Club t-shirt FREE)
- $250 Platinum Paddler★ (Receive AW's exclusive Patagonia Platinum Paddler Polo Shirt FREE)
- $65 2-Year Membership
- $150 5-Year Membership
- $750 Lifetime Membership

★ A portion of your contribution may be tax deductible. If you would like information about the tax deductibility of your contribution, please speak with an AW staff member.

ORGANIZATIONAL MEMBERSHIP TYPES

- $75 Affiliate Club (Join our growing network of paddling organizations across North America)
- $100 Paddling Community Partner

ADDITIONAL DONATION

$ _____

TURN OVER →

TRANSACTION TYPE

_____ Cash   _____ Credit Card   _____ Check #

AMOUNT

Membership subtotal _____

Donation subtotal _____

          TOTAL _____

CREDIT CARD

MC   Visa   Discover   AMEX

Card account # _____

Expiration date _____

Name as it appears on card _____

Signature _____

☐ I am interested in volunteering.
☐ DO NOT share my name with like-minded groups.

MAIL MEMBERSHIP FORM TO:

American Whitewater
46 Haywood Street, Suite 210
Asheville, NC 28801

1-866-262-8429
www.americanwhitewater.org